"The Chicks" Weekend

Sept. 20-22, 1991

Great Time!

Every chick needs a good rooster - and you're one to crow about!! Jan, Cathy, Ginnie and Betty - the best of friends. Its so great to have that special closeness - and an extra bonus is you, Dan. Thanks for being just you. Lotza Love
Betty

Dan -
Thanks for these days you are a Great tour guide. Thanks too for giving up a Sat. to wait on us - your one in a million. Come stay with us again this summer.
Love ya, Jan

Dan -
Great times, Great food, Great Friends. Your expertise is one to admire! Join us for another 'northern' Chicks week-end. Sorry to see this week-end end!
Love. G.

Pure & Simple

An InCircle Cookbook

Neiman Marcus

Published by Neiman Marcus InCircle

Dallas, Texas

Acknowledgments

Neiman Marcus InCircle would like to thank the people who believed in this project and who worked diligently to bring it to where it is today . . .

Our InCircle customers, who brought us these fun, creative, and unique recipes and stories.

Bob Jones, for his selection of recipes and coordination with our panel of judges and the Neiman Marcus restaurant staff.

Our international panel of judges for their interest in our book and their expertise in judging the recipes submitted:

Princess Marie-Blanche de Broglie
Anton Edelmann
Albert Kellner
Ferdinand Metz
James Villas

Stanley Marcus, who supported our project and proudly signed on to write the Foreword.

Laura Rivers, who wrote the editorial and the chapter introduction segments of the book.

Lucy Burton Johnson, for her precise editing of every page.

Clare Adams Kittle, project manager, who sought the talents of so many individuals.

Jack Unruh, for his illustrations, so essential to the theme of *Pure & Simple.*

The Neiman Marcus art directors, who designed our signature cover and the unifying icons throughout the pages.

Mary Homi, for her direction and talent in promoting the book.

Debby Posin from The Neiman Marcus Group, Inc., for her advice, knowledge, and work with tedious detail.

Published by Neiman Marcus InCircle, a division of The Neiman Marcus Group, Inc.

Printed by R.R. Donnelley & Sons Company.

Distributed in the United States and internationally by Independent Publishers Group, Chicago, Illinois.

Type set by Impressions, division of Edwards Brothers, Inc., Madison, WI.

Manufactured in the United States of America.
First Edition
10 9 8 7 6 5 4 3 2 1

ISBN 0-96294723-0-X

Library of Congress Catalog Card Number: 91-62049

Dedicated to those people whose discerning tastes set the standards for fine retailers and whose lifestyles inspired this book. You will recognize them on sight in Bergdorf Goodman, Neiman Marcus, and yes...Wal-Mart.

FOREWORD

In 1949, Neiman Marcus published *A Taste of Texas*, a cookbook containing the recipes of some of its customers, who at that time were mainly domiciled in Texas and the neighboring southwestern states. At that point in time, Neiman Marcus was a single store in downtown Dallas with a modest mail-order business.

Members of the organization suggested that it would be fun to produce a cookbook of Texas recipes from Neiman Marcus customers; so, with a minimum of knowledge of what compiling a cookbook entailed, I commissioned two bright Neiman Marcus executives to take on the task of putting it together.

Marihelen McDuff headed our public relations at Neiman Marcus and Jane Trahey was advertising director. They were the two who undertook the job and learned very quickly the numerous pitfalls involved.

After reading hundreds of recipes, they made a final selection of about 350. They balanced them out for good geographical distribution, eliminated duplications, and thought they were finished. The editor from the publisher, Random House, raised a new question that stunned them: "Who is going to test the recipes?"

"Test them?" they asked, aghast. "Of course," said the editor. "We couldn't publish a cookbook unless the recipes were all tested by a competent cook to prove that they will work." "But we don't have a kitchen," the two entrepreneurs replied in unison. "Well then, get one," was the editor's command. They did.

They found more-than-adequate testing facilities at the Texas State College for Women in Denton, Texas. "Into their capable hands we thrust the directions for jerked deer meat, for Hopkins County Stew that serves 50, and for curry powder pounded on stone. They became our guarantee that your stove wouldn't blow up when you tried our recipes," wrote Jane Trahey in her preface to the book.

A Taste of Texas contained recipes from the leading kitchens of Dallas, San Antonio, Brownsville, Nacogdoches, Houston, Fort Worth, and Waco; and a few from literary people like E.E. DeGolyer, the distinguished bibliophile and the world's eminent petroleum geologist, who gave his recipe for Chili Con Carne; J. Frank Dobie, Texas' most prominent author and teacher, who offered Frijoles à la Dobie; and Dave Cheavers of The Associated Press in Austin, who presented his recipe for Hopkins County Stew.

Cookbooks have become one of the most popular publications of the 20th century. There have been cookbooks by celebrities, symphonies, churches, college alumnae, and art museum groups, as well as those organized around topics like seafood, pasta, bread, dessert, hors d'oeuvre, soup, and salad.

Never before, to my knowledge, had a cookbook of contributors been bound together by the similarity of their shopping habits. Most participants did not know each other, but they were related by the fact that all were Neiman Marcus customers. That is a condition that could probably be duplicated by only a few institutions, and the ones that come to mind as having similar bonds with their customers are Porsche and the Range Rover automobiles.

Now, 42 years later, a second customers' cookbook has been published by Neiman Marcus. The contributors are members of InCircle, a program devised by Neiman Marcus to reward loyal and consistent patrons, which enables them to earn points that are redeemable for a series of rewards. The whole concept of customers contributing their favorite recipes for inclusion in a cookbook is carried a step further in this case, for a portion of the author royalties, earned from sales of the book, will be donated to the various charitable institutions designated by those whose entries have been accepted and published—another thing for sociologists in the 21st century to examine!

Pure & Simple is a splendid title for a cookbook in this day of increased culinary rivalry. Pure and simple should become the cooking trend for years to come.

In this book you will find recipes from all over the United States and from foreign countries, as well. This reflects the growth of Neiman Marcus into a series of 25 stores at the time of publication, with one aborning in Scottsdale. When *A Taste Of Texas* came out, there was only one store.

The names of some contributors will have a familiar ring—Lady Bird Johnson, Joan Lunden, Ed McMahon, Georgette Mosbacher, Texas Governor Ann Richards, and Randy Travis. Their pure and simple recipes have met the tests of a panel of judges in this country and abroad who know their business. They have been impressed, as they should be, by the recipes—not by the names.

Bon appétit!

Stanley Marcus
Chairman Emeritus
Neiman Marcus

INTRODUCTION

Survey the cookbooks in your favorite bookstore and you will find quick and easy recipes using packaged and processed ingredients, recipes for comfort foods, and esoteric, complicated recipes requiring a true culinary master.

Pure & Simple is very different. The title says it all: ingredients are all pure and largely fresh; methods are all simple.

The people who submitted the recipes are all very real. They are members of Neiman Marcus InCircle and lead active, social, community-oriented, and, yes, international lifestyles. They try to eat healthful foods; they enjoy the preparation of food and the planning of parties. Because they are, indeed, community-oriented, they have responded enthusiastically to the proposal from Neiman Marcus that for each recipe accepted for publication in the book, a portion of the royalties will be contributed to the charitable institution of the individual's choice. (Royalties for the recipes from Neiman Marcus' own files and the panel of judges will be distributed among the charities chosen by the InCircle customers.)

But, who are InCirclers? They are highly valued Neiman Marcus customers from all over the world. They enjoy little gifts from NM, such as hotel, restaurant, and travel perks and subscriptions to choice publications. They gather annually for the Private InCircle Shopping Night Parties, and, from time to time, enjoy each other's company on specially arranged travel experiences and at social events.

They are friends of Neiman Marcus, friends of each other, and through the publication of their recipes, it is hoped they will become recipe-exchanging friends of yours, too.

Billy J. Payton
Vice President, InCircle
Neiman Marcus

TABLE OF CONTENTS

MESSAGE

A recipe book by InCirclers has been a long-desired project at Neiman Marcus. It took some time to come up with what is a very unique concept and even more time to organize it. We asked each and every InCircler to submit a favorite recipe and to tell its history, or relate an anecdote about it (some did, some didn't). We were overwhelmed with the number of responses. Then our own restaurant professionals spent weeks culling the roster to 700 from the nearly 2,000 recipes submitted.

These 700 recipes were then judged by an international panel of food experts and chefs who made the final selection for publication. Next, the recipes were tested in our own kitchens (watch for our comments on some of them), and the dishes appeared at least once on our menus as a daily special. We augmented the final list of recipes with some of our own, which represent the most-requested dishes in our restaurants. The end result is not a coffee-table book, but a kitchen-counter book—a working manual for the way we will be cooking and eating throughout the 1990s. We expect every page to be well smudged!

R. Wray (Bob) Jones

Vice President, Food Services
Neiman Marcus

Princess Marie-Blanche de Broglie,
Princess Ere 2001 Cooking School, Paris

Cookbook author and founder of her renown cooking school, the Princess conducts classes in her home in Paris or her château in Normandy. She now enjoys a world-wide reputation as a popular guest speaker with appearances at the Culbertson Winery in California, at Neiman Marcus, and for the French-American Chamber of Commerce. Her honors include: Councilor to Gastronomic Communications Abroad for the Association Internationale des Maîtres-Conseils en Gastronomie Francaise, Commandeur de L'Ordre des Cordons Bleus, and Canardiere d'Honneur de l'Ordre des Canardiers de Rouen.

Anton Edelmann, Maître Chef des Cuisines and Director,
The Savoy Hotel, London

His career began at The Savoy as Commis Saucier in the early 1970s. He then gathered experience in Geneva, Düsseldorf, and Munich before returning to London and the Dorchester. From there, he worked as Premier Sous Chef at the Portman Intercontinental Hotel, and later as Head Chef at the Grosvenor House Hotel before returning to The Savoy as Maître Chef des Cuisines and Director. His kitchen is one of the busiest and most creative in London, gaining an Egon Ronay Star, an AA Rosette, and a Black Clover award in the *Ackerman Guide*. His book, *The Savoy Food and Wine Book*, was published in 1988.

Albert Kellner, Master Chef,
Brenner's Park-Hotel, Baden-Baden, Germany

At age 14, Chef Kellner was apprenticed to the kitchen of the Hotel Bayerischer Hof in Bavaria. His early career took him to the Hotel Eden au Lac in Montreux, Switzerland; the Hotel St. Gotthard in Zurich; and the Hotel Metrople in Monte Carlo. In these posts, he experienced every kitchen station appointment necessary to qualify him as Master Chef. He has occupied this position at Brenner's Park-Hotel since 1966 and oversees every aspect of food service, from the elegant restaurant to the dietary meals prepared especially for spa guests.

Ferdinand E. Metz, C.M.C., *The Culinary Institute of America*

In 1980, he was appointed president of The Culinary Institute of America after a broad career, including important positions with many of America's finest restaurants and 15 years as an executive with a major food industry company. He is the only Certified Master Chef in the United States with an M.B.A. Chef Metz has received numerous accolades, including the Medal of the French Republic, regarded as the highest recognition of culinary achievement.

James Villas, Food and Wine Editor, *Town & Country*

In his position at the magazine, he travels the world as a food and wine writer and restaurant critic, keenly interested in the hotel industry. He has authored five food books: *American Taste, The Town & Country Cookbook, James Villas' Country Cooking, Villas at Table*, and *French Country Cooking.* In addition, he has been published in numerous other publications and has appeared on many network and cable television programs. He holds a Ph.D. in Romance Languages and Comparative Literature and is a former professor at four major American universities. He is listed in the Seagrams-James Beard House *Who's Who.*

CHAPTER ONE

Quick Fixes & Hors d'Oeuvres

Gone are the groaning boards, gargantuan meals, and endless preparations. Smart people simply are not eating that way. Instead, the world has moved toward smaller, quicker, more frequent meals. For one thing, it's probably healthier. The Spaniards have known it for years; they call them *tapas* (little plates). Whatever you call them, the delectables in this category are giving new meaning to quick fixes—a bite after the theater, something to munch on while you watch a movie at home, and best of all, a big impression with little effort when guests drop by.

Sara Dunham—Marfa, TX
Donation to: National Foundation for Ileitis, and Colitis, Inc., New York, NY

Crab Quesadillas

Mrs. Dunham's home is a Texas landmark: the famed Barrel Springs Ranch, where the movie *Giant* was filmed in the fifties.

INGREDIENTS

- **⅓ cup** *butter*
- **¼ cup** *safflower oil*
- **1** *clove garlic*
- **½** *medium-sized onion, chopped*
- **2** *jalapeño peppers, stemmed, seeded, and finely diced*
- **1 pound** *lump crab meat, washed*
- **¼ cup** *mayonnaise*
- **1 teaspoon** *minced cilantro*
- **16** *flour tortillas*
- **4 ounces** *Monterey jack cheese, shredded*

DIRECTIONS

Heat butter and oil in medium-sized saucepan until butter is melted. Pour all but 2 tablespoons into a small cup and set aside. Add garlic and onion to the remaining oil mixture and sauté over medium heat 2 minutes until translucent. Remove from heat and add jalapeños, crab meat, mayonnaise, salt, and cilantro. Mix well and set aside. Heat a nonstick skillet over medium-high heat for about 3 minutes. Place 1 tortilla in the skillet, turning until soft. (If it starts to stick, spray skillet with PAM.®) Remove from skillet. Spread one spoonful of crab mixture over half the tortilla; top with cheese and fold over. Brush liberally with reserved oil mixture on both sides of tortilla. Repeat until all quesadillas are made. These may be prepared a day early. Refrigerate until ready to sauté. Heat a nonstick sauté pan over medium-high heat. Sauté 2 quesadillas at a time until golden brown on both sides, about 3 to 4 minutes. Cut each into 3 triangles. Or, quesadillas may be grilled 5 minutes on each side for a smokier taste.

Makes about 48 pieces.

Testing Notes: *Suggest serving with pico de gallo, sour cream, and guacamole.*

Elizabeth McCall—Piedmont, CA
Donation to: Children's Hospital Branches, Inc., Oakland, CA

Hot Salmon Fondue

I adapted a crab recipe to use more readily available ingredients.

INGREDIENTS

1 package *(8 ounce) cream cheese, softened*

2 jars *(5 ounces each) processed sharp American cheese*

1 can *(16 ounce) Alaskan salmon, skin and bones removed*

½ cup *half-and-half*

1 teaspoon *Worcestershire sauce*

½ teaspoon *garlic salt*

½ teaspoon *cayenne pepper or TABASCO® sauce*

DIRECTIONS

Combine cream cheese, American cheese, and salmon until well-blended in a food processor. Add remaining ingredients and continue to process until completely smooth. Heat in a chafing dish until very hot. Surround dish with bread cubes and a large supply of long bamboo skewers. Don't forget a bowl nearby for the used skewers. Very simple and quick to prepare.

Serves 12.

Richard Zappa—Dallas, TX
Donation to: AIDS Arms Network, Inc., Dallas, TX

Salmon Ball

INGREDIENTS

- **1 can** *(16 ounce) red salmon*
- **1 package** *(8 ounce) cream cheese*
- **1 tablespoon** *lemon juice*
- **2 teaspoons** *grated onion*
- **1 teaspoon** *prepared horseradish*
- **¼ teaspoon** *salt*
- **¼ teaspoon** *liquid smoke*
- **½ cup** *chopped pecans*
- **3 tablespoons** *snipped parsley*

DIRECTIONS

Drain and flake salmon; remove skin and bones. Combine salmon, cream cheese, lemon juice, onion, horseradish, salt, and liquid smoke. Mix thoroughly. Chill several hours. Combine pecans and parsley. Shape salmon mix into ball; roll in nut and parsley mixture. Chill well. **Serves 6 to 8.**

❧ *Serve with assorted crackers.*

Carol R. Cooper—West Bloomfield, MI
Donation to: Botsford General Hospital, Farmington Hills, MI (Memorial Fund)

Salmon Wellington

When I was president of a large women's organization, we hosted a group for three days and had to prepare lunch and dinner each day. Many pitched in, and as president, I felt it my duty to do my share; so, I made this recipe for lunch for nearly 100 people. They loved it, as had guests in our home.

INGREDIENTS

- ½ **cup** *kasha or cracked wheat*
- *Water*
- 1 **can** *(16 ounce) red salmon*
- ½ **cup** *sour cream*
- ¼ **cup** *melted butter or margarine*
- 1 **tablespoon** *lemon juice*
- ¼ **teaspoon** *salt*
- 1 **package** *refrigerated crescent rolls*
- 2 *hard-cooked eggs*

DIRECTIONS

Cook kasha in water, according to package directions. Drain, bone, and flake salmon. Combine salmon, cooked kasha, sour cream, butter, lemon juice, and salt in medium-sized bowl. Mix well. Unroll crescent dough, but do not separate into triangles. Roll out on lightly floured surface into a 15 x 10-inch rectangle; press dough together at seams. Place dough on baking sheet. Spoon half the salmon mixture down center of dough, leaving a 1-inch margin on each end. Place a row of overlapping egg slices down center of filling. Cover with remaining salmon mixture. To seal, bring up sides of dough over top of salmon and pinch edges and ends together. Place another baking sheet upside down on top of the roll. Flip over so roll is on new baking sheet. Remove top baking sheet. Bake 20 to 25 minutes at 375° until dough is browned. Slice and serve hot. **Serves 6.**

❧ *Served with a salad and vegetable, this is also a wonderful main dish.*

Mrs. William Terry Barbee—Weslaco, TX
Donation to: Make-A-Wish Foundation of the Texas Gulf Coast, Inc., Houston, TX

Torte du Fromage avec Saumon

Collecting recipes and cookbooks is a hobby of mine. This is my own recipe, derived from several related recipes. I tend to enjoy preparing and serving food that, although done ahead, lends itself toward unique and distinctive entertaining.

INGREDIENTS

1 jar *(3½ ounce) capers, chopped and drained, but reserve liquid*

16 ounces *Neufchâtel cheese, softened*

1 *red onion, finely chopped*

Vodka, peppered or plain

1 package *softened Boursin cheese, peppered variety*

8 *crêpes*

1 *small package whipped cream cheese*

6 ounces *smoked salmon*

DIRECTIONS

Mix capers with 8 ounces of Neufchâtel cheese. Add as much caper liquid as needed to this cheese mixture to make it spreadable. Set aside. Mix onion with remaining Neufchâtel cheese, thinning to spreading consistency with vodka. Set aside. Stir peppered Boursin cheese until pepper is well blended. Set aside. Place 1 crêpe on a plate and spread with ½ caper mixture. Top with another crêpe and spread with ½ onion mixture. Top with another crêpe and spread with ½ whipped cream cheese. Cover with 3 ounces smoked salmon. Top with another crêpe and spread with all of the Boursin cheese. Top with another crêpe and spread with the remaining whipped cream cheese. Cover with remaining smoked salmon. Top with another crêpe and spread with remaining onion mixture. Top with another crêpe and spread with remaining caper mixture. Top with the last crêpe. Place a flat object (pie or dinner plate) on top of torte and weight the flat object to compress torte firmly, yet slightly. Refrigerate several hours or overnight. Cut into small wedges. **Serves 8.**

❧ *Serve with champagne.*

Mrs. Joe B. Mullins—Dallas, TX
Donation to: Dallas Symphony Orchestra Guild, Dallas, TX

Black-Eyed Pea Dip

While planning a Mexican party for about sixteen people, I voiced a desire to find a different hors d'oeuvre; and a friend gave me this true Texas dip. I've served this to young, old, hot-food lovers and not–all love this one!

INGREDIENTS

- **2** *stalks celery, finely chopped*
- **1 can** *(8 ounce) whole jalapeño peppers, seeded and chopped*
- **¼ cup** *finely chopped green bell pepper*
- **1** *large onion, peeled and finely chopped*
- **1 teaspoon** *black pepper*
- **2 tablespoons** *TABASCO® sauce*
- **½ cup** *ketchup*
- **1 teaspoon** *salt*
- **3 cubes** *chicken bouillon, crushed*
- **¼ teaspoon** *nutmeg*
- **¼ teaspoon** *cinnamon*
- **3 cans** *(16 ounces each) black-eyed peas*
- **1 can** *(14½ ounce) tomatoes*
- **2** *cloves garlic, finely chopped*
- **8 slices** *bacon, browned*
- **½ cup** *bacon grease*
- **3 tablespoons** *flour*

DIRECTIONS

Combine celery, jalapeño pepper, bell pepper, onion, black pepper, TABASCO®, ketchup, salt, bouillon, nutmeg, and cinnamon in a stockpot. Bring to slow simmer. Slightly mash peas, being careful not to make a paste of them. (Two or three pulses in a food processor works best.) Add peas to sauce. Repeat the gentle mashing procedure with tomatoes. Add tomatoes and garlic to black-eyed pea mixture. Cook 30 minutes over moderate-heat, stirring occasionally. Fry bacon in a skillet, reserve ½ cup grease, and set bacon aside. Stir flour into the grease, mixing well. Add roux to the black-eyed pea mixture. Heat and stir 10 minutes. Remove from heat, crumble bacon on top, and stir. This is best served hot, but is also popular cold. It may be reheated and it freezes well. **Serves 14 to 16.**

❧ *Serve on tortilla chip rounds, or serve as a dip with dip-sized FRITOS®.*

Dean Fearing—Dallas, TX
Donation to: American Cancer Foundation, Dallas, TX

Warm Lobster Taco with Yellow Tomato Salsa

Our good friend Dean Fearing has come a long way from his early beginnings as a fry cook at a Holiday Inn in his native Kentucky. His reputation for innovative Southwestern cuisine is known the world over and this recipe from his first cookbook, *The Mansion on Turtle Creek Cookbook*, published by Grove Weidenfeld, is a perfect example. Dean says, "It's my signature appetizer, since the introduction in 1986."

INGREDIENTS

2 pints *yellow cherry tomatoes, or 1 pound yellow tomatoes*

1 *large shallot, very finely minced*

1 *large clove garlic, very finely minced*

2 tablespoons *fresh cilantro, finely minced*

1 tablespoon *champagne vinegar or white-wine vinegar*

2 *serrano chiles, seeded and minced*

2 teaspoons *lime juice*

Salt, to taste

1 tablespoon *maple syrup (only if tomatoes are not sweet enough)*

2 cups *sifted all-purpose flour*

1 teaspoon *baking powder*

½ teaspoon *salt*

½ teaspoon *sugar*

1 tablespoon *vegetable shortening*

½ cup *warm water, approximately*

4 *lobsters (1 pound each)*

3 tablespoons *corn oil*

1 cup *grated jalapeño jack cheese*

1 cup *shredded spinach leaves*

DIRECTIONS

Using the steel blade, process tomatoes until well-chopped in food processor. Do not purée. Or, for crunchier salsa, put tomatoes through the fine die of food grinder. Combine tomatoes and their juices with shallot, garlic, cilantro, vinegar, chiles, lime juice, and salt; mix well. Add maple syrup, if needed, to balance flavor and sweeten slightly. Cover and refrigerate yellow tomato salsa at least 2 hours but no more than 8. Sift together flour, baking powder, salt, and sugar. Cut in shortening until flour looks as though it has small peas in it. Add enough warm water to make soft dough. Mix well and knead on well-floured surface 3 to 5 minutes or until shiny and elastic. Cover dough and let rest 30 minutes, out of draft. Form dough into 2- to 2½-inch-diameter balls. On lightly floured surface, roll into 7-inch circles, ¼-inch-thick. Cook 2 minutes on hot, ungreased griddle or skillet until edges are lightly browned. Turn and cook 1 minute on other side until edges are brown. Tightly wrap 6 tortillas in foil and refrigerate. (Freeze remaining 4 or 5 for future use.) Preheat oven to 300°. Fill large stockpot with lightly salted water and bring to boil over high heat. Add lobsters and cook 8 minutes until just done. Drain and let lobsters cool slightly. Remove tortillas from refrigerator and place in oven 15 minutes until heated through. Keep warm. Remove meat from lobster tails, being careful not to tear meat. Cut meat into thin medallions (or medium-sized dice, if meat breaks apart). Heat oil in medium-sized sauté pan over medium heat. Sauté lobster medallions until just heated through. Spoon equal portions of warm lobster into center of each warm tortilla. Sprinkle with equal portions of cheese and spinach. Roll tortilla into a cylinder shape and place each on a warm serving plate, seam side down. Surround taco with salsa. **Serves 6.**

❧ *Serve with Sauvignon Blanc, Arbor Crest, 1985, a dry, medium-bodied wine with lemon-lime overtones in the nose and a crisp, melon citrus taste to enhance the lobster and its tart salsa.*

Susan Barnes—Phoenix, AZ
Donation to: John Wayne Cancer Clinic Auxiliary, Los Angeles, CA

Taco Appetizer

INGREDIENTS

- **1** *avocado, peeled*
- **1 package** *(8 ounce) cream cheese*
- **¾ cup** *sour cream*
- **2 teaspoons** *lemon juice*
- **½** *head lettuce, chopped*
- **1** *onion, chopped*
- **2** *tomatoes, chopped*
- **1 can** *(6 ounce) pitted olives, sliced*
- **2 packages** *(6 ounces each) shredded Cheddar cheese*

DIRECTIONS

Blend avocado, cream cheese, sour cream, and lemon juice in a blender or a food processor until smooth. Spread mixture in an 8-inch pie plate. Layer the remaining ingredients in the order listed. Refrigerate before serving. **Serves 10 to 12.**

❧ *Serve with DORITOS® or any type of taco chip. I usually serve this over Memorial Day weekend around the pool to kick off the summer.*

Carol Adamek—Dallas, TX
Donation to: Susan G. Komen Foundation, Inc., Dallas, TX

Kevin's Artichoke Dip

First served twelve years ago after a law-student neighbor suggested combining these ingredients, and people haven't stopped raving about it since. As a matter of fact, I had a call for this recipe two weeks ago from a sister of a friend.

INGREDIENTS

2 cans *(14 ounces each) non-marinated artichoke hearts, drained*

1 cup *mayonnaise, preferably homemade*

1 cup *freshly grated parmigiano-reggiano cheese*

3-4 *cloves garlic, minced*

2 tablespoons *sherry*

Dash of cayenne

Dash of paprika

DIRECTIONS

Mix and mash the drained artichoke hearts, the mayonnaise, and the Parmesan cheese with a fork. The mixture should be thoroughly mixed, but with a few lumps. Do not purée. Add garlic and sherry. Mix thoroughly. Put mixture in a small soufflé or casserole dish, and top with dash of cayenne and/or paprika. Bake uncovered 15 minutes at 300°. It will be eaten before it cools down. **Serves 6 to 8.**

❧ *Serve warm with toasted pita triangles, Melba toast, or crackers.*

Susanne McCoy—Washington, D.C.
Donation to: American Cancer Society, Inc., Washington, D.C.

Easy Food Processor Hummus

Because I am busy and like to cook, I often modify recipes for the food processor or microwave. I also like to combine different recipes, taking ideas from each. This hummus recipe is one I've adapted from several basic recipes and changed for the food processor. Hummus is the Middle Eastern name for this chick-pea dip, and it's a favorite snack or dip for us.

INGREDIENTS

1 can *(19 ounce) garbanzo beans*

2 *cloves garlic, peeled*

2/3 cup *tahini (sesame seed paste)*

1 tablespoon *olive oil*

5 tablespoons *fresh or frozen lemon juice*

1/4 teaspoon *salt (optional)*

DIRECTIONS

Drain garbanzo beans. Save a small amount of the liquid to add back in, if you prefer a creamier dip. Use food processor with metal blade. Turn on food processor and drop garlic cloves through the feed tube into the work bowl. Process until chopped. Add remaining ingredients. Turn on food processor (you may prefer pulsing on and off) until ingredients are well blended. The result will be a smooth, creamy spread. Add more salt, lemon juice, etc., to taste. Or, add bean liquid for even creamier consistency. Use immediately or refrigerate, covered. This will keep several days. **Makes 3 cups.**

❧ *Serve with crisp, thick slices of red bell pepper; cauliflower; broccoli; crackers; or pita bread, cut into small wedges.*

Inez Cohen—Winnetka, IL
Donation to: Children's Museum of the Desert, Rancho Mirage, CA

Brie with Sun-dried Tomatoes

I found this recipe in 1989, and it has been a favorite ever since.

INGREDIENTS

- **2 pounds** *Brie*
- **5 tablespoons** *minced parsley leaves*
- **5 tablespoons** *freshly grated Parmesan cheese*
- **10** *oil-packed sun-dried tomatoes, minced*
- **2½ tablespoons** *oil from tomatoes*
- **12** *cloves garlic, mashed*
- **2 tablespoons** *minced fresh basil*

DIRECTIONS

Brie should be well chilled before handling. Remove rind from top and place cheese on serving platter. Combine remaining ingredients and spread on top of cheese. Serve at once or refrigerate for later use. For the most flavor, allow Brie to stand 30 to 60 minutes at room temperature. If Brie is well chilled before preparation, it is possible to cut across and make 2 layers. **Serves 16.**

Serve with plain crackers.

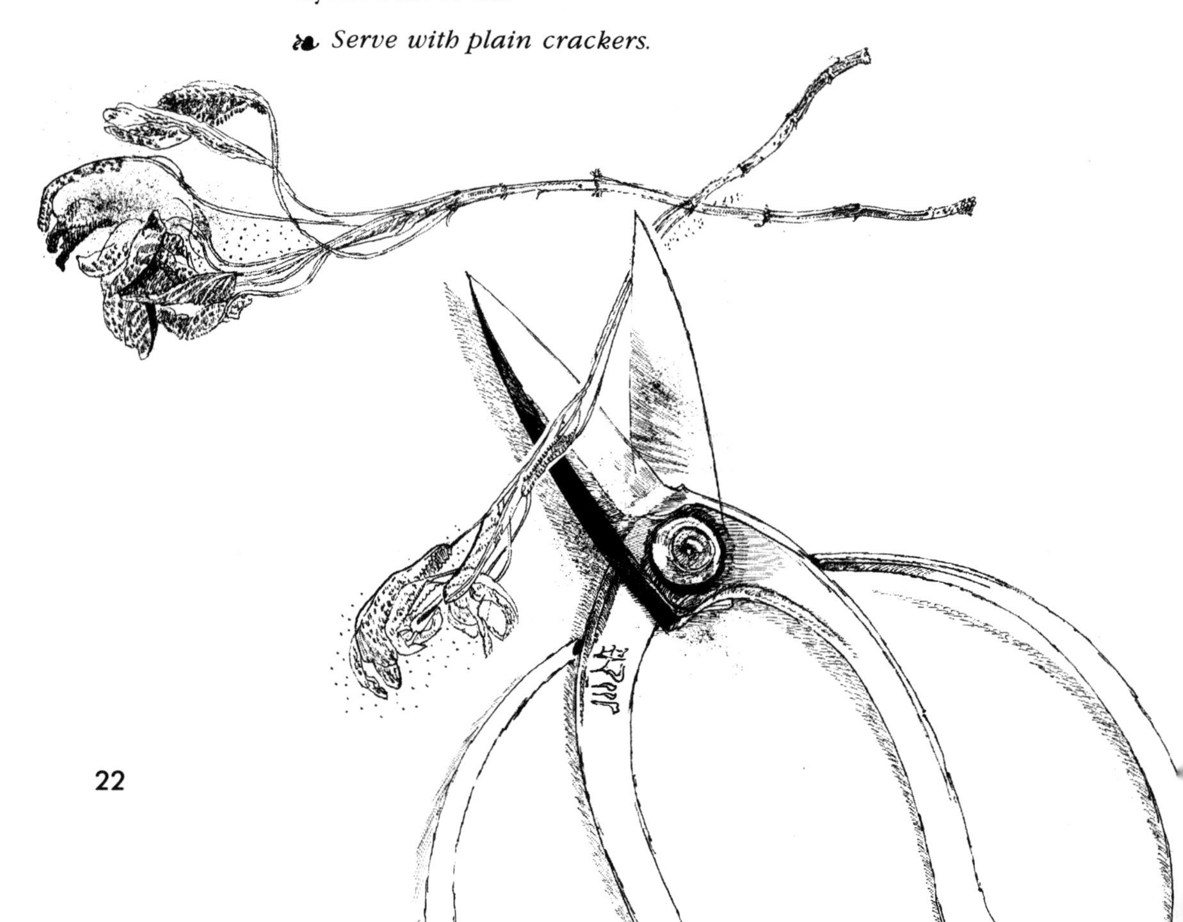

Beverly Wade (Mrs. Roy Lee) Aach—Baldwin, MO
Donation to: St. Louis Symphony Society, St. Louis, MO

Cheese Wiches

These dainty "dee-lish-us" tidbits evolved from years of making appetizers. Men love them, all ages eat at least six at one time, and my lady friends request a copy of this recipe.

INGREDIENTS

- **1 stick** *unsalted butter, softened*
- **2 jars** *KRAFT OLD ENGLISH® spread cheese*
- **½ teaspoon** *onion powder*
- **¾ teaspoon** *LEA & PERRINS® Worcestershire sauce*
- **¾ teaspoon** *dill weed*
- **½ teaspoon** *TABASCO® sauce*
- **1** *large loaf PEPPERIDGE FARM® thinly sliced white sandwich bread*

DIRECTIONS

Mix butter and cheese in food processor, then add the remaining ingredients except the bread. Cut crusts from bread and spread 3 slices of bread with cheese mixture. Stack them, as if for a sandwich, and cut sandwich two times one way; then two times the other way, making nine cheese wiches. Continue to make these delicious tidbits until you have used all the cheese mixture. You may freeze these on cookie sheets and store in plastic freezer bags for another day. I do this in order to have them on hand for special occasions. Bake 12 minutes at 350°. **Makes about 95.** Enjoy!

❧ *Serve with apéritifs or on any special occasion when you want to please guests with something special.*

Kit W. Harrison—Houston, TX
Donation to: M. D. Anderson Cancer Center Outreach Corporation, Houston, TX

Stuffed Mushrooms

This is an adaptation of a recipe from a Houston Junior League cookbook. These mushrooms are the quickest and best hors d'oeuvres you'll ever enjoy.

INGREDIENTS

1 package *(8 ounce) KRAFT® Philadelphia cream cheese with chives, softened*

1 teaspoon *curry powder*

⅓ cup *crumbled bacon bits*

24 *medium-sized mushrooms, stems removed*

DIRECTIONS

Mix cream cheese, curry powder, and bacon bits in a bowl. Stuff mushroom caps with mixture. Bake 10 to 15 minutes at 350°. Serve immediately. **Makes 24.**

❧ *Serve with drinks before dinner.*

Mrs. Patsy Cantrell—Cresson, TX
Donation to: Cook-Fort Worth Children's Medical Center, Fort Worth, TX

Hot Ryes

The first time I tasted these delicious hors d'oeuvres was on a pack/fishing trip in the mountains outside of Jackson, Wyoming. They were wonderful then and are just as good in the comfort of your living room now.

INGREDIENTS

1 cup *finely grated Swiss cheese*

¼ cup *cooked and crumbled bacon*

1 can *(4½ ounce) ripe olives, chopped*

¼ cup *minced green onions or chives*

1 teaspoon *Worcestershire sauce*

¼ cup *mayonnaise*

Party rye bread

DIRECTIONS

Mix together all ingredients, except bread. Spread on party rye or pumpernickel. Bake 15 minutes at 375° until browned. These may be frozen after baking and reheated. **Makes 36.**

Marne Davis Kellogg—Denver, CO
Donation to: Cleo Parker Robinson Dance Ensemble, Denver, CO

Jalapeño Roll-Ups for Dudes

In the summertime at our ranch, which is in the Colorado Rockies, this is one of the menus that gives our guests, and us, the most pleasure. We like to serve it down by the creek, and it is suitable for large and small parties. We live sophisticated city lives most of the time, so at the ranch, everyone especially enjoys simple food and strong whiskey. Flatlanders scream and yell with their first few bites, but then, they can't stop eating them!

INGREDIENTS

2 packages *(3 ounces each) cream cheese, softened*

2 cans *(2¼ ounces each) black olives, chopped and drained*

1 can *(4 ounce) jalapeños, chopped and drained*

8 *burrito-sized flour tortillas*

Salsa, medium-hot

DIRECTIONS

Mix cream cheese, olives, and jalapeños. Spread each tortilla with this mixture and roll up. There should be enough for 8 roll-ups, altogether. Put them in a plastic bag or wrap in wax paper; refrigerate at least 2 hours, if possible. Slice each roll-up into 1-inch slices and arrange on platter around a bowl of salsa. Low-fat, cholesterol-free cream cheese may be substituted with no effect on the flavor. **Serves 4 to 6.**

❧ *Serve with 8-ounce rib eye steaks; oven-roasted new potatoes with tarragon; salad with lettuce, tomatoes, scallions, cucumbers, avocados, and bleu cheese dressing; fresh strawberry shortcake; and Jordan Cabernet.*

Jan S. Kinsler—Atlanta, GA
Donation to: Georgia Special Olympics, Inc., Atlanta, GA

Stuffed Baked Brie

My daughter, Julie, has not only improved her artistic skills while in college, but her cooking talents as well. Her Brie appetizer is one of her most frequently requested recipes.

INGREDIENTS

- **1 carton** *(7 ounce) pesto*
- **1** *Brie wheel (2.2 pound), chilled*
- **1** *egg, beaten with 2 to 3 tablespoons water*
- **1 package** *(1 pound, 1¼ ounce) pastry dough, 2 sheets thawed 20 minutes*

DIRECTIONS

Drain excess oil from pesto. Cut Brie in half, horizontally, as if cutting layers for a torte. Remove top layer and set aside. Spread pesto on the top side of the bottom layer. Place other layer of Brie on top of pesto, cut side down. Slightly roll out thawed dough on top of paper provided with the pastry dough. Place entire Brie wheel on top of the pastry sheet. Brush corners and edges of dough with egg wash. Fold up edges. Brush top of Brie wheel with egg wash. Top with second sheet of pastry dough. Trim edges of this second sheet to make it more circular. Spread underside of dough edges with egg wash and press down so they overlap the bottom edges. Top pastry with egg wash and bake 25 minutes in a preheated 375° oven on a lightly greased cookie sheet. Let stand 25 to 30 minutes before serving. For decoration, use a cookie cutter to cut festive shapes from the extra pastry trimmings. Use egg wash to attach pieces before baking. **Serves 18 to 20.**

❧ *Serve with water crackers.*

Beth Donnell—Houston, TX
Donation to: Lupus Foundation of America, Inc., Dallas Chapter, Dallas, TX

Sunday Night Cheese

This quick and simple recipe is from my maternal grandmother, Tennyson Von Sain Ohron.

INGREDIENTS

Buttered bread
3 *eggs*
2 cups *milk*
1 teaspoon *Worcestershire sauce or PICKAPEPPA® sauce*
1 teaspoon *GREY POUPON® country Dijon mustard*
2 cups *grated mild Cheddar cheese*
1 teaspoon *salt (optional)*
½ teaspoon *white pepper*
½ teaspoon *paprika*
½ teaspoon *TABASCO® sauce*
½ teaspoon *mixed salad herbs*

DIRECTIONS

Line bottom and sides of a shallow 2-quart casserole with buttered bread, buttered side down. Blend all ingredients and pour into casserole. Bake 30 minutes at 350°. **Serves 8.**

❧ *Excellent with black grape, pear, and orange-slice fruit salad and NM's famous poppy seed dressing.*

Ferde Grofe—Malibu, CA
Donation to: Motion Picture & Television Fund, Woodland Hills, CA

Fernando's Breakfast Tortilla

We spend five months a year in an Andean colonial village, Villa de Leyua, founded in 1568. This is our California adaptation of a favorite local recipe, *Huevos Pericos.*

INGREDIENTS

1 tablespoon *sour cream*
2 tablespoons *white wine*
Dash hot-pepper sauce
¼ teaspoon *garlic powder*
Dash of salt
4 *large eggs*
1 *green onion, sliced*
4 tablespoons *chopped cilantro*
2 tablespoons *chopped green or red bell pepper*
1 slice *of tomato, chopped*
3 ounces *Swiss or sharp Cheddar cheese, cut in strips*
1 *large fresh mushroom, finely sliced*
6 *ripe black California olives, sliced*
Handful of crushed corn chips

DIRECTIONS

Combine sour cream, wine, hot sauce, garlic powder, and a dash of salt in a small bowl; mix with fork. Add eggs and beat. Add green onion, cilantro, bell pepper, and tomato. Mix. Heat slightly oiled, small omelet pan to very hot; then reduce to lowest flame or setting. Add egg mixture. Lay cheese, mushroom, black olives, and corn chips (FRITOS®) over top of tortilla. Cover pan and allow to cook slowly on low. It may take as long as 30 minutes to cook this way, but the tortilla rises, not unlike a quiche. Texture is light and fluffy. The tortilla is ready when the dish no longer bubbles and, yet, is still moist on top. **Serves 2.**

❧ *Serve with a side of bacon; sausage (chorizo) or ham; fruit juice; hot rolls; and coffee (Colombian, of course).*

Mrs. Susan Carroll—Elgin, IL
Donation to: American Cancer Society, Inc., Batavia, IL

Garden Quiche Lorraine

I was hosting a luncheon for my ladies' tennis team and I wanted to serve something different than the usual fruit or vegetable salad plates. I put this together using recipes from various cookbooks, plus some ideas of my own. Everyone at the luncheon really raved about it!

INGREDIENTS

- **6 slices** *bacon, cut into ½-inch pieces*
- ½ *small yellow onion, finely diced*
- **1 package** *(16 ounce) frozen broccoli, carrots, and cauliflower mixture*
- **1 package** *(8 ounce) cream cheese, softened*
- ½ **cup** *whipping cream*
- **3** *egg yolks*
- **1** *whole egg*
- ¼ **teaspoon** *salt*
- ¼ **teaspoon** *pepper*
- **1 9-inch** *deep-dish pie shell*

DIRECTIONS

Place cookie sheet in oven and preheat at 400°. Meanwhile, fry bacon in a skillet until browned and nearly crisp. Remove bacon and drain on paper towel. Cook onion in bacon grease until onion becomes translucent. Remove onion and drain on paper towel. Microwave vegetables, according to package directions. Beat cream cheese with cream, egg yolks, whole egg, salt, and pepper until smooth and fluffy. Stir bacon, onion, and vegetables into cheese mixture; put mixture into the pie shell. Bake 20 minutes. Reduce heat to 350° and bake 10 minutes. Let stand 2 to 3 minutes before cutting. **Serves 8.**

❧ *Serve with fresh spinach salad garnished with mandarin orange sections, sliced almonds, bacon bits, and sweet-and-sour dressing.*

Jan Querbes—Shreveport, LA
Donation to: California Special Olympics, Inc., Santa Monica, CA

Sausage Spinach Bread

I take pleasure in finding great new recipes. They don't all turn out to be divine, but this one is guaranteed to bring you rave reviews.

INGREDIENTS

2 loaves *frozen French bread dough (most contain 2 or 3 loaves per package)*

1 package *(10 ounce) frozen chopped spinach*

1 pound *hot pork sausage*

1 *egg, beaten*

12 ounces *grated mozzarella cheese*

½ cup *grated Parmesan cheese*

DIRECTIONS

Thaw the dough. Cook spinach, according to package directions. Drain well. Brown sausage and drain off fat. Add about half the beaten egg to the drained spinach and reserve the other half. Working with one loaf of bread at a time, roll dough into a 9 x 13-inch rectangle. Spread half the spinach, sausage, and mozzarella cheese over the dough. Sprinkle with half the Parmesan cheese. Roll up, jell-roll style, and tightly seal all edges so filling remains inside. Lightly score top. Brush with remaining beaten egg. Repeat with the second loaf. Bake 20 minutes at 375° until browned. Serve hot.

Each loaf serves 8.

❧ *This also makes a good addition to a brunch.*

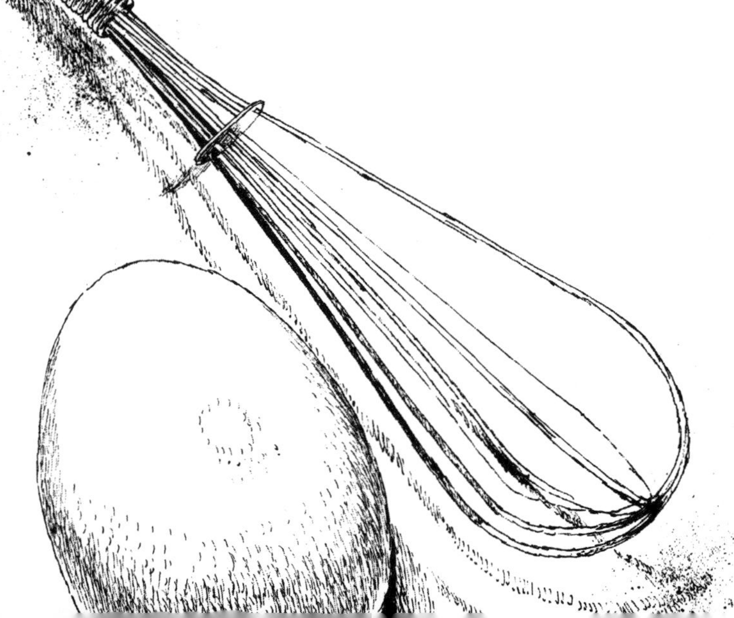

Joanna McDonald—Fort Worth, TX
Donation to: Save the Whales, Inc., Venice, CA

Armadillo Eggs

This recipe was given to me by a girlfriend, Joanie Bulmer, at a recipe shower before my marriage. It is a wonderful football party snack, as well as a real conversation starter.

INGREDIENTS

1 jar *mild whole jalapeño peppers*
12 ounces *grated Cheddar cheese*
1 pound *hot ground sausage*
10 *canned biscuits*

DIRECTIONS

Remove and discard pepper stems. Slit peppers lengthwise, rinse, and stuff with cheese. Pat sausage into thin patties and wrap patty around stuffed peppers, laying seam side down. Bake at 450° until sausage is cooked. Drain grease and set sausage-peppers aside. Roll out each biscuit, place a sausage-pepper at one end and roll up. Bake at 450° until biscuits are browned.
Serves 10.

Mrs. Paul (Lil) Mnoian—Arcadia, CA
Donation to: Visiting Nurse Association, Pasadena, CA

Cocktail Meatballs

This is my original recipe and is a very old favorite of mine. The meatballs are so good, and I serve them when I entertain or take a dish to a social function, like our Arcadia Tournament of Roses parties.

INGREDIENTS

1 *egg, slightly beaten*
1 pound *bulk sausage*
¼ pound *ground round*
½ cup *finely crushed soda crackers*
⅓ cup *milk*
½ teaspoon *sage*
½ cup *water*
¼ cup *ketchup*
1 tablespoon *soy sauce*
2 tablespoons *brown sugar*
¼ cup *barbecue sauce*

DIRECTIONS

Combine egg, sausage, ground round, crackers, milk, and sage until well-mixed. Shape into meatballs and brown in a small amount of oil in a large pot. Drain the meatballs and place in a baking dish. Combine water, ketchup, soy sauce, brown sugar, and barbecue sauce in a bowl. Stir until well-blended. Pour sauce over meatballs and bake 30 minutes at 325°.
Serves 8 to 12.

Marilyn M. Smith—Dallas, TX
Donation to: Ronald McDonald House, Dallas, TX

Libba's Picadillo

This recipe is from my dear friend, Libba Barnes, who's one of the best cooks I know and certainly the most fun.

INGREDIENTS

- **4 pounds** *lean ground meat*
- **1 can** *(16 ounce) ROTEL® tomatoes and green chiles*
- **1 pint** *jar salad olives, drained*
- **4 cups** *chopped black olives*
- **3 boxes** *(1½ ounces each) raisins*
- **2** *small jars cocktail onions, drained (juice optional)*
- **1 jar** *capers, drained (juice optional)*
- **1 can** *(16 ounce) sliced, new potatoes, including juice*
- **2 bags** *slivered almonds*
- **1 can** *(7 ounce) chopped green chiles*
- *Chili powder, to taste*
- *Garlic salt, to taste*
- *Lemon pepper, to taste*

DIRECTIONS

Cook meat until well-browned. Chop salad olives into medium-sized pieces. Add olives and remaining ingredients to meat. Simmer until well-blended. For added flavor, add onion and caper juice. Serve hot in chafing dish. **Serves 20.**

❧ *Serve with dip-sized FRITOS® or tostados.*

Joyce Baseman—Alexandria, VA
Donation to: Children's National Medical Center, Washington, D.C.

Roulades de Jambon (Ham Rolls)

I acquired this recipe in Europe over thirty years ago from a Belgian friend. It's been a favorite ever since.

INGREDIENTS

4 *hard-cooked egg yolks, sieved*

2 teaspoons *tarragon vinegar*

4 tablespoons *HELLMAN'S® mayonnaise*

2 teaspoons *Dijon-style mustard*

2 teaspoons *FRENCH'S® prepared mustard*

Freshly ground pepper

2 teaspoons *minced cornichon*

2 teaspoons *peeled and minced shallot*

8 thin slices *boiled ham, halved*

16 *asparagus spears, cooked and drained*

Boston lettuce

Watercress

DIRECTIONS

Mix first eight ingredients. Spread on each ham slice. Tightly roll two asparagus spears in each ham slice. Chill well. Serve on a platter of Boston lettuce garnished with watercress. **Makes 24 individual pinwheels.**

❧ *This may also be served as a small first course.*

Lisa J. Cave—Clearwater, FL
Donation to: Tampa Museum of Art, Inc., Tampa, FL

Stromboli with Mustard Sauce

I learned this from my good friend, Chef Miles Norris, at a Junior League of Tampa cooking class.

INGREDIENTS

- **1 can** *PILLSBURY PIZZA CRUST®*
- *Basil, to taste*
- **¼-½ pound** *thinly sliced ham*
- **2 pounds** *shredded mozzarella cheese*
- **1** *egg*
- **1** *clove garlic, crushed*
- **3** *different-tasting mustards (sweet, FRENCH'S®, etc.)*
- *Fines herbes*

DIRECTIONS

Roll out pizza dough, according to package directions. Sprinkle with small amount of basil. Cover ¾ of dough with sliced ham and top with cheese. Make sure stuffing does not overlap edges. Roll dough, lengthwise, and place on greased baking sheet, seam side down. Combine egg and garlic in a bowl; beat thoroughly. Brush top of dough with egg and crushed garlic. Bake 25 minutes at 400° until golden brown. Mix 3 mustards and add Fines herbes. After the Stromboli cools, slice into 1- to 1½-inch pieces and serve with mustard sauce, for dipping. **Serves 4 as an appetizer, or 2 as a meal.**

❧ *Serve with cocktails as an appetizer, or with marinara sauce as a meal.*

Marcia Strauss—Houston, TX
Donation to: American Cancer Foundation, Houston, TX

Water Chestnut and Pineapple Roll-Ups

These are a special favorite of children at Christmas time. They love to prepare them and devour them as quickly as they are served.

INGREDIENTS

Bacon (minimum 1 slice per person), cut into thirds
Water chestnuts, sliced
Canned pineapple chunks, drained
Soy sauce

DIRECTIONS

Wrap bacon slice around a chunk of pineapple and a slice of water chestnut. Secure with a toothpick. Broil, turning once or twice, until bacon is crisp. Drain on paper towel. Put on rack in shallow baking pan and sprinkle with soy sauce. Just before serving, reheat 5 minutes in a preheated 350° oven.

❧ *Serve with hot apple cider before Christmas dinner to ward off hunger pangs.*

Mrs. Julius Falkoff—Union City, TN
Donation to: Hickman County Literacy Council, Inc., Centerville, TN

Estelle Dobson's Chopped Liver Pâté

This is my mother's handed-down recipe for chopped liver. I can see her, now, making it.

INGREDIENTS

1 pound *chicken or calf livers*
2 *onions, minced*
Chicken fat
3-4 *hard-cooked eggs*
Salt, to taste
Pepper, to taste
Garlic salt, to taste (optional)

DIRECTIONS

Boil, broil, or sauté livers, according to personal preference. Sauté onions in chicken fat until lightly browned. Mix liver, onions, and eggs together; or put through a meat grinder. Add enough fat to hold mixture together and mix well. Add seasonings. Chill before serving. **Serves 8 to 10.**

Testing Notes: *Livers should be finely chopped.*

CHAPTER TWO

Soups

We're talking a lot more than a cup of broth here. We're talking hearty—the kinds of soup that make a meal when combined with crusty bread, salad, and dessert. (Once again, an example of how we are beginning to eat lighter in the nineties.) Some of the recipes that follow border on being more stew than soup, but all exemplify the importance of increasing our intake of vegetables and using meats sparingly. From one of our informal InCircle surveys, we learned that soup parties are catching on like wildfire all across the United States. (Look for sales of antique tureens to soar next.)

Judith Enright—Brighton, MI
Donation to: Founder's Society, Detroit Institute of Art, Detroit, MI

Irish Tomato Soup

I am not fond of tomato soup. When my husband and I were in Ireland, celebrating our twenty-fifth wedding anniversary, we stopped for dinner at a little pub on the Irish Sea. There was only one choice for dinner, and it included tomato soup. I inwardly groaned, but much to my surprise, it was one of the best soups I had ever tasted. Ever since then, I have been trying to perfect the recipe. Here are my results.

INGREDIENTS

- **4 tablespoons** *unsalted butter*
- **2** *yellow onions, peeled and chopped*
- **1** *small carrot, peeled and chopped*
- **2** *medium-sized potatoes, peeled and chopped*
- **1 can** *(49 ½ ounce) chicken broth*
- **7-8** *ripe plum tomatoes*
- **1½ tablespoons** *basil leaves*
- *Salt and pepper, to taste*
- **2 cups** *low-fat milk*

DIRECTIONS

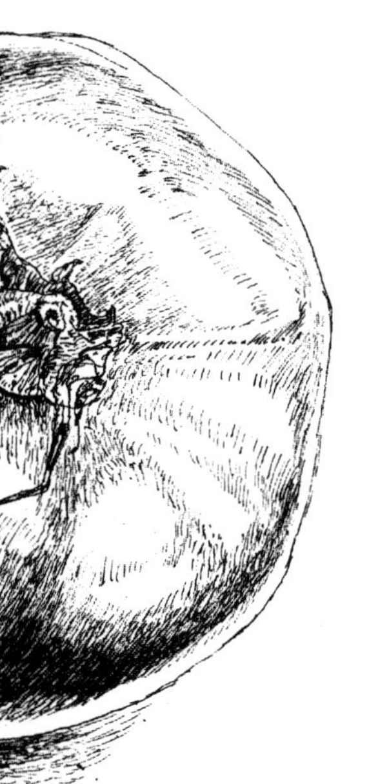

Melt butter in a soup pot. Add onions and carrot; cook 5 minutes. Add potatoes; stir briefly. Add chicken broth. Blanch tomatoes in saucepan of boiling water 30 seconds. Remove from water; peel and discard skin. Add tomatoes to soup. Simmer 1 hour. Add basil, salt, pepper, and milk. Heat 5 minutes. **Serves 4.**

❧ *Serve with fish.*

Testing Notes: *After peeling tomatoes, run through food processor for 10 seconds. Recommend only 1 tablespoon basil.*

Mrs. Sharon H. Dewberry—Dallas, TX
Donation to: Presbyterian Hospital of Dallas, Dallas, TX

Potage Crème de Tomates (Cream of Tomato Soup)

This is my father's recipe, and he started making it with home-grown tomatoes from his garden.

INGREDIENTS

4 tablespoons *sweet butter*
1 tablespoon *olive oil*
1 *yellow onion, peeled and thinly sliced*
¼ teaspoon *minced garlic*
3 *ripe tomatoes (4 to 5, if small), coarsely chopped*
3 tablespoons *tomato paste*
4 tablespoons *all-purpose flour*
2½ cups *chicken stock*
½ teaspoon *granulated sugar*
Salt
½ teaspoon *thyme (don't use basil)*
Freshly cracked white pepper
1 cup *heavy cream*

DIRECTIONS

Heat 2 tablespoons butter with olive oil in saucepan. Add onion and garlic; sauté 5 minutes. Stir in tomatoes and tomato paste. Cook 2 to 3 minutes. Add flour and mix with wooden spatula. Add stock, sugar, salt, thyme, and white pepper. Simmer 15 minutes. Pour into electric blender and blend a few seconds. Strain through a fine sieve. Pour in saucepan. Add cream and bring to boil. Reduce heat and simmer 2 to 3 minutes.
When ready to serve, stir in remaining butter, bit by bit.
Serves 6 to 8.

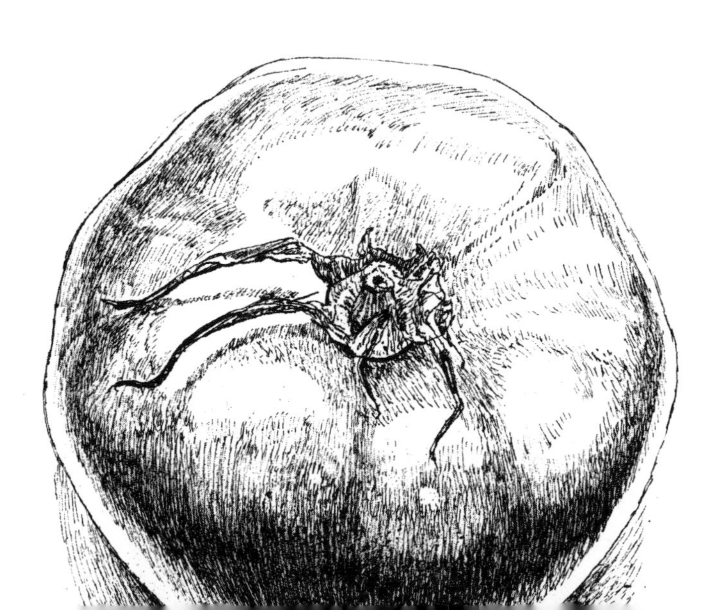

Gwen Cupp—Hot Springs, AR
Donation to: Hot Springs Art Center, Hot Springs, AR

Black-Eyed Pea Soup

Several years ago, while vacationing in upper New York State, our group ordered the Soup du Jour for lunch. It turned out to be a soup that was delicious, attractively presented, and not at all what one would expect to find in that part of the country. All of us enjoyed it so much that we asked the waiter to prevail upon the chef for the recipe. In a few minutes, he returned with a list of ingredients (no proportions) and skimpy directions handwritten on a scrap of paper. Needless to say, it has taken me several tries to get the right taste.

INGREDIENTS

1 package *(16 ounce) dried black-eyed peas*

1 *large white onion, finely chopped*

2 *large carrots, finely chopped and peeled*

1 cup *ground smoked ham*

3 *stalks celery, finely chopped*

2 *cloves garlic, minced*

1 cup *Burgundy wine (red)*

1 teaspoon *salt*

½ teaspoon *pepper*

½ teaspoon *ground coriander, to taste*

1 quart *chicken stock*

Salsa

Sour cream

Green onions, chopped

DIRECTIONS

Soak peas overnight in water to cover. Change water and cook 1 hour. Sauté onion, carrots, ham, celery, and garlic until softened. Add wine. Add peas, salt, pepper, coriander, and stock. Simmer about 1 hour until peas are mushy. Purée, if desired. Thin with stock, if necessary. Serve hot. Top with a tablespoon of salsa, a teaspoon of sour cream, and a sprinkle of chopped green onions. **Serves 6 to 8.**

❧ *Serve this hearty, winter dish with grilled-cheese sandwiches, dill pickles, olives, make-your-own-sundaes, and cookies for a complete, easy, and satisfying lunch.*

Testing Notes: *Use finely diced (not ground) ham and fresh chopped tomatoes.*

Trish Ballard—Atlanta, GA
Donation to: Scottish Rite Hospital for Crippled Children, Inc., Atlanta, GA

Brownwood Texas Black Bean Soup

This was served at a dinner party on my first visit to Brownwood, Texas. A winner!

INGREDIENTS

- **2 pounds** *black beans*
- **2 quarts** *chicken stock (or canned broth)*
- **½ pound** *bacon, chopped*
- **1** *large onion, chopped*
- **1** *large green bell pepper, chopped*
- **1 ounce** *olive oil*
- **1 teaspoon** *oregano*
- **1** *clove garlic*
- **1½ teaspoons** *cumin*
- **1 ounce** *red-wine vinegar*

DIRECTIONS

Wash and soak beans overnight in water to cover. Drain beans; add chicken stock and bacon to beans. Bring to boil; simmer 2 hours until beans are tender. (Add water as needed.) Sauté onion and bell pepper in olive oil; add to the bean mixture. Add oregano, garlic, cumin, and vinegar. Cook 1 to 1½ hours. May be served over cooked rice in soup mugs. **Serves 6 to 8.**

❧ *Offer chopped onions, grated Cheddar cheese, and sour cream for toppings. Serve with jalapeño cheese bread or garlic bread.*

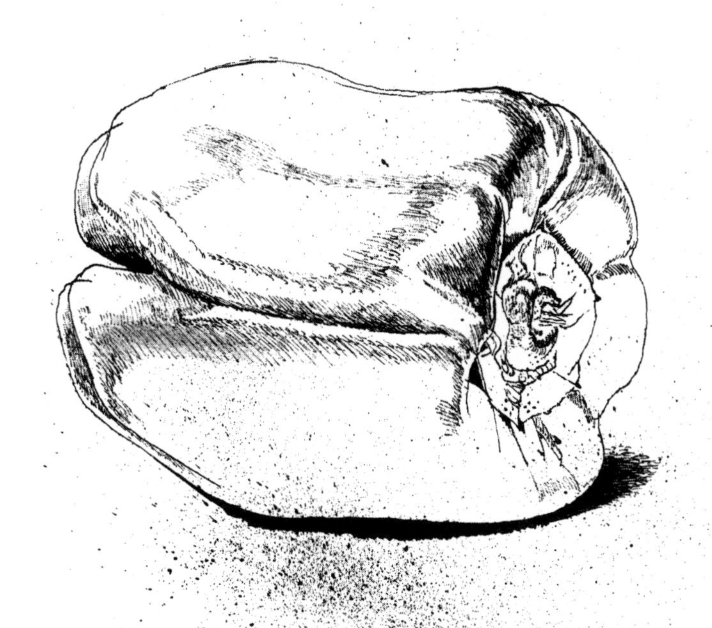

Nancy Lasser—Winnetka, IL
Donation to: Alzheimer's Association, Inc., Chicago, IL

Lentil Soup Supreme

This is based on a recipe from *Gourmet Magazine.* I changed it to suit my family and used ingredients that I usually have on hand.

INGREDIENTS

1 ½ cups *chopped onions*
1 ½ cups *chopped celery*
6 *cloves garlic, minced*
2 tablespoons *olive oil*
3 cans *(28 ounces each) tomatoes*
½ teaspoon *pepper*
1 ½ teaspoons *oregano*
12 cups *water*
12 *beef bouillon cubes*
1 package *(16 ounce) washed lentils*
Parmesan cheese, freshly grated

DIRECTIONS

Sauté onions, celery, and garlic in olive oil in a stockpot 5 minutes until tender. Drain and chop tomatoes, reserving liquid. Add tomato liquid, tomatoes, pepper, and oregano to the stockpot. Simmer 5 minutes. Add water, bouillon cubes, and lentils. Cover and simmer 40 minutes. Sprinkle Parmesan cheese on top of each serving. **Serves 14 to 16.**

❧ *This tastes supremely good with garlic bread and a salad, or before any meal.*

Neiman Marcus—THE MERMAID BARSM NorthPark, Dallas
Donation to: combined charities

Chili con Queso Soup (Tortilla)

Some of the regulars know it as "tortilla soup." It's so popular Maureen Hagerty, Restaurant General Manager, makes sure it's on the menu every Saturday.

INGREDIENTS

1 *large onion, finely chopped*

6 tablespoons *unsalted butter*

3 cans *(4 ounces each) mild green chiles, drained, seeded, and finely chopped*

4 cans *(14½ ounces each) plum tomatoes, drained, seeded, and finely chopped*

4 packages *(3 ounces each) cream cheese, cut into bits*

2 cans *(14½ ounces each) chicken broth*

3 cups *half-and-half*

8 teaspoons *fresh lemon juice, or to taste*

Cayenne, to taste

Salt, to taste

Julienned tortilla strips, finely chopped

Green onions, chopped

Monterey jack cheese, grated

DIRECTIONS

Cook onion in butter over moderately-low heat in a saucepan, stirring occasionally until onion is softened. Add chiles and tomatoes. Cook mixture 8 to 10 minutes over moderate heat until liquid evaporates, stirring occasionally. Stir in cream cheese. Maintain moderate-to-low heat until cheese melts. Stir in chicken broth, half-and-half, lemon juice, cayenne, and salt. Heat soup over moderate heat until hot, but do not boil. Sprinkle tortilla strips, green onions, and Monterey jack cheese over individual servings. **Makes 8 cups.**

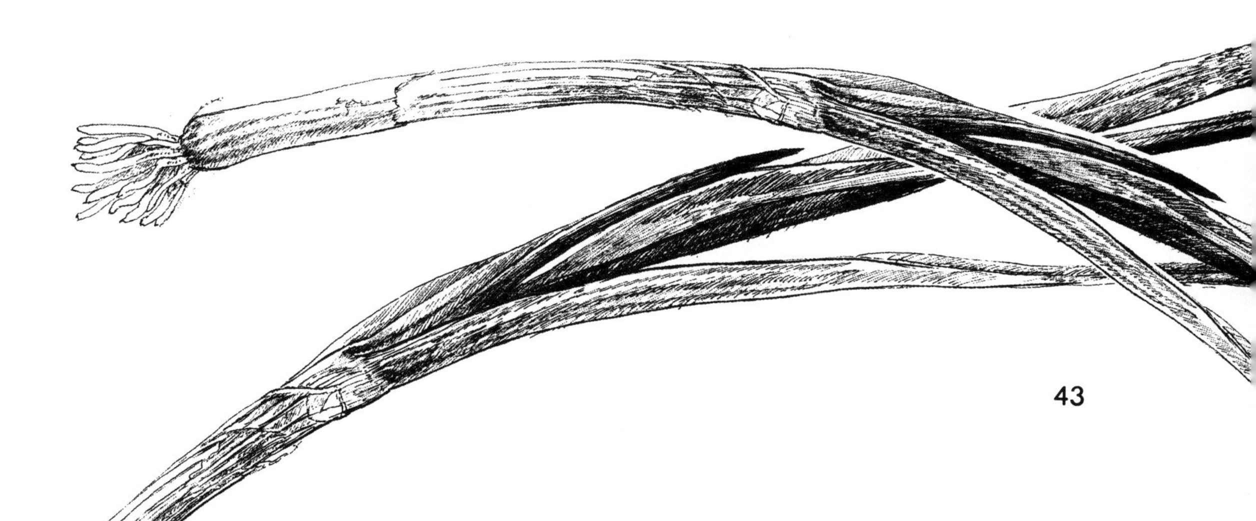

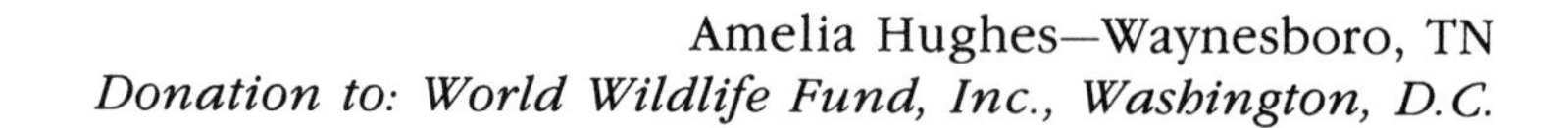

Amelia Hughes—Waynesboro, TN
Donation to: World Wildlife Fund, Inc., Washington, D.C.

Chili Bean Soup

This is an easy-to-prepare recipe, which I recently concocted. It's a soup with lots of flavor, yet low in fat, and a wonderful substitute for chili.

INGREDIENTS

1 package *(12 ounce) dried red kidney beans*

3 cans *(14½ ounces each) chicken stock*

½ cup *water*

2 *onions, chopped*

2 *cloves garlic, minced*

1 tablespoon *olive oil*

1 *red bell pepper, chopped*

1 *green bell pepper, chopped*

2 cans *(28 ounces each) tomatoes*

2 tablespoons *white-wine vinegar*

1½ tablespoons *chili powder*

¼ teaspoon *cumin powder*

1 *bay leaf*

Pinch of thyme

Salt and black pepper, to taste

Red-pepper flakes, to taste

Sour cream

Chives, chopped

DIRECTIONS

Wash and soak beans overnight in water to cover. Drain beans; add chicken stock and ½ cup water to beans. Simmer 2 hours until tender. Sauté onions and garlic in olive oil until softened. Add bell peppers; sauté 2 minutes. Add this mixture to soup pot. Add remaining ingredients, except sour cream and chives, and simmer 1½ to 2 hours. Remove from heat and cool slightly. Remove bay leaf. Purée in batches in blender. Reheat. Thin with a little chicken stock, if necessary. Serve in soup bowls; garnish with sour cream and chives. **Serves 6.**

❧ *Serve with avocado salad and a warm loaf of crusty French bread.*

Testing Notes: *Also, good over white rice. Recommend using 4 cups chicken stock.*

Nancy Harrell—Houston, TX
Donation to: Texas Heart Institute, Houston, TX

Creole Corn Chowder

Some recipes are passed down through family, but some are passed through good friends.

INGREDIENTS

2 cups *finely diced bacon*
2 cups *finely diced onion*
2 cups *finely diced green bell pepper*
2 cups *finely diced red bell pepper*
2 cups *finely diced ham*
4 cups *corn*
3 cups *diced tomatoes*
½ cup *tomato juice*
1 teaspoon *oregano*
1 teaspoon *basil*
1 teaspoon *thyme leaves*
2 teaspoons *crushed red pepper*
1 teaspoon *black pepper*
2 cups *milk*
¼ cup *flour*
¼ cup *oil*
2 cups *cream*

DIRECTIONS

Sauté bacon in heavy pan until crisp. Add onion and bell peppers; cook until limp. Add ham, corn, tomatoes, tomato juice, and seasonings. Simmer 30 minutes. Bring milk to boil in a saucepan. Make a roux with the flour and oil in another saucepan. Add roux to corn mixture and mix well. Add milk. Simmer 15 to 20 minutes. When ready to serve, add cream and cook until hot. **Serves 10 to 12.** This recipe can easily be cut in half.

❧ *Serve with boiled lobster or any fish entrée.*

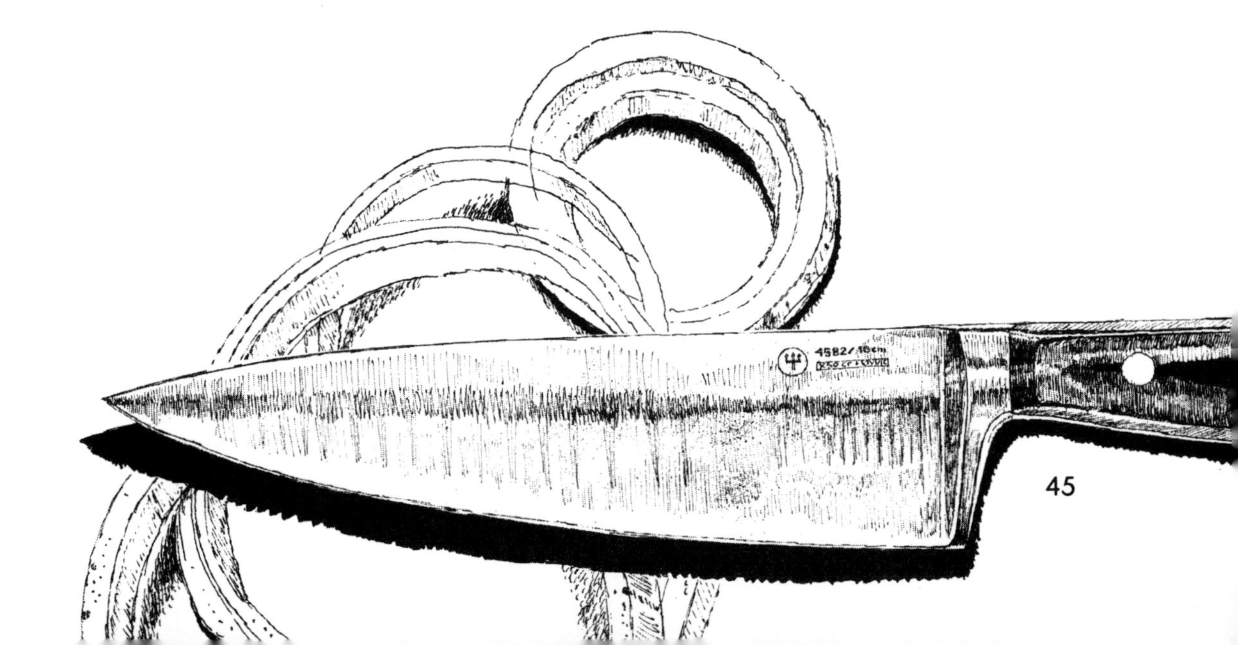

Susan Z. Diamond—Melrose Park, IL
Donation to: Lyric Opera of Chicago, Chicago, IL

Shrimp Gumbo

My creation is made up of bits and pieces from a number of gumbo recipes.

INGREDIENTS

- **3** *strips bacon*
- **3 tablespoons** *flour*
- **1¾ pounds** *(approximately) fresh or frozen okra, sliced*
- **1** *large onion, chopped*
- **1** *clove garlic, minced*
- **2 cups** *tomato juice*
- **1 can** *(16 ounce) Italian-style tomatoes, chopped*
- **4 cups** *water*
- **3-4** *bay leaves*
- **1 teaspoon** *salt*
- **¼-½ teaspoon** *crushed red pepper*
- **2 tablespoons** *Worcestershire sauce*
- **1 tablespoon** *pickling spice*
- **¼-½ teaspoon** *lemon pepper*
- **1 teaspoon** *thyme*
- **½ teaspoon** *dried sweet chile pepper*
- **½ cup** *chopped green bell pepper*
- **2** *stalks celery, chopped*
- **2 pounds** *raw shrimp, cleaned*

DIRECTIONS

Fry bacon in large pot; remove bacon and set aside. Stir flour into bacon grease and cook, stirring until light brown. Add okra, onion, and garlic. Cook until light brown. Add everything else, except shrimp and cooked bacon. Simmer 1 to 2 hours. Add shrimp and crumbled bacon. Cook until shrimp curl and turn pink. **Serves 6 to 8.**

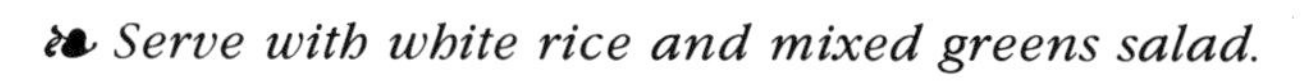

❧ *Serve with white rice and mixed greens salad.*

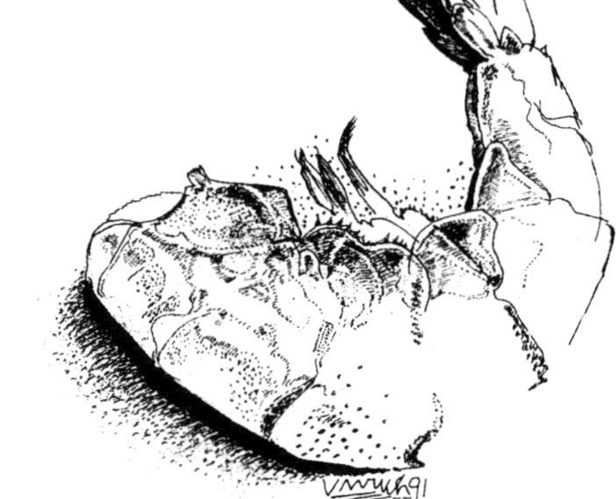

Bonnie Baker—Playa del Rey, CA
Donation to: Gymnastics Olympica USA, Inc., Van Nuys, CA

Gazpacho de Blanco

Fabulous in summer. I received this recipe from my sister in Texas, and she would serve it on hot evenings. Everybody flips over it.

INGREDIENTS

- **3** *medium-sized cucumbers, peeled*
- **3 cups** *CAMPBELL'S® chicken broth*
- **1** *clove garlic, minced*
- **3 tablespoons** *white vinegar*
- **1 tablespoon** *salt*
- **2 cups** *sour cream*
- *Tomatoes, chopped*
- *Scallions, sliced*
- *Fresh parsley, chopped*
- *Almonds, dry-roasted*
- *Avocados, peeled and chopped*
- *Cilantro (optional)*

DIRECTIONS

Blend cucumbers, broth, and garlic in blender or food processor. Add vinegar, salt, and sour cream. Refrigerate 24 hours. Serve in chilled bowls and garnish with tomatoes, scallions, parsley, almonds, avocados, and cilantro. May be made 2 to 3 days in advance of party. **Serves 8.**

Testing Notes: *Use ½ tablespoon salt instead of 1 tablespoon.*

Ellen Rosenbach—N. Palm Beach, FL
Donation to: American Cancer Society, Inc., N. Palm Beach, FL

Cece's Vegetable Soup

This is my aunt's recipe for an all-natural, no-fat, all-vegetable soup. Great for dieters!

INGREDIENTS

1 cup *dried baby lima beans*

1 cup *marrow beans (or navy, pinto, or any interesting combination of beans)*

5 *onions (3 whole and 2 chopped)*

3 *stalks celery*

4-5 *carrots, thinly sliced*

Handful of washed barley

Handful of split peas

Handful of lentils

1 can *(14½ ounce) stewed tomatoes*

Salt and pepper, to taste

Basil leaves, to taste

Parsley, to taste

Garlic powder, to taste

DIRECTIONS

Boil the lima beans and marrow beans in a large pot, according to package directions. In another large pot, cook remaining ingredients in water to cover. When lima and marrow beans are soft and thick, remove from heat and cool. Purée 75 percent of the beans in a blender, and add to the other pot to thicken the soup. For variety, add one of the following on top before serving: grated Parmesan cheese, grilled onions, or sautéed mushrooms. **Serves 12.**

❧ *Serve with French bread and salad.*

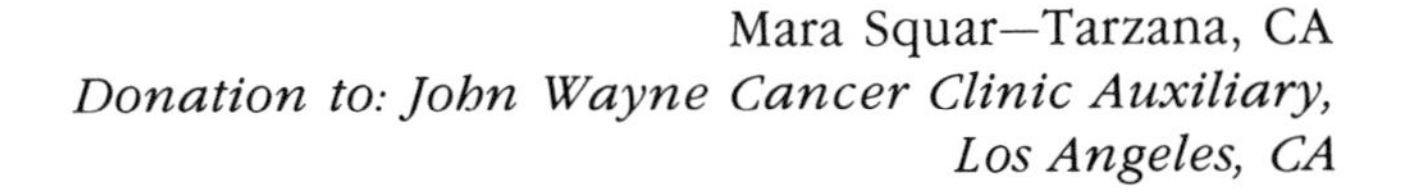

Mara Squar—Tarzana, CA
Donation to: John Wayne Cancer Clinic Auxiliary, Los Angeles, CA

Minestrone

I have been making and giving out this recipe for at least a dozen years. I found the original in a magazine, and have since adapted it to my taste. I'm sure everyone to whom I give the recipe changes it a little. As with any great soup, the recipe is a base to work from—just use a little imagination.

INGREDIENTS

½ pound *Italian sweet sausage*

½ pound *Italian hot sausage*

3 tablespoons *very good quality olive oil*

3 *large onions, diced*

3 *cloves garlic, finely minced*

1 *bunch carrots, diced*

2 teaspoons *basil*

2-3 *zucchini, sliced*

1 can *(28 ounce) Italian-style tomatoes, including liquid*

2 cans *(10 ounces each) beef bouillon*

1 *small head cabbage, finely shredded*

Salt and pepper, to taste

1 can *(16 ounce) white kidney beans, including liquid*

1 can *(16 ounce) red kidney beans, including liquid*

½ cup *rice*

Parmesan cheese, freshly grated

Fresh parsley, chopped

DIRECTIONS

In a large stockpot, brown and scramble both sausages in olive oil. Add onions, garlic, carrots, and basil; cook 5 minutes. Add zucchini, tomatoes (with liquid), bouillon, cabbage, salt, and pepper. Bring to boil; reduce heat, cover, and simmer 1 hour. Add beans (with liquid) and rice. Cook 20 minutes. For a thinner broth, add more bouillon. Serve, topped with Parmesan cheese and parsley. The soup may be made ahead and reheated. It may also be frozen, but the texture changes a bit.
Serves 8 to 10.

❧ *Serve with hot, crusty Italian bread.*

Irene Kuzyk—Kew Gardens, NY
Donation to: Cancer Research Institute, Inc., New York, NY

Curried Carrot Soup

My friend gave me this recipe in the summer as a great, refreshing start to a meal. It may be served cold or hot.

INGREDIENTS

1 *onion, coarsely chopped*
2 tablespoons *butter*
4-6 *medium-sized carrots, diced*
4 cups *chicken stock*
¼ teaspoon *lemon peel*
1 teaspoon *sugar*
½ teaspoon *salt*
⅛ teaspoon *white pepper*
1 teaspoon *curry*
3 tablespoons *sherry (optional)*
Sour cream
Dill

DIRECTIONS

Sauté onions until translucent. Add all ingredients, except sherry, sour cream, and dill. Cover and simmer until carrots are cooked, but not mushy. Cool. Put in blender; blend until smooth. Add sherry and chill. Before serving, garnish with a dollop of sour cream and sprinkle of dill. **Serves 4 to 6.**

Testing Notes: *Add an additional cup of chicken stock.*

Mrs. Eustace K. Shaw—Newton, IA
Donation to: Iowa Natural Heritage Foundation, Des Moines, IA

Green and Gold Soup

I created this soup and usually serve it to my bridge club.

INGREDIENTS

2 pounds *carrots*
1¼ pounds *potatoes*
1 *medium-sized onion*
4 cans *(10½ ounces each) chicken broth, or 5¼ cups homemade*
1½ cans *water (almost 2 cups)*
2 cups *half-and-half*
Salt, to taste
Pepper, to taste
Nutmeg, to taste
¾ cup *chopped raw spinach*

DIRECTIONS

Slice carrots, potatoes, and onion in food processor. Cook in broth and water. Purée in food processor. Season with salt, pepper, and nutmeg. Purée spinach with 1 cup soup. Add to rest of soup. **Serves 12 to 14.**

Serve with a green salad, cheese wafers, wine, and dessert.

Reidun V. Gann—Beverly Hills, CA
Donation to: American Cancer Society, Inc., Beverly Hills, CA

Black Forest Potato Soup

This recipe was given to me by my husband's aunt. She was born in the Black Forest, and came to Chicago, Illinois, as a young girl. There was not much money in the family at that time, so they used vegetables from the farm for all meals. This aunt was the best cook, and I loved to be invited to her house.

INGREDIENTS

1 ½ cups *thinly sliced leeks, washed*

1 ¼ cups *thinly sliced onions*

4 tablespoons *unsalted butter*

2½ tablespoons *flour*

5-6 cups *chicken stock (or canned broth)*

1 ½ pounds *potatoes, peeled and thinly sliced*

Sour cream, to taste (optional)

Salt and pepper, to taste

Toasted bread crumbs or croutons

DIRECTIONS

Put leeks and onions in a large saucepan with butter. Cover with buttered wax paper to "sweat," or braise, the vegetables. Place a lid on the saucepan and cook over medium heat until very soft. Discard paper, stir in flour, and cook about 4 minutes. Add chicken stock and whisk hard. Add potatoes. Bring to boil, cover, and simmer 30 minutes. The potatoes should be soft. Purée soup in blender or food processor. Transfer back to saucepan. Whisk in sour cream, salt, and pepper. Simmer until heated. Do not boil. A few drops of MAGGI® seasoning will also enhance the flavor of this soup, but is not necessary. Sprinkle bread crumbs or croutons on top when served.
Serves 8.

❧ *Serve a good, fresh bread.*

Testing Notes: *Recommend only a minimum amount of sour cream, perhaps a little bacon. Sweating vegetables is not necessary.*

Sandra Krusoff—Sherman Oaks, CA
Donation to: World Wildlife Fund, Inc., Washington, D.C.

Wild Rice Soup

INGREDIENTS

1 ⅓ cups *wild rice*
2 cups *salted water*
2 *large leeks, chopped including green tops*
8 *large mushrooms, sliced*
½ cup *butter or margarine*
1 cup *flour*
8 cups *hot chicken broth*
Salt, to taste
Pepper, to taste
1 cup *half-and-half*

DIRECTIONS

Wash wild rice thoroughly. Place in a heavy saucepan with salted water. Bring to boil. Cover and simmer 45 minutes until tender, but not mushy. Uncover. Fluff with fork. Simmer 5 minutes. Drain excess liquid. Sauté leeks and mushrooms in butter 3 minutes until softened. Sprinkle in the flour, stirring and cooking until flour is cooked but not browned. Add chicken broth slowly, stirring until flour mixture is well blended. Add rice, season to taste, and heat thoroughly. Stir in half-and-half and heat gently. Do not boil. **Serves 12.**

❧ *Serve with crusty bread, a glass of wine, and a roaring fire.*

Testing Notes: *Add 1 cup of wine and serve with Parmesan cheese toast.*

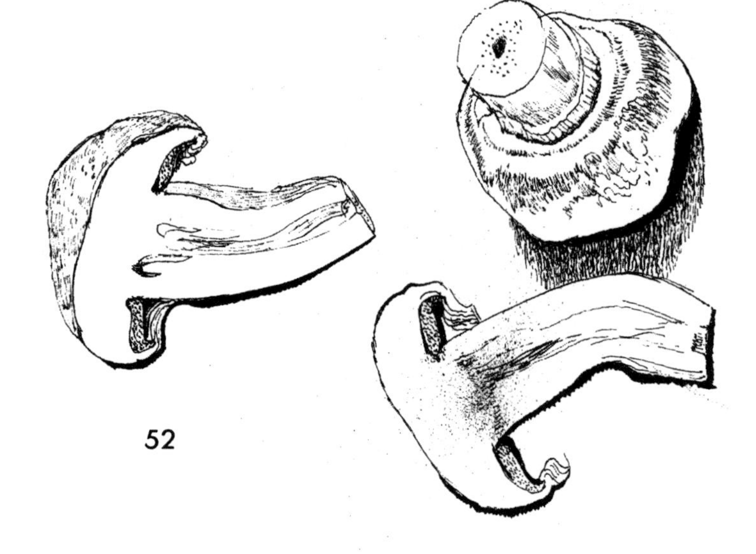

Mrs. Robert Zarchen—Miami, FL
Donation to: American Heart Association, Inc., Miami, FL

Nanny's Chicken Soup

This is from my grandmother, Nanny Neiditch, the most wonderful cook ever!

INGREDIENTS

2 quarts *chicken broth*
1 *whole chicken breast with ribs*
4 *stalks celery with leaves, cut into 4-inch pieces*
4 *carrots, peeled and halved*
4 *parsnips, peeled and halved*
½ *large bunch dill*
½ *large bunch parsley*
1 *large yellow onion (or 2 small)*
Salt and pepper, to taste

DIRECTIONS

Put all ingredients in a large stockpot; bring to boil. Turn down heat and simmer 2 hours until all vegetables are soft. Remove chicken. Remove skin and remove bones. Place chicken and vegetable mixture in small batches in the CUISINART® and purée. Return everything to the stock; stir and season with with salt and pepper. **Serves 8 to 10.**

❧ *My grandmother sometimes served this meal-in-a-bowl with matzo balls or homemade croutons, freshly baked challah, pumpernickel rolls, and salad.*

Mrs. Claude R. Erickson—Livingston, MT
Donation to: Livingston Memorial Hospital League, Livingston, MT

Turkey Barley Soup

This recipe is from my grandmother, a Montana pioneer in the late 1800s.

INGREDIENTS

- **1** *meaty turkey carcass from a 16-pound bird*
- **9** *stalks celery, cut into ½-inch-wide pieces*
- **1½ pounds** *carrots, peeled, halved lengthwise, and cut into 1-inch-wide pieces*
- **2** *medium-sized onions, peeled and cut into ½-inch-thick rounds*
- **6** *large cloves garlic, peeled and chopped*
- **1 pound** *parsnips, peeled and cut into ½-inch-thick rounds*
- **2 cups** *chopped dill*
- **1 cup** *chopped parsley*
- **1 tablespoon** *salt*
- **2 teaspoons** *ground pepper*
- **10 quarts** *water*
- **1 cup** *barley*

DIRECTIONS

Place turkey carcass, vegetables, 1 cup dill, seasonings, and water in a large stockpot. Bring to boil, reduce heat, and simmer 3 hours. Skim foam, as it cooks. Remove carcass; cool and shred meat. Return meat to stockpot; add barley. Simmer 40 minutes. Add remaining dill, stir, and serve hot. This may be frozen, too. **Serves 8, generously.**

❧ *Serve with hot bread.*

CHAPTER THREE

Salads

Did you know salads comprise 65 percent of the choices on menus in seated restaurants today? That's because they've become a lot more than just lettuce. With the addition of protein in the form of beans, cheese, eggs, or meat, some salads are a whole meal. And, the most innovative of the lot mix icy-cold greens with warm slices of grilled meats. Of course, greens alone can be interesting with the proliferation of various lettuces that used to be available only to California salad makers.

Mrs. J. A. Cronic—Griffin, GA

Donation to: National Wildlife Federation, Washington, D.C.

Gourmet Spinach Salad with Sweet-and-Sour Dressing

My daughter serves this at gourmet club dinners for the University of South Carolina faculty members.

INGREDIENTS

- **4 packages** *raw spinach*
- **1½ cups** *WESSON® oil*
- **1 cup** *HEINZ® salad vinegar or malt vinegar*
- **1 cup** *sugar*
- **1 cup** *ketchup*
- **1 teaspoon** *salt*
- **1 package** *GOOD SEASONS® Italian salad dressing*
- **10** *hard-cooked eggs, chopped*
- **1 pound** *bacon, fried crisp*
- **1** *large red onion, sliced into rings*

DIRECTIONS

Wash spinach and dry thoroughly between layers of paper towels. Refrigerate for desired crispness. Mix oil, vinegar, sugar, ketchup, salt, and dry salad dressing in a bowl. Refrigerate. Prepare eggs, bacon, and onion; toss with spinach. Garnish with a few onion rings. Pour sweet-and-sour dressing over the top before serving. **Serves 10 to 12.**

❧ *Serve with beef stroganoff.*

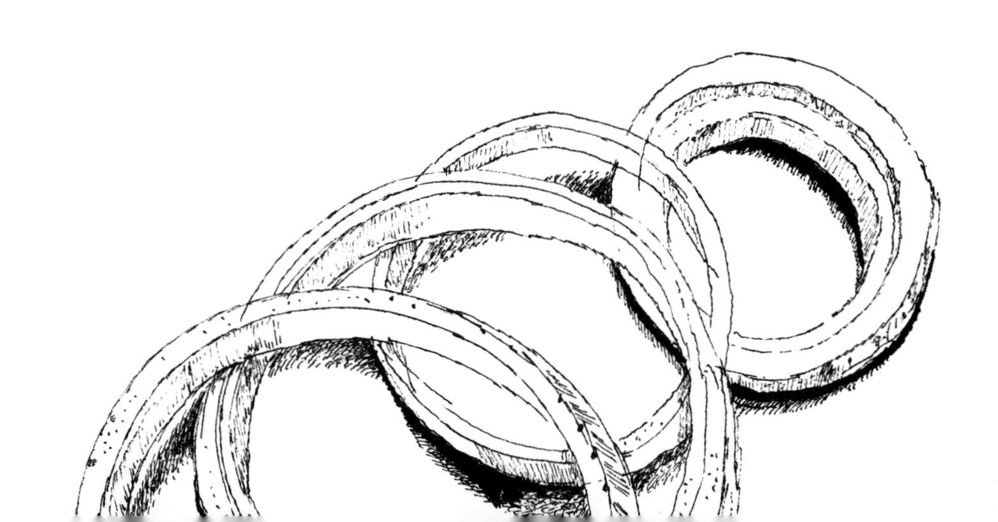

Salad Broccoli with Sour Cream

Not to name names, but those who have publicly sworn off broccoli might be tempted.

INGREDIENTS

2 pounds *fresh broccoli (or two 10-ounce packages frozen broccoli spears)*

3/4 teaspoon *salt*

1 cup *sour cream*

2 tablespoons *tomato paste*

1/4 teaspoon *dry basil*

2 teaspoons *minced drained capers*

DIRECTIONS

Discard some of the larger leaves and a little of the stalk from the fresh broccoli. Cook broccoli, covered, 10 to 15 minutes in 1 inch of boiling, salted water. (Cook frozen broccoli according to package directions.) Drain and refrigerate. Mix salt, sour cream, tomato paste, basil, and capers; chill. Serve sauce over cold, cooked broccoli. **Serves 8.**

Christine Fluor—Newport Beach, CA
Donation to: South Coast Medical Center, South Laguna, CA

Harvest Salad

I needed a quick salad for an impromptu dinner. The dining table centerpiece of a bowl of autumn fruits and nuts provided an ideal Harvest Salad.

INGREDIENTS

- **2** *bunches watercress, stems removed*
- **1** *pomegranate*
- **1** *red apple, cored and cut into bite-sized pieces*
- **1** *green apple, cored and cut into bite-sized pieces*
- **1** *yellow pear, cored and cut into bite-sized pieces*
- **1** *red pear, cored and cut into bite-sized pieces*
- **½ cup** *chopped walnuts*
- **4 teaspoons** *lemon juice*
- **2 teaspoons** *honey*
- **¼ cup** *finely chopped crystallized ginger*

DIRECTIONS

Rinse watercress and pat dry. Remove pomegranate seeds, discarding skin and white pulp. The removal of pomegranate seeds takes a little patience. Wear an apron and be prepared for slightly brown fingers, as the juice stains. (Surgical gloves, available at drugstores, may be used.) Do not be discouraged. The beauty and refreshing flavor of this fruit are well-worth the effort. (If necessary, ½ cup finely chopped cranberries may be substituted.) Place pomegranate seeds in a medium-sized bowl and gently stir in apples, pears, and walnuts. In a separate bowl, mix lemon juice and honey until combined. Add ginger and stir. Pour honey dressing over fruit mixture. Chill up to 2 hours. Serve salad on beds of watercress on individual salad plates. **Serves 6.**

❧ *It's especially nice served with holiday goose, chicken, or other poultry.*

Testing Notes: *Remember, pomegranates are available only in autumn.*

Princess Marie-Blanche de Broglie—Founder, Princess Ere 2001 Cooking School Paris, France

Donation to: combined charities

Fromage de Chevre Chaud aux Pommes

INGREDIENTS

3 *Granny Smith apples*

3 *crotins de Chavignol*

2 teaspoons *oil*

8 slices *pain grille*

3 tablespoons *crème fraîche, or heavy cream*

1 teaspoon *TABASCO® sauce*

8 *pieces fresh thyme*

DIRECTIONS

Chavignol is a creamy, semi-aged goat cheese sold in small, round discs, measuring about 2 inches in diameter and 2 inches in height. If not available, choose any number of other kinds of fresh goat cheese. Prepare the *pain grille* (crisp toast) by toasting crustless, thick slices of white bread under the broiler. Set aside. Preheat oven to 375°. Peel and core apples. Slice each into 4 thick, horizontal slices, ½-to ¾-inch-thick. Lightly coat a baking sheet with oil, arrange the *pain grille* on the baking sheet, and top each with an apple slice, followed by a cheese slice. Mix TABASCO® with cream and spoon a little over the top of each cheese slice. Bake 10 minutes until cheese is soft, but not melted. Sprinkle lightly with thyme and serve warm. This warm goat cheese with apples is a pleasant alternative to the hot goat cheese salad that is ubiquitous on French menus. **Serves 4.**

❧ *Serve with a green salad.*

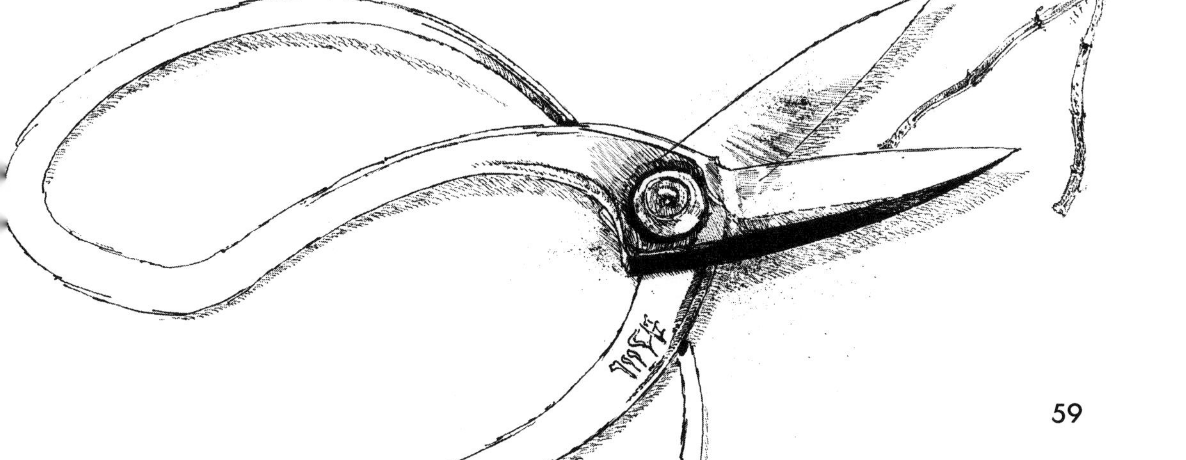

Nicki Mendelson—Boca Raton, FL
Donation to: American Cancer Society, Inc., Boca Raton, FL

Layered Southwestern Salad

This is a great layered salad for entertaining outdoors or poolside. It's tasty, as well as colorful.

INGREDIENTS

- **1 cup** *black beans*
- **1 cup** *salsa (I like DESERT ROSE®, spiced medium-hot)*
- **3 tablespoons** *fresh lime juice*
- **2 tablespoons** *olive oil*
- **½ teaspoon** *salt*
- **2** *medium-sized green onions, minced*
- **1** *medium-sized jalapeño pepper,seeded and minced*
- **1** *large yellow bell pepper, seeded and cut into ½-inch cubes*
- **1** *large green bell pepper, seeded and cut into ½-inch cubes*
- **2 cups** *cubed, smoked turkey (about 1 pound)*
- **1 cup** *diced Monterey jack cheese*
- **2 cups** *peeled, diced jicama (about 1 pound)*
- **4** *medium-sized plum tomatoes, sliced*
- **1 cup** *plain low-fat yogurt*
- **¼ cup** *light mayonnaise*
- **½ teaspoon** *ground cumin*
- **½ teaspoon** *red-hot pepper sauce*
- **1 can** *(4¼ ounce) black olives, chopped*
- **½** *lime, cut into slices*

DIRECTIONS

Cover beans in 3 times their amount of boiling water and soak 1 hour. Drain and combine in large saucepan with 4 cups water; heat to boil. Reduce heat; cook 1 hour until tender. Drain and cool. Combine salsa, lime juice, olive oil, and salt in food processor. Process until blended. Stir 4 tablespoons of this dressing into the cooled beans; add green onions and jalapeño. Set aside. Combine bell peppers with 2 tablespoons of salsa dressing. Set aside. Layer salad in a deep, clear bowl in this order: beans, turkey, cheese, peppers, and jicama. Drizzle with remaining dressing, and lay sliced tomatoes across the top. Cover and refrigerate 6 hours or overnight. Stir yogurt, mayonnaise, cumin, and hot sauce until well-blended. Cover and refrigerate. Remove salad from refrigerator 20 minutes before serving. Spoon yogurt dressing over salad, sprinkle with black olives, and garnish with lime slices. **Serves 10.**

Serve with pitchers of iced tea and margaritas and bowls of regular or blue corn chips.

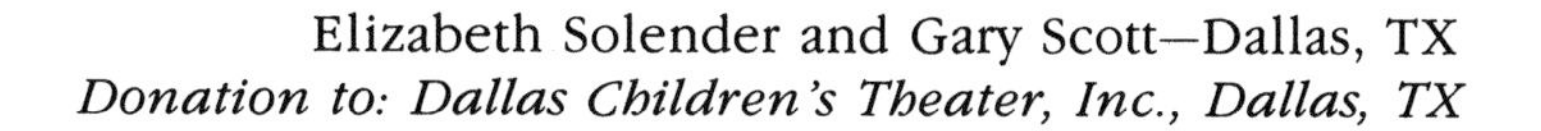

Elizabeth Solender and Gary Scott—Dallas, TX
Donation to: Dallas Children's Theater, Inc., Dallas, TX

Fontina Cheese and Sweet Red Pepper Salad

This version is based on a recipe in the July, 1978, issue of *BON APPÉTIT*. We discovered a dramatic difference in the salad when we used Italian fontina cheese and when we used Danish fontina cheese. The Italian is better for antipasto, and the Danish cheese is better for salad.

INGREDIENTS

2 tablespoons *red-wine vinegar*

2 teaspoons *Dijon-style mustard*

1/8 teaspoon *freshly ground pepper*

6 tablespoons *olive oil*

1 *head iceberg lettuce, torn into bite-sized pieces*

1 *small bunch green onions, finely sliced*

1/4 cup *chopped fresh chives*

1/4 cup *diced celery*

4-5 *anchovy strips, diced*

4 ounces *Italian fontina cheese, cubed (approximately 1 cup)*

1 jar *(8 ounce) roasted, sweet red peppers, cut into 1/4-inch-wide slices*

DIRECTIONS

Make a vinaigrette dressing by combining first 3 ingredients in a small bowl and adding oil gradually. Beat (or whisk) constantly until emulsified. In a large bowl, toss lettuce with onions, chives, celery, anchovies, and vinaigrette dressing. Place equal portions of this mixture on each salad plate. Place cheese cubes on top of the salad in the center. (You may substitute Danish fontina cheese for a slightly different, more mild flavor.) Arrange pepper slices around the cheese. **Serves 6.**

❧ *We enjoy this dish with breaded red snapper with a tomato sauce.*

Neiman Marcus—THE ZODIAC® Michigan Avenue, Chicago
Donation to: combined charities

Shanghai Salad

"This is one of the most popular daily specials on the menu," says Regional Food Supervisor, Michael Grasso.

INGREDIENTS

- **8 ounces** *mayonnaise*
- **2 ounces** *pommery mustard*
- **2 teaspoons** *superfine sugar*
- **2 teaspoons** *Worcestershire sauce*
- **4 teaspoons** *sesame seeds*
- **10 ounces** *cooked chicken breast meat, cut into ½-inch cubes*
- **2 ounces** *bean sprouts*
- **2 ounces** *diced scallions, green part only*
- **1 ounce** *finely diced onions*
- **3 ounces** *sliced water chestnuts*
- **3 ounces** *sliced bamboo shoots*
- **5 ounces** *shredded red cabbage*
- **20 pieces** *julienned red bell pepper*
- **20 pieces** *julienned green bell pepper*
- **20 pieces** *julienned carrots*
- **20 pieces** *julienned zucchini*
- **20 pieces** *blanched snow peas*
- **20 pieces** *julienned yellow squash*
- **4 pieces** *blanched broccoli florets*
- **4 pieces** *blanched cauliflower florets*
- **8 pieces** *leaf lettuce*
- *Alfalfa sprouts*

DIRECTIONS

Combine mayonnaise, mustard, sugar, Worcestershire sauce, and sesame seeds thoroughly in a small bowl. Combine chicken, bean sprouts, scallions, onions, water chestnuts, and bamboo shoots in a large mixing bowl. Add mayonnaise dressing and toss well. Set aside. Arrange leaf lettuce on each salad plate. Scoop 8 ounces of chicken salad onto center of each plate. Around that, arrange 1 ounce of red cabbage, 5 pieces each of the peppers, squashes, and snow peas; and 1 floret each of broccoli and cauliflower. Garnish with small pinch of alfalfa sprouts on top. Serve a dressing for the vegetables. **Serves 4.**

Dorothy Longoria—Laredo, TX
Donation to: Cancer Patients Services, Inc., Laredo, TX

Rice, Avocado, and Corn Salad

As a senior citizen trying to cut out unhealthy foods, I have really tried to switch to a macrobiotic diet, which is basically grains and vegetables. I improvised on this "practically macrobiotic" rice salad. All my junk-food friends love it.

INGREDIENTS

- **3 cups** *cooked brown rice*
- **1** *avocado*
- **2** *ears of corn, cooked*
- **½ cup** *toasted almonds*
- **1** *onion, finely chopped*
- **1 teaspoon** *lemon juice*
- **1 teaspoon** *olive oil*
- **1 teaspoon** *brown-rice vinegar*
- **1 teaspoon** *tamari soy sauce*
- **4** *young lettuce leaves, washed and finely sliced*

DIRECTIONS

Cook brown rice, according to package directions. Peel and pit avocado; slice and mash with the rice. Scrape corn from the cob and add to the mixture. Add almonds and onion. Mix lemon juice, oil, vinegar, and tamari sauce. Pour over salad. Refrigerate. Serve chilled over lettuce. **Serves 4.**

Norma Sue Davis—Arlington, TX
Donation to: Mission Arlington Health Clinic, Arlington, TX

Garden Salad with Almonds and Oranges

This recipe was given to me by a friend in Colorado, who got it from a friend in Arkansas. It is an unusual green salad. My family loves it!

INGREDIENTS

- **1** *head iceberg lettuce*
- **1** *head romaine lettuce*
- **1 cup** *sliced or slivered almonds*
- **½ cup** *sugar*
- **1 cup** *vegetable oil*
- **¼ cup** *vinegar*
- **1 teaspoon** *salt*
- **1 tablespoon** *parsley flakes*
- *Dash black pepper*
- *Dash red pepper*
- **6** *green onion tops, thinly sliced*
- **1 can** *(22 ounce) mandarin oranges, drained and chilled*

DIRECTIONS

Wash and tear lettuce into bite-sized pieces. Refrigerate. Combine almonds and ¼ cup sugar in saucepan, stirring over medium heat until sugar browns. Cool caramelized almonds on an ungreased cookie sheet. Break into tiny pieces and set aside. Combine oil, vinegar, salt, parsley, black pepper, red pepper, and the remaining sugar in a bowl. Refrigerate. Before serving, combine lettuce, green onions, almonds, and oranges. Toss with desired amount of dressing. **Serves 10.**

❧ *This salad is good with a chicken casserole and warm rolls.*

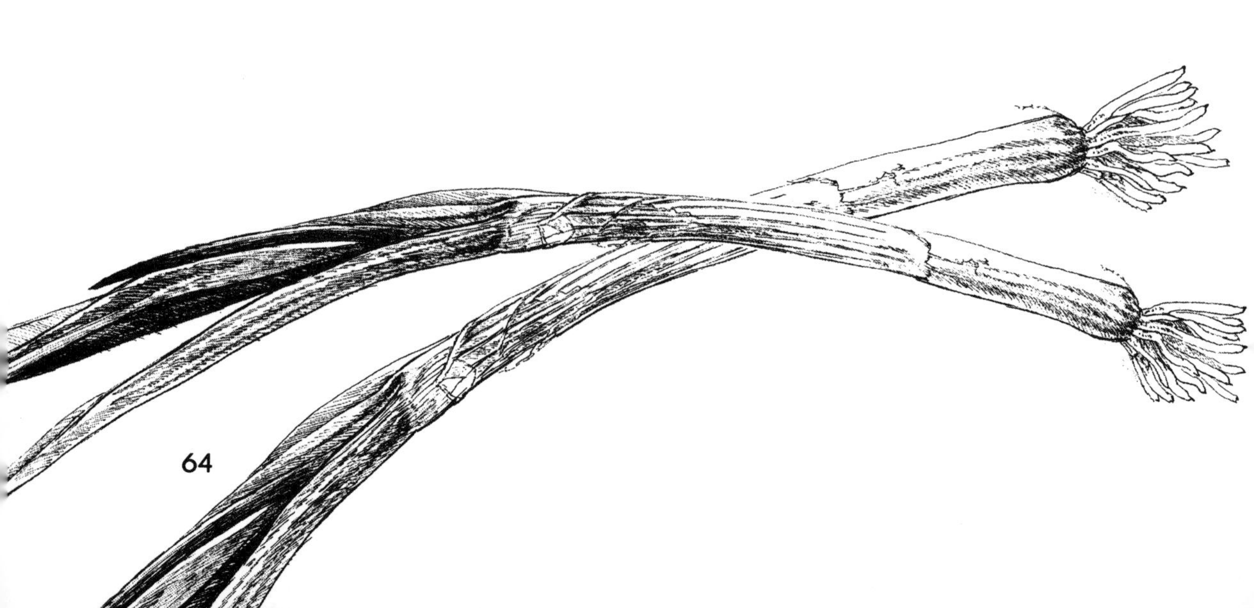

Jody E. White—Atlanta, GA
Donation to: High Museum of Art, Atlanta, GA

Peanut Salad

While traveling in Kenya this past summer, we had lunch on the shore of Lake Naivasha. This salad was served by a wonderful cook, Milcah Hg'ethe.

INGREDIENTS

- **8 ounces** *dry-roasted peanuts, unsalted*
- **2** *medium-sized leeks, finely chopped*
- **2** *heads Boston lettuce*
- **1 heaping tablespoon** *light, plain-Italian dressing*

DIRECTIONS

Combine peanuts and leeks. Arrange on lettuce leaves. Add dressing just before serving. **Serves 4.**

❧ *It's delicious with all meats.*

Neiman Marcus—CLASSIC
Donation to: combined charities

Carrot-Pineapple Salad Mold

Back in the sixties, Thursday night buffets at NM were a family affair, and this salad was on almost every buffet plate.

INGREDIENTS

- **2 packages** *(3 ounces each) lemon-flavored gelatin*
- **2 cups** *boiling water*
- **1 can** *(16 ounce) crushed pineapple, including liquid*
- **1 cup** *grated carrots*
- **1 cup** *grated Cheddar cheese*
- **¾ cup** *chopped pecans*

DIRECTIONS

Dissolve gelatin in boiling water. Drain liquid from canned pineapple and add enough water to liquid to make 2 cups. Stir in the gelatin. Refrigerate until partially congealed. Stir in pineapple, carrots, cheese, and pecans. Pour into a 2½-quart mold or individual molds. Chill until firm. **Serves 12.**

Mrs. A. T. Salmeri—Laguna Beach, CA
Donation to: Hoag Hospital Foundation, Newport Beach, CA

Fatoosh (Lebanese Salad)

Summers were hot in Arizona before air conditioning. Mother would make fatoosh and bring melon, and we'd go to the river for a cool afternoon.

INGREDIENTS

2 *hard-toasted pita bread rounds*

½ *head romaine lettuce*

½ *head iceberg lettuce*

3 *pickling cucumbers, peeled and thinly sliced*

4 *ripe tomatoes, chopped*

1 cup *diced fresh mint*

4 *green onions, diced*

Salt, to taste

⅓ **cup** *olive oil*

⅓ **cup** *cider vinegar*

DIRECTIONS

Turn oven to 225°, place pita bread on flat pan, and leave 2 hours, turning once or twice. Cool and cut into fairly large pieces. Meanwhile, wash, tear, and drain lettuce. Place in large salad bowl. Add cucumbers, tomatoes, mint, onions, and salt. Blend oil and vinegar in a small bowl. Season salad with oil-and-vinegar dressing. Mix well. Place pita bread on top of the salad. **Serves 6 to 8.**

❧ *Serve with lentil soup.*

Fran Scher—Atlanta, GA
Donation to: Deborah Hospital Foundation—Sonia Sobelman Chapter, Browns Mills, NJ

Chinese Chicken Salad

Twelve years ago in Atlanta, I took a cooking class taught by a Japanese woman. This recipe is from that class—long before Chinese chicken salads became fashionable. It is still the best!

INGREDIENTS

- **1 pound** *boneless chicken breasts*
- **2 cups** *water*
- **5** *whole green onions (1 halved; 4 thinly sliced on the diagonal)*
- **1 slice** *of fresh ginger (1/4-inch-thick), crushed*
- **1 tablespoon** *dry sherry or rice-wine vinegar*
- **1 teaspoon** *salt*
- **1 1/2 teaspoons** *pepper*
- **2 ounces** *maifun (rice sticks)*
- **1** *small head lettuce*
- **1** *cucumber, seeded and thinly sliced on the diagonal*
- **2 tablespoons** *toasted sesame seeds*
- **1 teaspoon** *dry mustard*
- **3 tablespoons** *sugar*
- **1/2 cup** *vegetable oil*
- **2 tablespoons** *sesame oil*
- **6 tablespoons** *rice-wine vinegar*

DIRECTIONS

Place chicken in a stockpot with water, 1 whole green onion (halved), ginger, sherry, and 1/2 teaspoon each of salt and pepper. Bring to boil; cover and simmer 20 minutes. Remove from heat and cool. Strain broth and save for soup. Shred chicken and refrigerate. Pour some vegetable or peanut oil into a wok and heat until hot. Add small bunches of maifun and fry until crisp. Drain on paper towels. Shred lettuce into salad bowl and add cold chicken, cucumber, sesame seeds, and remaining onions. Top with fried maifun. Just before serving, mix together mustard, sugar, vegetable oil, sesame oil, rice-wine vinegar, and remaining salt and pepper. Shake well, pour over salad and toss gently. **Serves 6 to 8.**

❧ *Serve with cold soup and fresh bread.*

Neiman Marcus—THE ZODIAC Northbrook, Chicago
Donation to: combined charities

Club Salad

It debuted at the Thursday night buffets and turns up regularly in every restaurant.

INGREDIENTS

1 cup *mayonnaise or salad dressing*

¼ cup *tarragon vinegar*

¼ cup *finely chopped parsley*

2 tablespoons *finely chopped green onion*

2 tablespoons *snipped chives*

½ teaspoon *dry mustard*

¼ teaspoon *salt*

⅛ teaspoon *pepper*

2 quarts *bite-sized, crisp salad greens*

3 cups *cooked, cubed, and chilled chicken*

2 *tomatoes*

5 *slices bacon, cooked and crumbled*

DIRECTIONS

Combine first 8 ingredients and mix well. Cover and refrigerate several hours or overnight. (Bottled green goddess salad dressing may be substituted.) Just before serving, place greens in salad bowl. Place chicken in the center of greens. Add dressing and toss to thoroughly coat chicken and greens. Garnish with tomato slices and bacon. **Serves 8.**

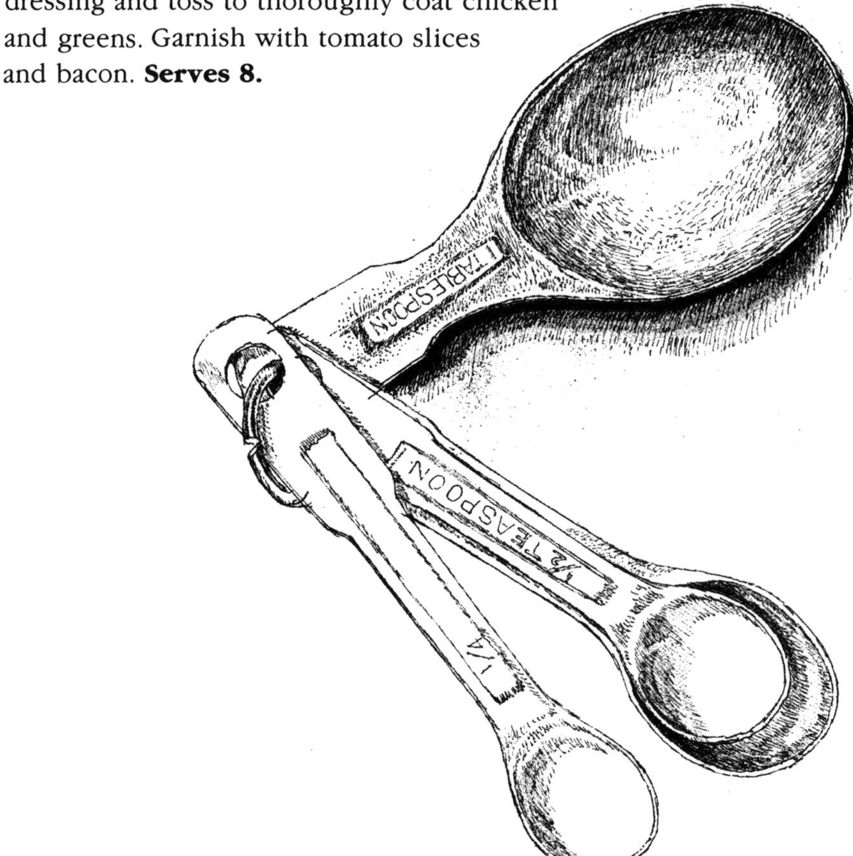

Ed McMahon—Burbank, CA
Donation to: St. Jude's Ranch for Children, Inc., Boulder City, NV

Curried Chicken Salad

Imagine our excitement when we received a letter from Ed! But, no, we were not sweepstakes winners. However, this chicken salad recipe from Johnny's long-time sidekick is a winner in its own way.

INGREDIENTS

4 *whole chicken breasts*
1 *stalk plus* **½ cup** *chopped celery*
2 tablespoons *butter*
1 cup *blanched almonds*
2 *red apples*
2 tablespoons *fresh lemon juice*
½ pound *bacon*
1-1½ cups *mayonnaise*
2-3 tablespoons *curry powder*
2 *heads Bibb lettuce, separated*
Watercress
Parsley sprigs

DIRECTIONS

Place chicken breasts in large saucepan with water to cover. Add whole celery stalk to chicken and simmer 25 to 30 minutes. In a small skillet, melt butter. Add almonds and sauté 3 to 4 minutes, stirring constantly. Remove almonds from skillet and place on paper towels. Peel, core, and chop apples into fine pieces. Place in bowl and sprinkle with lemon juice. Skin and bone cooked chicken; cut into bite-sized cubes. Set aside. Fry bacon until crisp; crumble. Set aside. Mix mayonnaise and curry powder until well-blended. Combine chicken pieces, almonds, apples, ½ cup chopped celery, and curry mayonnaise. Toss lightly to coat. Serve on beds of lettuce. Garnish with crumbled bacon, watercress, and sprigs of parsley.

Testing Notes: *Add ¼ cup Dijon-style mustard to dressing.*

Sylvia Hilton—Beverly Hills, CA
Donation to: Concern Foundation, Los Angeles, CA

Hot Mah-Jongg Chicken Salad

Our Mah-Jongg group meets weekly in each other's home, with the hostess furnishing a light luncheon. We had long-tired of the usual tuna fish, egg salad, or cottage cheese-with-fruit dishes. One day I concocted a surprise: something easily prepared ahead of time, popped into the oven at the right moment, and ready for lunch after the end of the first game. Off to the dining room we went, to devour what became the "hit" of our group. I'm always reminded to serve it.

INGREDIENTS

3 cups *cooked chicken from 2 large whole breasts, cut into large chunks*

2 teaspoons *lemon juice*

1 tablespoon *soy sauce*

¼ cup *chopped scallion*

1 cup *chopped celery*

1 can *(6½ ounce) sliced water chestnuts, drained*

½ pound *bean sprouts, washed*

¼ teaspoon *seasoned salt*

½ cup *snow peas (or green peas or string beans)*

3 *shiitake (or large brown) mushrooms, sliced (or 1 jar whole button mushrooms, drained)*

1 cup *mayonnaise*

1 cup *small macaroni noodles, cooked al dente*

1 teaspoon *sesame seed*

½ cup *chow mein noodles*

DIRECTIONS

Sprinkle chicken with lemon juice and soy sauce. Chill 2 hours or longer. Add scallion, celery, water chestnuts, bean sprouts, salt, snow peas, mushrooms, and mayonnaise. Mix lightly but thoroughly. Place a thin layer of chicken mixture in a greased 2-quart casserole; arrange cooked macaroni on top. Top with remainder of chicken mixture. Cover and bake 30 minutes at 350°. Uncover. Sprinkle with sesame seed and chow mein noodles. Bake uncovered 5 minutes. **Serves 6 to 8.**

❧ *Serve this with a fresh fruit platter.*

Testing Notes: *Recommend bow-tie pasta.*

Marsha Goldstein—Northbrook, IL
Donation to: Women's American ORT, Skokie, IL

Sweet-and-Sour Chicken Salad

My mother served this luncheon item, and it was a favorite of ours.

INGREDIENTS

4 *chicken breasts, skinned and boned*

Teriyaki sauce

8 *won tons, cut in ¾-inch strips*

½ cup *sugar*

½ cup *vinegar*

1 teaspoon *salt*

¼ cup *vegetable oil*

Ground black pepper, to taste

1 tablespoon *sweet-and-sour sauce*

1 *head lettuce, torn*

1 tablespoon *toasted sesame seeds*

Green onions, to taste

DIRECTIONS

Marinate chicken breasts in teriyaki sauce for several hours. Bake or microwave chicken until cooked. Cut into cubes. Fry won ton and drain. Boil sugar, vinegar, salt, oil, pepper, and sweet-and-sour sauce. Cool. Mix lettuce with chicken, sesame seeds, and green onions. Add dressing and won tons immediately before serving. **Serves 6.**

❧ *Serve with rolls and a gelatin mold.*

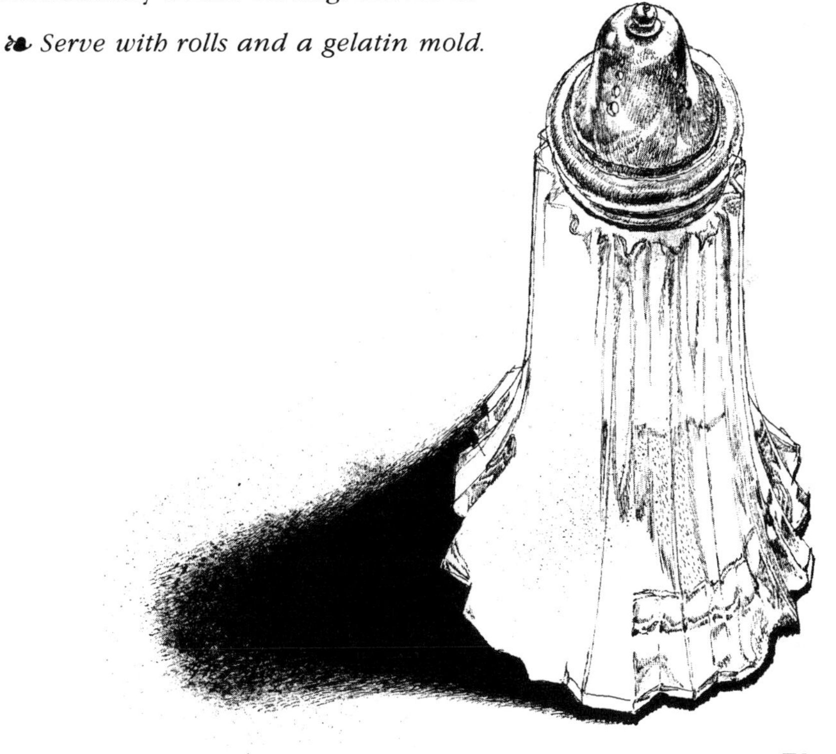

Ellen G. Chamberlin—Corona del Mar, CA
Donation to: Newport Harbor Art Museum, Newport Beach, CA

Cold Lettuce and Hot Noodle Salad

INGREDIENTS

8 ounces *noodles*

3 cups *fresh asparagus, cut into 1-inch pieces*

1 cup *chopped bell pepper, any color*

5 cups *iceberg lettuce, torn into bite-sized pieces*

2-3 *tomatoes, coarsely chopped*

Salt and pepper, to taste

1/3-1/2 cup *canned beef broth, undiluted*

2 tablespoons *olive oil*

1 *large clove garlic, pressed*

Parmesan cheese

DIRECTIONS

Place noodles in a large kettle of boiling water and cook, according to package directions. Two minutes before noodles are done, add asparagus and bell pepper. Meanwhile, put lettuce and tomatoes in a large bowl and sprinkle with salt and pepper. Set aside. Put broth, oil, and garlic in microwaveable bowl. Heat in microwave until hot. When noodles are cooked, drain with vegetables. Heap on top of lettuce, pour hot-oil dressing over the mixture, and toss well. Add Parmesan cheese on top of each serving. **Serves 3 to 4** as a main course.

Carole Loetscher—Dubuque, IA
Donation to: Finley Hospital, Dubuque, IA

Top Ramen Noodle Salad

My sister Nancy, who lives in Oregon, sent me this recipe. My friends beg for the recipe.

INGREDIENTS

- **1** *medium-sized head cabbage, finely chopped*
- **4** *green onions, chopped*
- **4 cups** *diced, cooked chicken*
- **1 cup** *oil*
- **4 tablespoons** *sugar*
- **6 tablespoons** *rice vinegar*
- **2 teaspoons** *salt*
- **1 teaspoon** *pepper*
- *Seasoning from ramen noodle packages*
- **2 packages** *chicken-flavored ramen noodles, uncooked and crumbled*
- **4 tablespoons** *toasted sesame seeds*
- **4 tablespoons** *toasted sliced almonds*

DIRECTIONS

Mix cabbage, onions, and chicken; refrigerate overnight. Combine oil, sugar, rice vinegar, salt, pepper, and noodle seasoning. Stir well and add to salad. Toss with noodles. Before serving, garnish with sesame seeds and nuts. **Serves 8.**

❧ *Serve with rolls.*

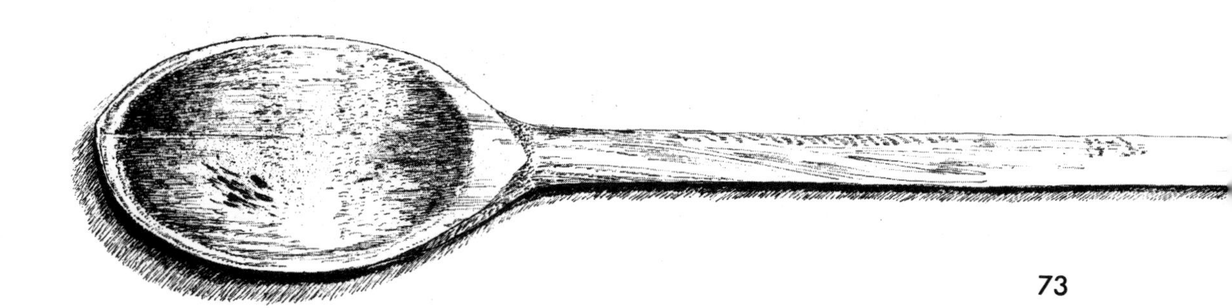

Sonia Williams—Las Vegas, NV
Donation to: American Cancer Society, Inc., Las Vegas, NV

German Potato Salad

This recipe came to me from my mother, my grandmother and the "old country."

INGREDIENTS

6-8 *medium-sized potatoes, boiled and peeled*
3 *green onions, diced*
1 *stalk celery, finely chopped*
¼ *green bell pepper, chopped*
¼ teaspoon *celery seed*
8 slices *bacon*
2 tablespoons *flour*
¼ cup *vinegar*
½ cup *water*
1 tablespoon *sugar*

DIRECTIONS

Boil potatoes and put in large bowl with green onions, celery, bell pepper, and celery seed. Set aside. Cut bacon into small pieces and fry until crisp. Do not drain. Add flour gradually, stirring constantly, until thickened. Add vinegar, water, and sugar, stirring until smooth. Immediately pour this mixture over the potatoes and mix well. **Serves 12.**

Testing Notes: *Add salt and white pepper, to taste.*

Yolanda Vrechek—Fort Lauderdale, FL
Donation to: Roye Levin Adopt-A-Pet, Miami, FL

Yolanda's Potato Salad

This has been a favorite of mine for years. It's so easy to make and tastes delicious.

INGREDIENTS

3 *medium-sized red potatoes*
1 teaspoon *sugar*
1 teaspoon *white vinegar*
2-3 *stalks celery, sliced*
1 *small onion, finely diced*
¼ cup *chopped gherkin*
1 teaspoon *celery seed*
¾ cup *mayonnaise*
3 *hard-cooked eggs, sliced*

DIRECTIONS

Cover potatoes with water in a covered pot; cook 25 minutes. Drain, peel, quarter, and slice. Add sugar and vinegar. Add celery, onion, pickle, and celery seed. Stir. Add mayonnaise and sliced eggs. Serve chilled. **Serves 4 to 6.**

Serve with grilled beef or chicken.

Mrs. Thomas S. Beyt—New Iberia, LA
Donation to: New Iberia Humane Society, Inc., New Iberia, LA

All-Purpose Louisiana Crayfish Salad

I wanted to use crayfish in a sandwich filling, so I just used my chicken salad procedures to arrive at my crayfish recipe.

INGREDIENTS

- **1 pound** *raw crayfish tails, peeled*
- **1 1/2 teaspoons** *salt*
- **3** *hard-cooked eggs, chopped*
- **1/4 cup** *minced celery, heart and leaves*
- **1/3 cup** *hand-sliced green onion, tops and bottoms*
- **2 tablespoons** *grated carrot (optional)*
- **1/8 teaspoon** *ground red pepper*
- **1/2 cup** *mayonnaise (more if creamier consistency is desired)*
- **3 tablespoons** *GREY POUPON® Dijon mustard*

DIRECTIONS

Season raw crayfish tails with salt. Cover and steam crayfish tails. Cook 4 to 6 minutes, stirring twice. Cool. Chop crayfish tails in food processor. In a mixing bowl, combine chopped crayfish, eggs, celery, green onion, carrot, and red pepper. Toss to mix thoroughly. Add mayonnaise and mustard. Mix well. Refrigerate before serving. If a food processor is used to chop eggs, be careful not to over-process. Do not use a food processor to chop green onions. Shrimp may be substituted when crayfish is not in season. Use as a filling for sandwiches, a spread for crackers, or a stuffing for fresh tomatoes or avocado. If the latter, reserve some steamed crayfish tails for garnish. **Serves 4.**

❧ *The stuffed tomato or avocado is ideal on a summer luncheon plate served with marinated fresh carrots, mushrooms, and green beans.*

Shirley Copeland—Grants Pass, OR
Donation to: American Cancer Society, Inc., Portland, OR

Bread Salad with Shrimp

I received this recipe thirty years ago from a friend.

INGREDIENTS

1 *large loaf of sandwich bread*

4 *hard-cooked eggs, finely chopped*

1 *large sweet onion, finely chopped*

1 pint *BEST FOODS® mayonnaise*

1 teaspoon *horseradish (optional)*

Chopped olives (optional)

2 pounds *small shrimp, cooked, shelled, and deveined*

1-2 *tomatoes, quartered*

DIRECTIONS

Remove crusts from bread, then butter and cube. Mix eggs, onion, mayonnaise, horseradish, olives, and bread cubes. This may be made a day ahead and stored in refrigerator. Just before serving, combine this mixture with shrimp. Mound on platter and surround with quartered tomatoes. **Serves 12.**

❧ *Serve with tomatoes and hot dog buns, which have been buttered, sprinkled with Parmesan cheese, and broiled.*

Testing Notes: *Substitute cheese buns for sandwich bread.*

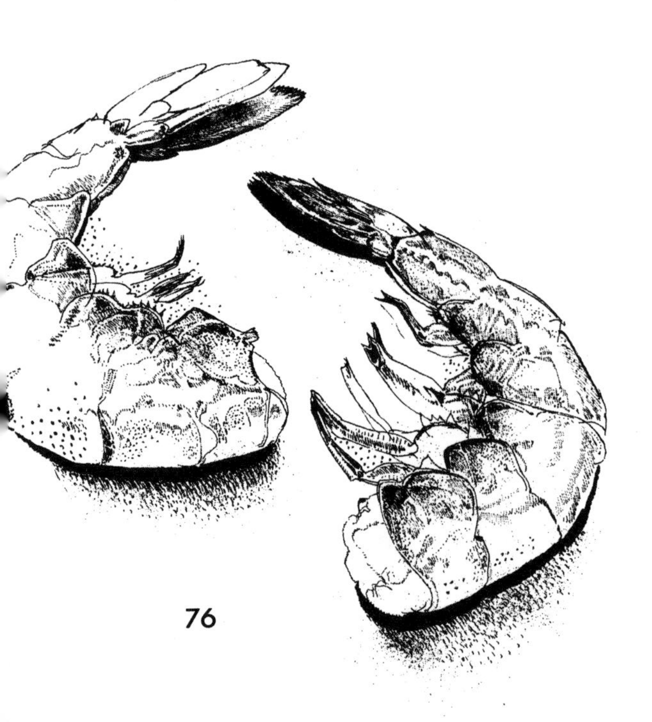

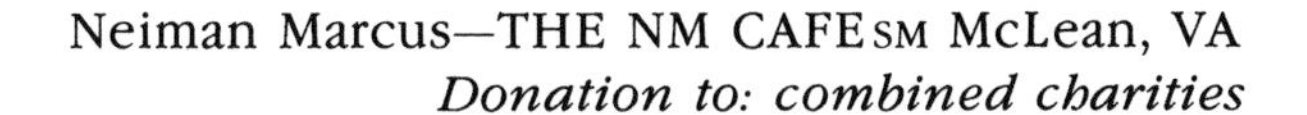

Neiman Marcus—THE NM CAFE℠ McLean, VA
Donation to: combined charities

Cold Crab Curry Salad

This one was created for one of NM's French Fortnights years ago.

INGREDIENTS

- **1** *apple, peeled, cored, and sliced*
- **4** *shallots, chopped*
- **¼ cup** *butter*
- **1 tablespoon** *curry powder*
- **1 teaspoon** *crushed coriander seed*
- **1 teaspoon** *flour*
- *Milk*
- **2 cups** *mayonnaise*
- *Lemon juice, to taste*
- **3 cups** *cold, cooked crab meat*
- **4 cups** *cold, cooked rice*

DIRECTIONS

Sauté apple and shallots in butter until softened; add curry powder, coriander seed, and flour. Add just enough milk to make a thick paste. Cool paste and stir it into mayonnaise. Add a little lemon juice and adjust the seasoning. Place crab meat on a bed of rice. Mask it with the curry sauce. **Serves 8 to 10.**

Mrs. Francis P. Osborne—Rancho Mirage, CA
Donation to: St. Elizabeth's Hospice Medical Center, Yakima, WA

Mom's Shrimp or Crab Salad

My husband's mother served this at her special luncheons. The recipe is over seventy-five years-old.

INGREDIENTS

- **1 cup** *celery, thinly sliced*
- **2** *sweet pickles, thinly sliced*
- **1 tablespoon** *cucumber, thinly sliced*
- **3** *hard-cooked eggs, diced*
- **¼ pound** *shrimp or crab meat*
- **1 package** *CREAMETTE® macaroni rings, cooked*
- **⅓-⅔ cup** *cider vinegar*

DIRECTIONS

Marinate celery, pickles, cucumber, eggs, shrimp or crab meat, and macaroni. Beat with whisk until well mixed. (Do not use a mixer.) Add cider vinegar slowly. Mix well. Keeps for weeks in refrigerator. **Serves 6 to 8.**

❧ *Serve with spiced crab apples or fresh fruits, hot homemade rolls, and Edna Valley Chardonnay wine.*

Mrs. Ronald Goldstein—Atlanta, GA
Donation to: Children's Wish Foundation International, Inc., Atlanta, GA

Cold Salmon Mousse

A friend of mine created this recipe.

INGREDIENTS

- **1 envelope** *unflavored gelatin*
- **½ cup** *boiling water*
- **1 cup** *mayonnaise*
- **¼ teaspoon** *paprika*
- **1 teaspoon** *dried dill*
- **1 can** *(16 ounce) salmon, skin and bones removed*
- **1 cup** *heavy cream*
- **1 tablespoon** *capers*
- **2 tablespoons** *plus* **1½ teaspoons** *lemon juice*
- **½ teaspoon** *TABASCO®*
- **½** *cucumber, diced*

DIRECTIONS

Dissolve gelatin in water in a blender. Add and blend ½ cup mayonnaise, paprika, dill, and salmon. Add cream slowly to salmon mixture while blender is on. Add capers, 2 tablespoons lemon juice, and TABASCO®; blend until smooth. Pour into oiled mold and chill 6 hours. Stir cucumber and the remaining lemon juice and mayonnaise until well-blended. Unmold salmon on plate and spoon sauce on top. Or, serve sauce in a separate bowl on the side. This salad may be made ahead. **Serves 6 to 8.**

❧ *Serve with thin, black bread; crackers; or crisp raw vegetables.*

Testing Notes: *Garnish with avocado and cherry tomatoes. Add salt and pepper to taste.*

Anneliese Eisenberg—Des Plaines, IL
Donation to: The Women's Board of The Lincoln Park Zoological Society, Chicago, IL

Italian Herring Salad

This recipe has been in the family for generations. My great-grandmother created it in 1860. It has been traditionally served on New Year's Day.

INGREDIENTS

12 *medium-sized potatoes, boiled*

5 *medium-sized apples, diced*

2 *medium-sized onions, diced*

2 cans *(16 ounces each) drained carrots, chopped*

2 cans *(16 ounces each) drained beets, chopped*

2 *hard-cooked eggs, chopped (optional)*

1 pound *sirloin tip, boiled and chopped*

2 *salt herrings, skinned, boned, and chopped*

2 *dill pickles, chopped*

White vinegar, to taste

Salt and pepper, to taste

DIRECTIONS

Chill, peel, and dice potatoes. Mix all ingredients together in large bowl and refrigerate overnight. The salad will turn completely red and flavors will marry. **Serves 18 to 20.**

❧ *Serve with smoked ham or cold ham sandwiches.*

Testing Notes: *Suitable for buffet. Halve the recipe for individual service.*

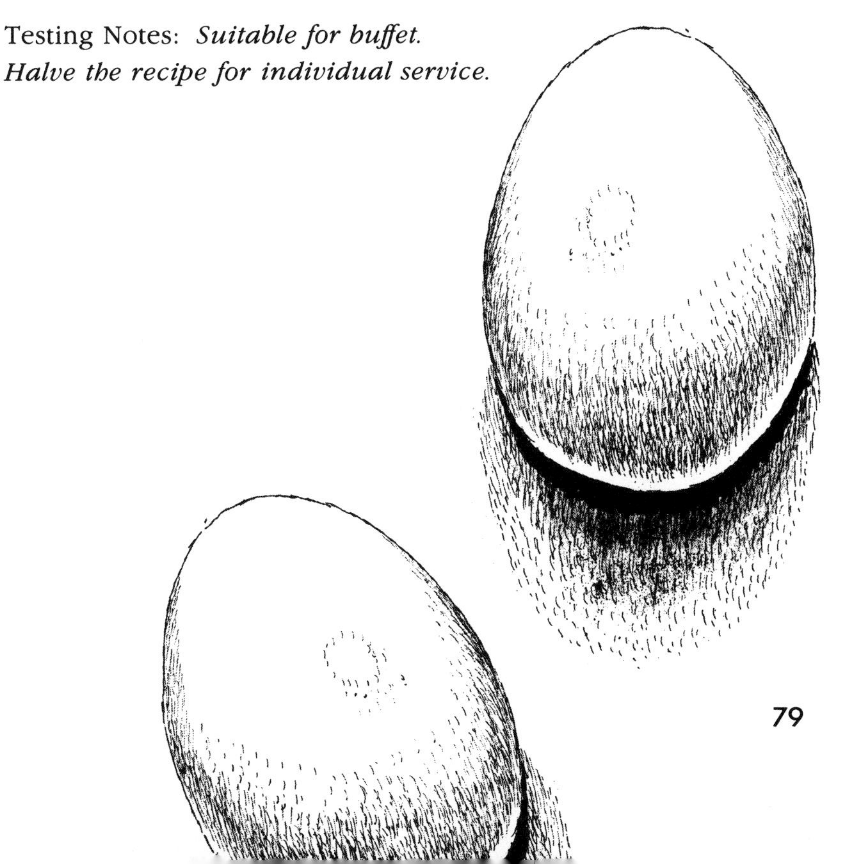

Mrs. L. E. Caraway—Houston, TX
Donation to: American Heart Association, Inc., Houston, TX

Vegetable Salad

This recipe is from my mother, Mrs. J. D. Liles.

INGREDIENTS

1 cup *sugar*

½ cup *canola oil*

¼ teaspoon *black pepper*

1 teaspoon *salt*

½ cup *white vinegar*

1 can *(16 ounce) French-style green beans*

1 can *(16 ounce) white-kernel corn*

1 can *(8 ounce) LESUEUR® small peas*

1 jar *(2 ounce) pimientos*

2 *small bunches green onion, finely chopped (tops included)*

1 cup *finely chopped celery*

1 cup *finely chopped bell pepper*

DIRECTIONS

Mix the sugar, oil, black pepper, salt, and white vinegar in saucepan. Bring to boil. Cool. Drain green beans, corn, peas, and pimientos; and mix with the green onions, celery, and bell pepper. Then, mix with the cooled sauce. Refrigerate 2 to 3 hours before serving. **Serves 4.**

❧ *Serve with beef or pork dishes.*

Testing Notes: *Use ½ cup sugar and red-wine vinegar, not white.*

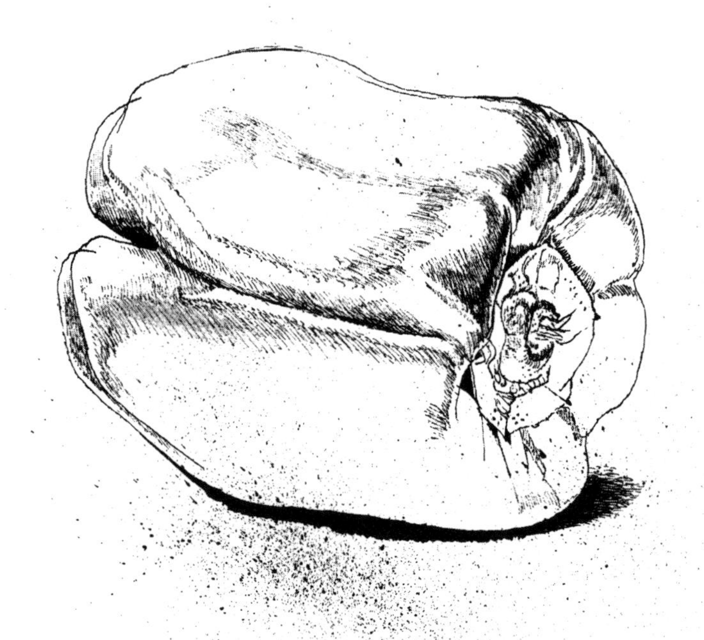

Donation to: combined charities

Vegetable Perfection Aspic

No buffet is complete without a tart, crunchy, molded salad like this one.

INGREDIENTS

3 ounces *unflavored gelatin*
1 cup *cold water*
1 quart *boiling water*
¼ cup *mild vinegar*
¼ cup *lemon juice*
¼ tablespoon *salt*
4 ounces *sugar*
10 ounces *chopped cabbage*
3 ounces *chopped celery*
1 ounce *chopped pimientos*
1 ounce *chopped green bell pepper*
½ teaspoon *paprika*

DIRECTIONS

Sprinkle gelatin over cold water. Soak 10 minutes. Add boiling water and stir until gelatin dissolves. Add vinegar, lemon juice, salt, and sugar; stir until sugar dissolves. Chill. When liquid begins to congeal, add cabbage, celery, pimientos, bell pepper, and paprika. Pour into a 12 x 20-inch pan. Refrigerate until congealed. **Serves 12.**

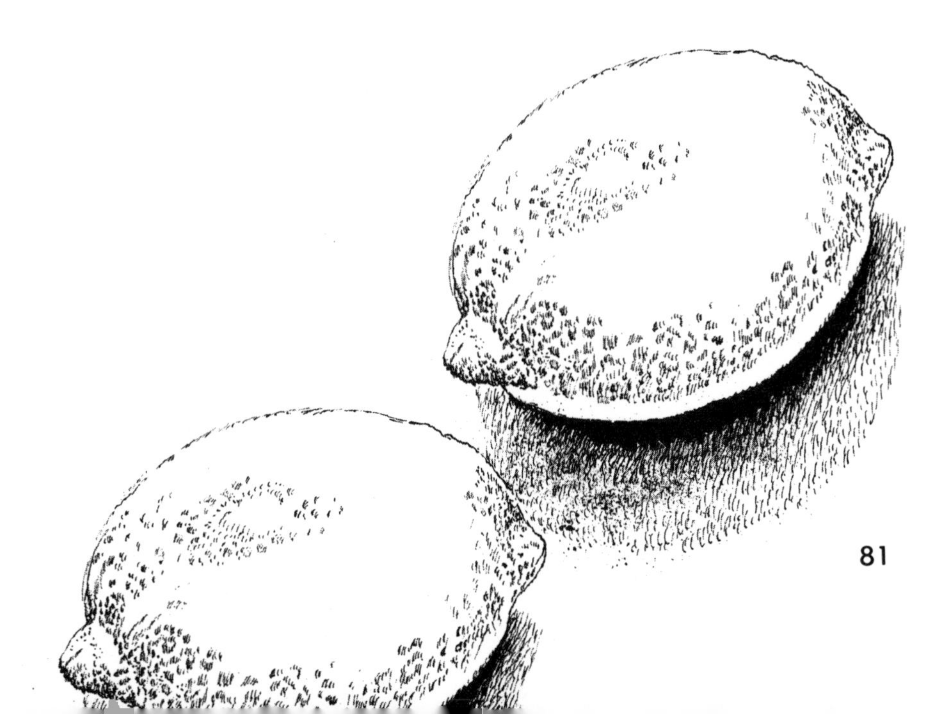

CHAPTER FOUR

Sandwiches

Here's where InCirclers shine: everything from dainties to Dagwoods. Nothing works better when it's time to entertain at lunch or tea, or serve as dinner-in-the-hand when the Super Bowl or World Series come around. Properly planned (as you'll see in these recipes), a sandwich can be a very nutritious, quick meal, with the bread supplying complex carbohydrates, and the filling, important protein. And, there's no reason to settle for boring breads with all the diversity you can find to buy in even the most average bakery today.

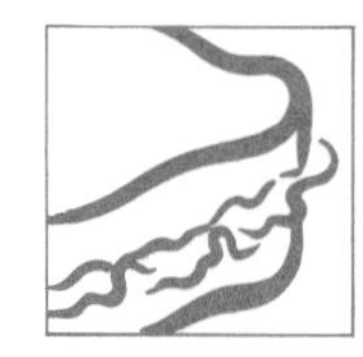

Mrs. Marilyn L. Reisel—St. Louis, MO
Donation to: The Salvation Army, St. Louis, MO

Avocado Bleu Cheese Sandwich

Several years ago, I had a bridge foursome at my home for lunch. Using a favorite dip recipe, I created this sandwich by making a few changes and adding the avocado. It's been a favorite ever since.

INGREDIENTS

8 ounces *bleu cheese*
2 tablespoons *mayonnaise*
1 tablespoon *milk*
2-3 slices *bacon, fried crisp and crumbled*
8-12 slices *whole-wheat toast*
1 *avocado, peeled and sliced*

DIRECTIONS

Mix cheese, mayonnaise, milk, and bacon until spreadable. Spread on whole-wheat toast. Place avocado slices on top and cover with toast. **Serves 4 to 6.**

❧ *Serve with a cup of split-pea soup.*

Testing Notes: *Bleu cheese has a tendency to overpower avocado if not used sparingly. Use food processor to blend bleu cheese, mayonnaise, and milk. Then, fold in bacon. Spread bleu cheese on toast, and add 3 whole slices of cooked bacon and a generous amount of avocado slices.*

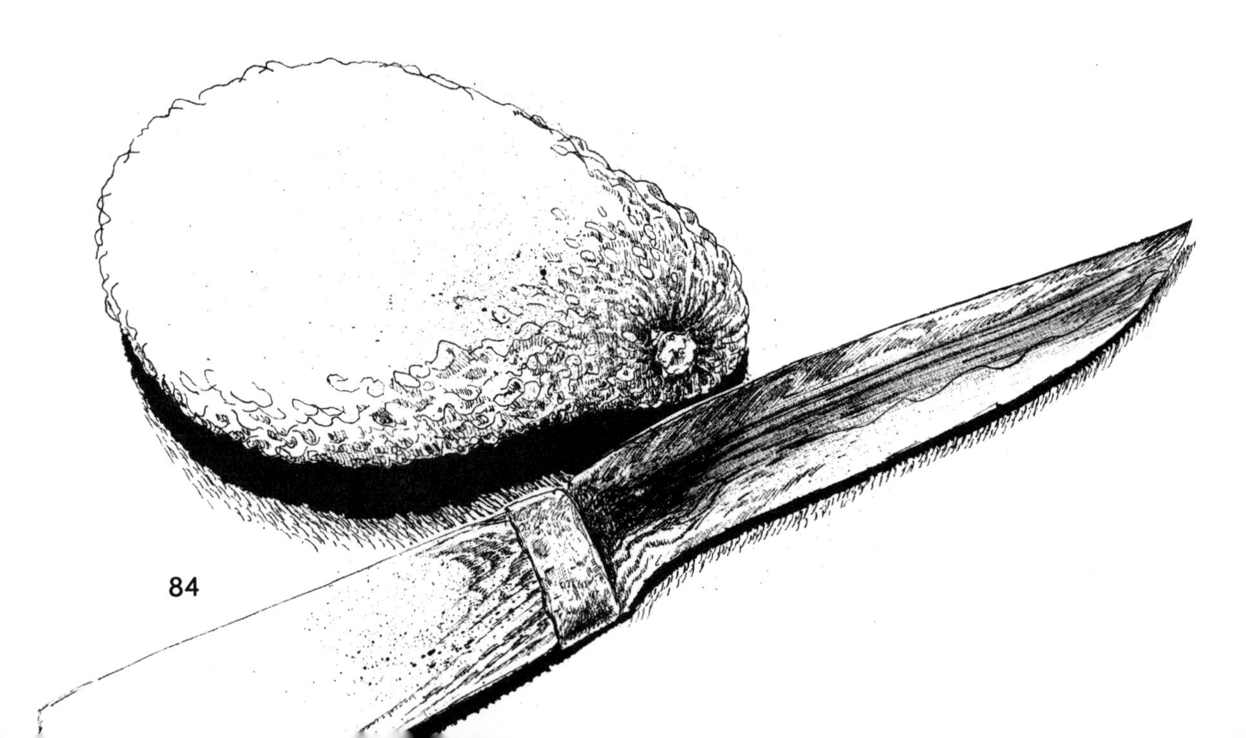

Neiman Marcus—THE NM CAFE Newport Beach
Donation to: combined charities

Avocado Shrimpwich

If ever there were two things meant for each other, it's avocados and shrimp.

INGREDIENTS

3 *medium-sized (or 2 large) avocados*

1 package *(8 ounce) cream cheese, softened*

2 tablespoons *mayonnaise*

2 tablespoons *prepared mustard*

¼ teaspoon *salt*

¼ teaspoon *dill weed*

1 tablespoon *chopped green onion*

6 slices *of rye bread, toasted*

18 *shrimp or scallops*

DIRECTIONS

Cut avocados in half, remove seeds, slice into rings, and gently remove rind. Set aside. Beat cream cheese, mayonnaise, mustard, salt, dill weed, and green onion until well-blended in an electric mixer. Spread each slice of toast with about 3 tablespoons of cream cheese mixture. Top with shrimp and avocado rings. Garnish with a sprinkle of dill. The spread may be made ahead and refrigerated. If you do this, let spread stand at room temperature 10 to 15 minutes to soften before spreading. **Serves 6.**

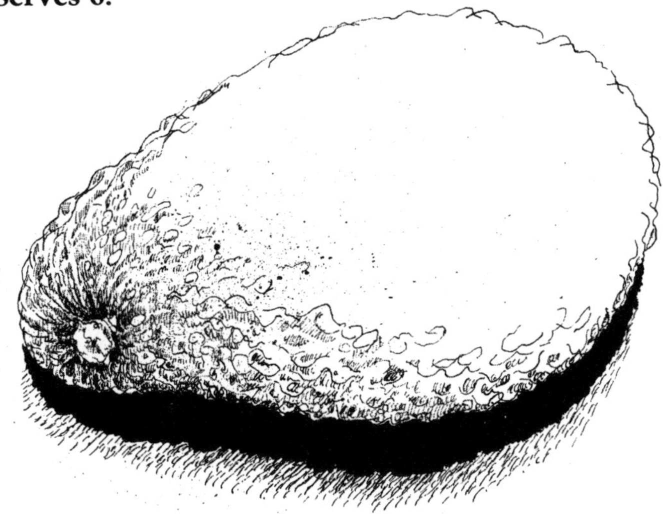

Mrs. Hayden Hatcher—Fort Worth, TX
Donation to: Make-A-Wish Foundation of the Texas Gulf Coast, Inc., Houston, TX

Asparagus Finger Sandwiches

This is from a family friend and is served for luncheons and bridal and baby showers.

INGREDIENTS

1 can *(8 ounce) asparagus tips, drained*

4 packages *(3 ounces each) cream cheese*

2 *hard-cooked eggs*

1 teaspoon *LAWRY'S® season salt*

2 loaves *PEPPERIDGE FARM® white bread, crusts removed*

Melted butter

Freshly grated Parmesan cheese

DIRECTIONS

Blend first 4 ingredients in blender and spread on bread. Cut into finger sandwiches. Dip each sandwich into melted butter. Roll in Parmesan cheese. (The sandwiches may be frozen now for later use.) Broil sandwiches on both sides. Serve warm. **Serves 24.**

❧ *Serve with raw vegetables, fruit, and chicken salad.*

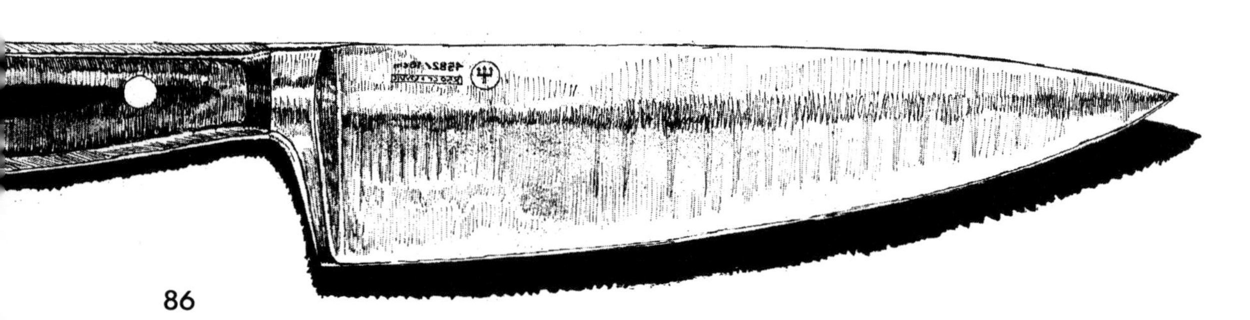

Carmen M. de Alejos—Miami, FL
Donation to: Aldeas Infantiles, S.O.S., Mixco, Guatemala

Santander Sandwiches

This recipe is an invented one. When I have a baby shower, a school reunion at home, or a child's birthday party, I usually serve these sandwiches and everybody loves them.

INGREDIENTS

- **18 slices** *of white bread, crusts removed*
- **12 ounces** *chopped chicken (white meat only) or tuna*
- **4 ounces** *chopped celery*
- **1 tablespoon** *chopped onion*
- **2 tablespoons** *chopped fresh pimientos*
- **6 tablespoons** *mayonnaise*
- **1 teaspoon** *mustard*
- **½ teaspoon** *salt*
- **½ teaspoon** *pepper*
- **¾ cup** *milk*
- **2 cups** *shredded Cheddar cheese*
- **1 can** *(16 ounce) whole asparagus, drained*
- *Whole pimientos, cut into strips*

DIRECTIONS

Divide the bread into 6 stacks (3 bread slices per stack). Mix chicken, celery, onion, pimientos, mayonnaise, mustard, salt, and pepper in a bowl. Remove the top bread slice from a stack, place on work surface, and spread top side with chicken mixture. Remove second slice from the stack, spread one side with chicken mixture and place, mixture side up, on the first slice. Top with the third slice and move the sandwich to a shallow baking pan. Repeat process for remaining sandwiches. Place milk in saucepan and add cheese, stirring constantly. As soon as thoroughly melted, ladle cheese mixture over sandwiches. Let cheese dry. Place on plates and decorate each with asparagus and a strip of pimiento. **Serves 6.**

❧ *Serve with your favorite salad or chips.*

Mrs. G. A. Hawkins—Graham, TX
Donation to: The Graham Public Library, Graham, TX

Deviled Ham Omelet Sandwich

The original recipe came from a magazine years ago, and I have added various ingredients.

INGREDIENTS

- ½ **stick** *butter*
- **6-8** *eggs, beaten*
- ¾ **cup** *milk*
- **1 tablespoon** *chopped parsley*
- **1 can** *(4¼ ounce) deviled ham*
- ½ **cup** *chopped green onion*
- **1 can** *(4 ounce) chopped green chiles (optional)*
- *Salt and pepper*
- *Cheddar cheese*
- **16 slices** *PEPPERIDGE FARM® thinly sliced wheat bread*

DIRECTIONS

Melt butter in an 8-inch-round skillet. Combine eggs, milk, parsley, deviled ham, green onion, green chiles, salt, and pepper. Cook on medium until sides set. Using two spatulas, carefully turn over and cook 3 more minutes. Cut into pie-shaped wedges. Put 4 butter-sized pats of Cheddar cheese on each bread slice. Toast until melted. Place wedges of omelet between slices of toast and add small green onions, if desired. **Serves 6 to 8.**

❧ *Delicious with chocolate milk for a Sunday-night supper.*

Testing Notes: *Green chiles are essential.*

Mrs. Patsy Machin—Longview, TX
Donation to: Good Shepherd Foundation, Longview, TX

Ham and Cheese Surprise

My mother made these. I don't know where the recipe originated.

INGREDIENTS

5 tablespoons *butter, melted*
Course-grained mustard
48 slices *of cocktail rye bread*
3/4 pound *deli-shaved baked or boiled ham, trimmed to fit bread*
1 1/2 cups *sauerkraut, drained and squeezed dry*
1/2 pound *deli-shaved Swiss cheese*

DIRECTIONS

Line 2 cookie sheets with foil; lightly brush each with 1 tablespoon butter. Spread mustard on one side of each bread slice. Arrange 24 slices, mustard side up, on cookie sheets. Top each with ham, 1 tablespoon sauerkraut, and cheese. Cover with remaining butter. Preheat oven to 425°. Bake uncovered 10 minutes until bottoms are browned. Remove any melted cheese from foil. Turn sandwiches with spatula. Return to oven and bake 5 minutes. Serve warm or at room temperature. (These may be prepared 6 to 8 hours in advance. Cover tightly with plastic wrap and refrigerate.) **Serves 12 to 16, generously.**

❧ *Serve with a green salad and cold beer.*

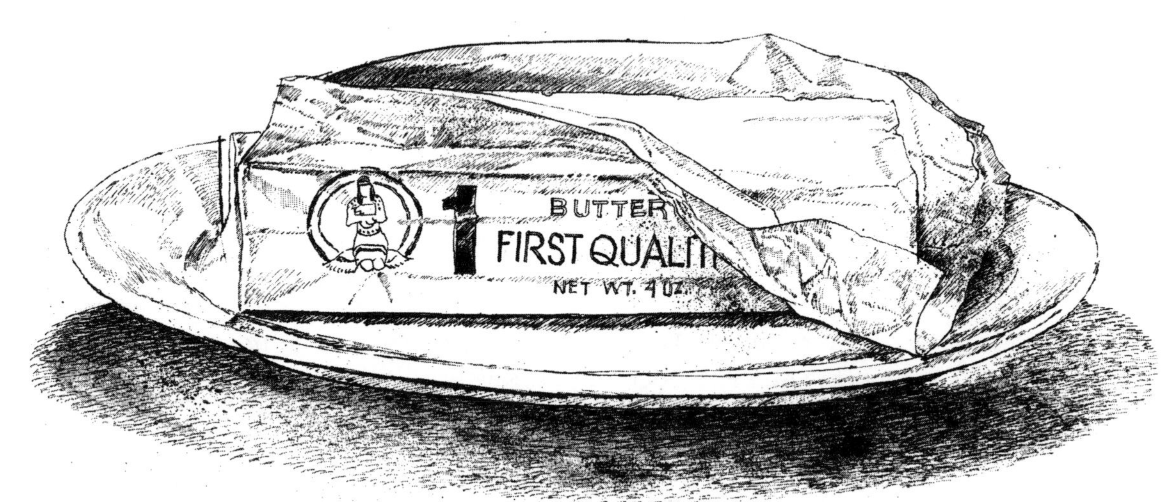

Blanche L. Rapoport—Scarsdale, NY
Donation to: Harlem Valley Psychiatric Center, Wingdale, NY

Sandwich Soufflé

My mother helped me prepare this for a lunch for my college friends. All twelve of them loved it.

INGREDIENTS

2 slices *of white bread*
2 slices *of ham*
1 *egg white*
2 tablespoons *mayonnaise*
Freshly ground pepper, to taste

DIRECTIONS

Lightly toast bread, crusts included. Place ham on toast slices. Beat egg white and fold in mayonnaise. Spread mixture on top of ham. Preheat oven to 350°. Bake open sandwiches until lightly browned and egg white rises. **Serves 2.**

❧ *Serve with a big green salad.*

Testing Notes: *Use 2 slices of ham per slice of bread.*

Neiman Marcus—THE NM CAFE Prestonwood, Dallas
Donation to: combined charities

Full-House Sandwich

NM sandwich creators designed this one to appeal to man-size appetites.

INGREDIENTS

2 slices *of bread*
Mayonnaise
Beef slices
Cheddar cheese slices
Ham slices
Swiss cheese slices
Pickle relish

DIRECTIONS

Toast bread. Lightly spread mayonnaise on 1 slice of toasted bread. Place beef on the mayonnaise. Place Cheddar cheese on beef. Place ham on the cheese. Place Swiss cheese on the ham. Spread pickle relish on top of Swiss cheese. Broil in oven until cheese melts. **Serves 1.**

Mrs. Martin Tobey—Fort Worth, TX
Donation to: Fort Worth Symphony Orchestra, Fort Worth, TX

Marty's Meatball Sandwiches

This was my husband's one recipe that he brought to our marriage. He created it and made it frequently.

INGREDIENTS

- **1 pound** *ground beef*
- *Salt and pepper, to taste*
- **1 tablespoon** *bread crumbs*
- **1** *medium-sized onion, sliced*
- **1** *green bell pepper, thinly sliced into rings*
- **1 bottle** *hot, spicy ketchup*
- **1 teaspoon** *sugar*
- **4** *poor-boy rolls*
- **4** *provolone cheese slices (optional)*

DIRECTIONS

Mix ground beef, salt, pepper, and bread crumbs. Form into 1-inch balls. In large saucepan, sauté onion and bell pepper in small amount of oil until tender. Add 1 bottle of ketchup and a ketchup bottle full of water to saucepan. Add sugar. Bring to boil; add meatballs. Reduce heat and cover. Simmer, covered, 30 minutes. Serve on poor-boy rolls with onion and bell pepper. Add slices of cheese and melt, if desired, under broiler or in microwave. **Serves 4.**

❧ *Serve with Italian salt and chips.*

Mary M. Harvey—Houston, TX
Donation to: Houston Foto Fest, Inc., Houston, TX

Sausage-Stuffed French Loaves

After relocating to Europe, I dedicated myself to the pursuit of wonderful recipes. I finally had time to spare.

INGREDIENTS

2 *fat, long loaves of French bread*

8 ounces *bulk pork sausage*

8 ounces *ground beef chuck*

1 *medium-sized yellow onion, diced*

1 teaspoon *Dijon-style mustard*

1 *egg*

¼ cup *chopped fresh Italian parsley*

¼ teaspoon *fennel seeds*

Salt, to taste

Freshly ground pepper, to taste

2 tablespoons *unsalted butter*

2 *cloves garlic, crushed*

DIRECTIONS

Preheat oven to 400°. Cut off the ends of the loaves, reserve the ends, and hollow out the loaves with your fingers. Process the soft bread to coarse crumbs in a food processor fitted with a steel blade. Brown sausage in a heavy skillet over medium heat. Add beef and onion; cook until beef is lightly browned. Combine bread crumbs, meat mixture, mustard, egg, parsley, fennel, salt, and pepper in a large bowl. Spoon mixture into bread shells; attach the bread ends with small skewers. Melt butter over medium heat, add garlic, and sauté 30 seconds. Brush loaves with garlic butter and wrap in separate pieces of aluminum foil, leaving the foil open slightly at the top. Bake 15 to 20 minutes until heated through. Cut each loaf into 4 pieces foı **8 main-course servings.** (This recipe makes 36 appetizers, if cut into 1-inch squares.)

❧ *Serve with salad and a nice wine.*

Testing Notes: *Add 4 ounces of mozzarella or provolone cheese to sausage-and-beef mixture.*

Marilyn Harbison—Dallas, TX
Donation to: Dallas Museum of Art, Dallas, TX

Mom Sandwiches

INGREDIENTS

2 tablespoons *butter*
Thousand Island dressing
8 slices *of pumpernickel bread*
3/4 pound *grilled pastrami*
1/2 pound *baby Swiss cheese, sliced*
1/2 pound *bacon, cooked crisp*
4 *eggs, fried with semi-hard yolks*
1 *tomato, sliced*

DIRECTIONS

Melt butter in a large skillet. Spread Thousand Island dressing over 4 bread slices. Place bread in skillet, dressing side up. Layer each bread slice with pastrami, cheese, bacon, egg, and tomato slice. Add bread on top and flip sandwich. Put lid on skillet and cook until cheese melts and bread is lightly browned. **Serves 4.**

Testing Notes: *We suggest you eliminate the fried egg.*

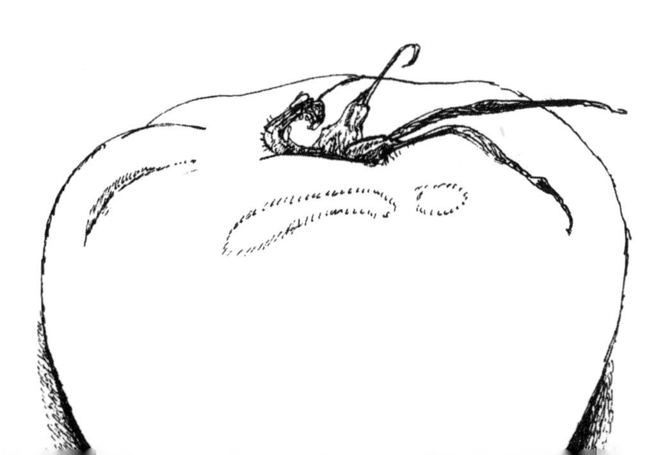

Diane M. Cummins—Columbus, OH
Donation to: AIDS Research Institute, San Francisco, CA

Salade de Homard en Petits Pains

This ultra-elegant recipe for lobster salad on little breads is an adaptation of a similar meal served at L'Oasis, near Cannes on the French Riviera.

INGREDIENTS

1 cup *water*

1 bottle *Reisling (or similar white wine)*

¼ cup *sea salt*

¼ cup *peppercorns*

2 *crushed bay leaves*

2 *sliced lemons*

6 *lobster tails*

¼ cup *Dijon-style mustard*

2 tablespoons *aged red-wine vinegar (try BEAUFORD® champagne vinegar)*

2 tablespoons *extra-virgin olive oil*

2 *egg yolks*

1 *clove garlic, crushed*

Pinch or two of freshly ground sea salt, to taste

Freshly ground white pepper, to taste

2 tablespoons *prepared horseradish, drained*

¼ cup *homemade mayonnaise (or HELLMAN'S®)*

6 *petits pains* (small French breads) or any small French-, Italian-, or Kaiser-style rolls

1 tablespoon *English thyme (or any fresh thyme)*

1 tablespoon *chopped parsley*

1 tablespoon *chopped chives*

Kalamata olives, sliced

8 ounces *slivered almonds, toasted*

Watercress, fresh spinach, or romaine lettuce

Truffles (optional)

DIRECTIONS

Prepare court bouillon by combining the first 6 ingredients in a stockpot. Cook 20 minutes. Add lobster and simmer 15 minutes until barely cooked. Remove from heat and cool. Whisk mustard into vinegar, add oil slowly to make an emulsion, and continue to whisk. Add egg yolks, one at a time, until well-incorporated. Add garlic, pinch of sea salt, white pepper, horseradish, and mayonnaise; stir well. Remove lobster from shell; cut into 1-inch chunks. Add to dressing, but do not leave in the dressing more than 30 minutes; otherwise, lobster will be tough. Use only the amount of dressing needed to incorporate the lobster. (The amount depends on the size of the lobster tails. Leftover dressing can be used in salads.) Slice *petits pains* in half, lengthwise, and scoop out most of the dough. Set aside. Add thyme, parsley, chives, olives, and almonds to the lobster-and-dressing mixture. Line each sandwich with watercress (no stems, please), top with lobster mixture, and garnish with a few truffle slices. **Serves 6.**

❧ *It is a spectacular offering when served with a strawberry borscht (just follow a good beet borscht recipe and substitute strawberries for beets; top with a little crème fraîche or sour cream), and perhaps some fruit sorbet or a fruit tart.*

Neiman Marcus—THE MERMAID BAR Fort Lauderdale
Donation to: combined charities

Hawaiian Surfwich

No matter how far inland you are, when you order this sandwich, you can hear waves . . . of approval.

INGREDIENTS

12 slices *of white bread*
Butter, softened
1 cup *sour cream*
½ cup *diced green bell pepper*
2 tablespoons *minced onion*
½ cup *chopped pimiento*
2 tablespoons *wine vinegar*
1 tablespoon *sugar*
1 teaspoon *salt*
¼ teaspoon *pepper*
3 cups *finely shredded cabbage*
1 can *(9¼ ounce) white tuna, drained and flaked*
6 *pineapple slices*
12 *thin tomato slices*
12 *thin (1 ounce each) Cheddar cheese slices*

DIRECTIONS

Toast and butter bread. Combine sour cream, bell pepper, onion, pimiento, vinegar, sugar, salt, and pepper. Fold in cabbage and tuna. Spread mixture equally on 6 slices of toast and top with a pineapple slice. Cut remaining toast diagonally in half and place a half at each side of sandwich. Place tomato slices on each toast triangle. Arrange 2 cheese slices to cover entire open-faced sandwich. Broil about 6 inches from heat until cheese bubbles. Serve at once. **Serves 6.**

❧ *Garnish with a papaya half and lime slices on a bed of lettuce.*

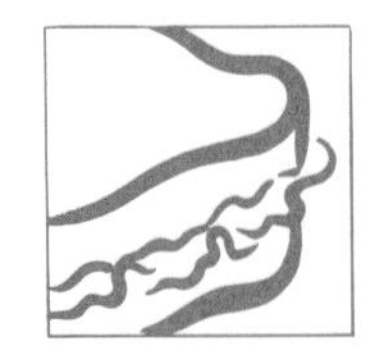

Mrs. Michael (Tamara) Silvestri—Dallas, TX
Donation to: Easter Seals Society for Children, Carrollton, TX

Hot Crab Sandwiches

A variation of a favorite recipe.

INGREDIENTS

2 *individual-portion French rolls*

Butter

1 *clove garlic*

1 tablespoon *olive oil*

1 cup *flaked crab meat (or lobster or shrimp)*

1 *egg*

Cayenne, to taste

TABASCO®, to taste

Dash salt

1 tablespoon *milk*

DIRECTIONS

Cut rolls in half, horizontally. Spread with butter. Broil until golden brown. Keep warm. Sauté garlic in olive oil until toasty brown. Add crab meat and mix well over low heat. In small bowl, beat egg gently and stir in cayenne, TABASCO®, salt, and milk. Add to crab meat mixture, stirring until crab begins to "hold together." Divide into 2 portions and place on hot buttered rolls. Serve at once. **Serves 2.**

❧ *Serve with an artichoke or pasta salad and lots of fresh vegetables.*

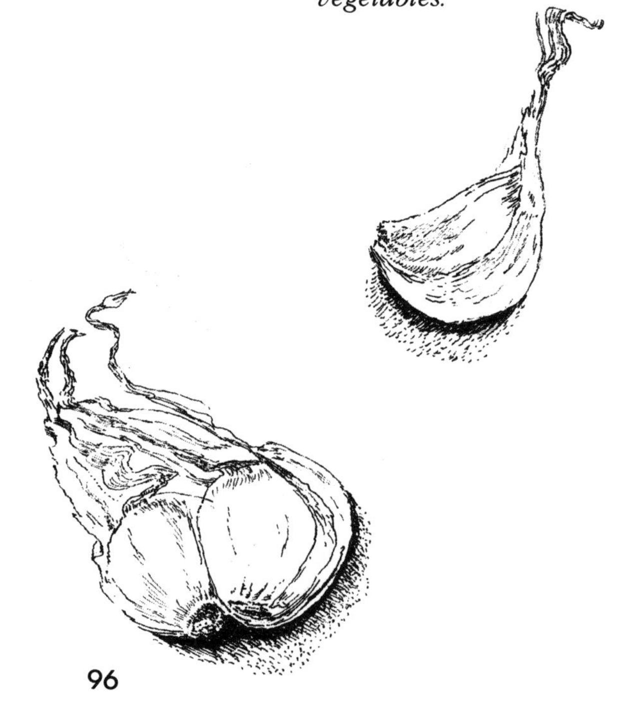

Sandy Mallin—Las Vegas, NV
Donation to: Nathan Adelson Hospice, Inc., Las Vegas, NV

Lavash Sandwich

A gourmet version of lox and cream cheese.

INGREDIENTS

Large lavash cracker bread
1 **package** *(8 ounce) cream cheese, softened*
1 *head Boston lettuce*
1 *tomato, thinly sliced (optional)*
1 *Bermuda onion, thinly sliced (optional)*
1 **pound** *nova salmon, thinly sliced*

DIRECTIONS

Moisten cracker bread between 2 damp towels about 45 minutes until soft and pliable. Remove paper towels and spread cream cheese over one side of the cracker. On first third of cracker nearest you, place lettuce slices. On middle third, place tomato and onion. On last third, place salmon slices. Tightly roll lavash away from you. Wrap in plastic wrap and refrigerate overnight. Slice in quarters. **Serves 6 to 8.**

Neiman Marcus—CLASSIC
Donation to: combined charities

Duke of Windsor Sandwich

Probably the oldest item on any NM menu, it was created by the late Helen Corbitt and inspired by a luncheon menu she prepared for the Duke of Windsor on his visit to Texas in the fifties.

INGREDIENTS

1 **canned** *pineapple ring*
2 **slices** *of white bread, toasted*
1½ **ounces** *YE OLDE LONDON TAVERN® sharp Cheddar cheese spread*
1 **tablespoon** *Major Grey's chutney*
2 **ounces** *thinly sliced turkey*
1 *lettuce leaf*

DIRECTIONS

This recipe must be made to order; it cannot be made in advance. Sauté pineapple ring in butter and cut in half. Spread cheese spread on bottom slice of toasted bread. Spread chutney on cheese spread. Place pineapple halves on top of chutney; add turkey and, then, add lettuce. Top with other slice of toasted bread. Trim crusts gently and cut sandwich into two pieces. **Serves 1.**

Vanessa L. Williams—Los Angeles, CA
Donation to: Schomburg Center for Research in Black Culture, New York, NY

Grilled Turkey and Cheese Sandwich

This is basically a twist on the basic grilled ham and cheese sandwich, which I used to prepare in college. It has evolved as my taste and diet have.

INGREDIENTS

1 stick *butter, softened*

8 ounces *mushrooms, sliced*

1 tablespoon *finely chopped scallion*

1 tablespoon *chopped onion*

Ground pepper, to taste

12 slices *of whole-wheat bread*

8-10 ounces *Monterey jack cheese, grated*

12 ounces *sliced turkey breast (smoked, if desired)*

DIRECTIONS

Melt 1 tablespoon butter in sauté pan. Add mushrooms, scallion, and onion. Sauté to perfection; add pepper. Heat stove-top grill, or place frying pan or heavy cast-iron skillet over medium-to-high heat. Butter bread evenly on one side and place six slices, buttered side down, on grill. Arrange about ¾ ounce of cheese on each bread slice, being careful not to spill cheese on grill. Quickly, but carefully, arrange turkey on top of cheese. Do not heap. Cover turkey with mushrooms. Top with remaining grated cheese and bread, buttered side up. Immediately, turn and flatten sandwich with spatula. By now, sandwiches should be browned on one side. Turn after 3 to 5 minutes. Heat each side an additional 1 to 2 minutes to melt cheese thoroughly. **Serves 6.**

❧ *Serve with sautéed vegetables or your favorite fruit.*

Joanna Shelby Lofton—Federal Way, WA
Donation to: Virginia Mason Medical Association, Seattle, WA (Virginia Mason Society)

Monte Cristo

Lost in time, but being a favorite of mine (and not a common menu item), I devised my own recipe. I prefer this without the usual confectioners' sugar or jam.

INGREDIENTS

1 cup *milk*
2 *eggs, beaten*
8 thick slices *of bread*
¾-1 pound *sliced turkey breast*
8 slices *Monterey jack or Swiss cheese*

DIRECTIONS

Stir milk and eggs together. Dip bread slices into mixture, and fry in butter or oil on both sides until golden brown. Remove and cool for a few minutes. Distribute turkey generously over 4 slices of the French toast, add 2 cheese slices to each sandwich and top with remaining toast slices. Microwave, or warm in 325° oven, until cheese melts. **Serves 4.**

❧ *Serve with Chenin Blanc or iced tea, vichyssoise, and Key lime pie.*

Neiman Marcus—THE FRESHMARKET CAFE℠
Town and Country, Houston
Donation to: combined charities

Turkey and Ham Salad-Wiches Plate

A perennial favorite, perfect for light summer meals and small party menus.

INGREDIENTS

1 slice *of bread*
1 slice *of ham (1 ounce)*
2 slices *of turkey (1 ounce each)*
1 *lettuce leaf*
1 scoop *potato salad*
1 ring-slice *of green bell pepper*
1 *small pimiento slice*
1 *cherry tomato*

DIRECTIONS

Slice bread into 3 finger-length portions. Roll ham and turkey slices. Place on bread fingers. Place lettuce leaf on plate; place potato salad in center of lettuce leaf. Place pepper ring around potato salad, and place a slice of pimiento on top. Arrange bread fingers on the plate. Garnish with cherry tomato. **Serves 1.**

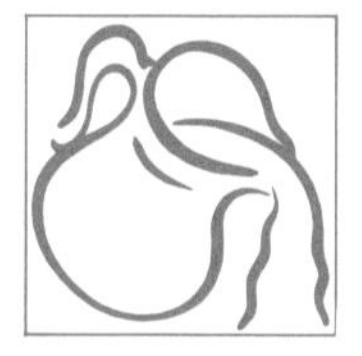

CHAPTER FIVE

Sauces & Dressings

This is where InCirclers became really creative, and now their secrets are yours. Sauces and dressings offer lots of opportunity for experimentation. (We were amazed at the patience of some cooks who pursued variations for months before reaching sauce nirvana!) For centuries, the chef assigned to make the sauces was the star of the kitchen, a man of mystery. But, if you would like to have sauces and dressings demystified, check page 304 for *Pure & Simple* definitions of basic sauces. Then, try these recipes before you venture on your own.

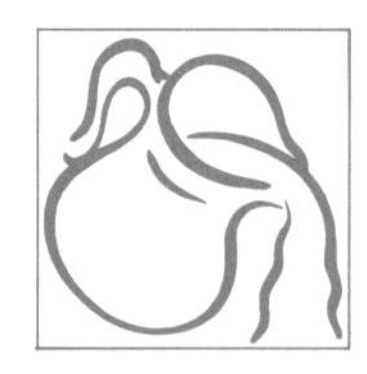

Cissy Brottman—Northfield, IL
Donation to: The Ark, Chicago, IL

Caesar Salad Dressing

INGREDIENTS

3 *cloves garlic*

1 can *(2 ounce) anchovy fillets*

6 tablespoons *fresh lemon juice*

3 tablespoons *red-wine vinegar*

1 *large egg*

1½ cups *olive oil*

Salt and freshly ground pepper, to taste

DIRECTIONS

Turn on food processor or blender. Drop in garlic cloves and mince. Add anchovy fillets that have been patted dry on a paper towel. Add lemon juice, red-wine vinegar, and egg. Purée. With machine running, add oil through the top in a thin, steady stream. Blend until dressing is creamy and smooth. Season with salt and pepper. This dressing will keep for weeks in the refrigerator. **Makes 1½ pints.**

❧ *Serve over romaine lettuce. Garnish with garlic croutons and grated Parmesan cheese.*

Carla Cotropia—Galveston, TX
Donation to: Galveston Arts Center, Inc., Galveston, TX

Carla's Killer Caesar Salad Dressing

I made this dressing every night for one month until perfected. The fish sauce is the secret discovery. This is my only original recipe and it is unique.

INGREDIENTS

2 tablespoons *safflower oil*

2 tablespoons *red-wine vinegar*

2 tablespoons *soy sauce*

1 *egg*

2 *cloves garlic, pressed*

⅛ teaspoon *Oriental fish sauce (don't exceed amount)*

Pinch dried mustard

DIRECTIONS

Mix all ingredients thoroughly. The fish sauce may be purchased in Oriental grocery stores or select supermarkets. **Makes 6 ounces.**

❧ *Serve over ice-cold, crisp romaine lettuce leaves. Garnish with mushrooms, cheese, and croutons.*

Saundra R. Shapiro—Marietta, GA
Donation to: Scottish Rite Hospital for Crippled Children, Inc., Atlanta, GA

Spanish Sauce

This is how Mummy used to wake us up on Sunday morning–with a Spanish omelet.

INGREDIENTS

1 *onion, finely diced*

3-4 *stalks celery, finely diced*

1 tablespoon *margarine or butter*

½ *green bell pepper, finely diced*

1-1½ cups *ketchup*

1 *fresh tomato, chopped*

Salt, to taste

Pepper, to taste

Chile peppers, to taste

DIRECTIONS

Sauté onion and celery with margarine in a saucepan. Add remaining ingredients; cover and simmer. Once vegetables just lose crispness, sauce is ready. **Makes 2 generous servings.**

❧ *Delicious filling for a Spanish omelet with cheese.*

Testing Notes: *This may be used on fish, as well.*

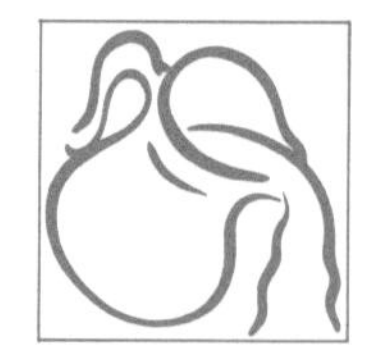

Julie Paulson—Califon, NJ
Donation to: Upper Raritan Watershed Association, Gladstone, NJ

French Dressing

This recipe has been in my mother's family a long time. I always have a jar of it on hand, just as my mother did. It is simple, but good. I never had quite the same dressing anywhere else until we were in France. Imagine my surprise when the salad, served with a beautiful steak for lunch, was dressed with this dressing. The restaurant was Les Trois Marches in Versailles.

INGREDIENTS

1 cup *vegetable oil (WESSON® canola oil may be used)*
Juice of 1 medium-sized lemon
2 tablespoons *cider vinegar*
1 teaspoon *salt*
1 teaspoon *sugar*
1 *clove fresh garlic, split*

DIRECTIONS

Combine everything in a jar and shake. Make the day before using. When dressing the salad, start with a little dressing. Toss. Then, if necessary, add a little more, to taste. Keeps 3 months in the refrigerator. **Makes 1½ cups.**

❧ *Serve with a lettuce, avocado, and tomato salad.*

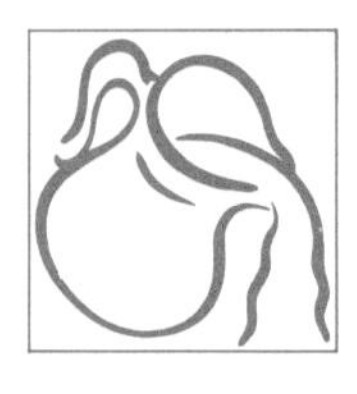

Mrs. Eddie (Betty) Williams—Arlington, TX
Donation to: Cancer Research Foundation of North Texas, Arlington, TX

Keilty Dressing

Pat Keilty, a friend who lives in Virginia, gave me this recipe.

INGREDIENTS

½ cup *red-wine vinegar*
1 tablespoon *Worcestershire sauce*
6 tablespoons *sugar*
1 teaspoon *dry mustard*
1 teaspoon *paprika*
¼ teaspoon *black pepper*
1 teaspoon *salt*
⅛ teaspoon *garlic powder*
1 cup *salad oil*
1 teaspoon *celery seed*

DIRECTIONS

Blend vinegar, Worcestershire sauce, sugar, mustard, paprika, black pepper, salt, and garlic powder. Add oil slowly. Blend well. Stir in celery seeds. **Makes 1 pint.**

❧ *As a main course for lunch, this dressing is wonderful served over a salad of fresh spinach, mandarin oranges, avocados, and sliced almonds. The salad is also good with any meat.*

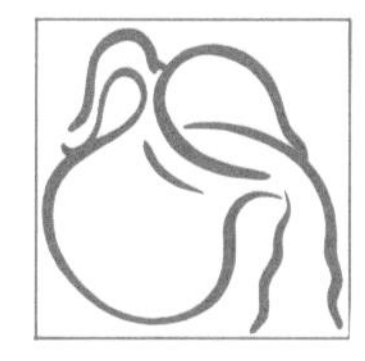

Patricia Giard Kaiser—St. Louis, MO
Donation to: St. Louis Symphony Orchestra, St. Louis, MO

Granny's Red Dressing

Our Granny, Ida M. Kaiser, my husband's paternal grandmother, was one of the great treasures of our life. When she spent the weekends with us, she kept Tom, myself, and our two boys spellbound with stories of growing up on the farm in Wisconsin. From going on her first date in a horse and buggy to shearing sheep for winter's wool, we were her eager and willing audience for hours. Her Red Dressing is just like she was—colorful and piquant! Traditionally, we serve it every year with Christmas-night supper. I am submitting this recipe to celebrate her memory. 1990 would have been Granny's 100th year. P.S. I can't make German potato salad (I've tried) and I never ate bratwurst growing up in Dallas living off Sonny Bryan's famous barbecue, but the Red Dressing I've mastered.

INGREDIENTS

- **1** *onion, chopped*
- **½ cup** *sugar*
- **1 teaspoon** *salt*
- **1 teaspoon** *paprika*
- **1 teaspoon** *plus a pinch of ground black pepper*
- **1 tablespoon** *prepared mustard*
- **1 tablespoon** *Worcestershire sauce*
- **1 bottle** *(14 ounce) ketchup*
- **¾ cup** *vinegar*
- **1 scant cup** *salad oil*

DIRECTIONS

Blend everything, except the oil, in a blender on high until smooth. Stop; stir. Replace lid. Turn on blender, remove plug from the lid, and add salad oil in a steady stream through opening in lid until well-blended. Stop; stir. Pour into storage jar with tight cap and refrigerate. Make at least 24 hours before serving. Shake well. **Makes 4 cups.**

❧ *Great served on or with tossed greens; spinach salad; fresh grapefruit sections; fresh-water fish; or seafood.*

Peggy Jane Miller—Dallas, TX
Donation to: American Heart Foundation, Des Moines, IA

My Salad Dressing

This is my creation and everyone loves it.

INGREDIENTS

- **¼ cup** *red-wine vinegar*
- **¾ cup** *oil*
- **⅛ cup** *KIKKOMAN® soy sauce*
- **2 tablespoons** *ketchup*
- **1 tablespoon** *garlic powder*
- **1 tablespoon** *curry powder*
- **1 tablespoon** *dried parsley*
- **½ teaspoon** *salt*
- **½ teaspoon** *red-pepper flakes*
- **3 tablespoons** *sugar*
- **3 tablespoons** *water*

DIRECTIONS

Pour vinegar in a large jar; add oil slowly. Stir in remaining ingredients. Store in refrigerator. **Makes 2 cups.**

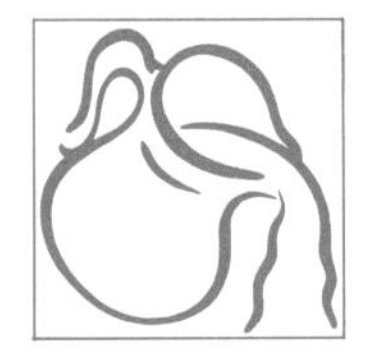

Lois S. Kennedy—St. Louis, MO
Donation to: American Heart Association, Inc., St. Louis, MO

Nonfat Salad Dressing

I made up this recipe for nonfat, low-salt cooking.

INGREDIENTS

- **2¼ cups** *DANNON® nonfat yogurt*
- **¼ cup** *cider vinegar*
- **1 packet** *EQUAL® sweetener*
- **2 tablespoons** *Dijon-style mustard*
- **2 tablespoons** *lemon juice*
- **2** *large cloves garlic, crushed*
- **1 teaspoon** *dill weed*

DIRECTIONS

Mix all ingredients thoroughly and chill.
Makes 3 cups.

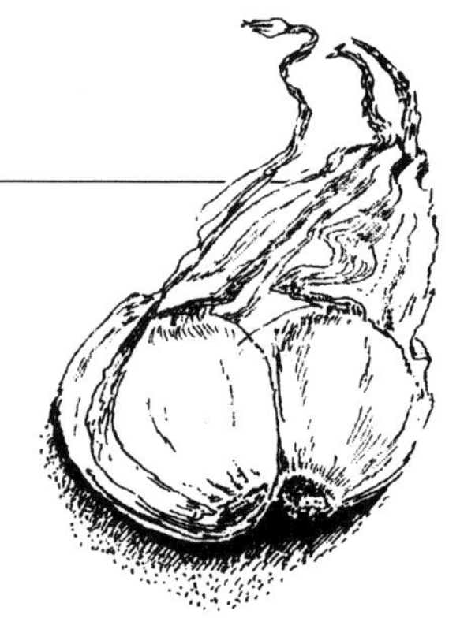

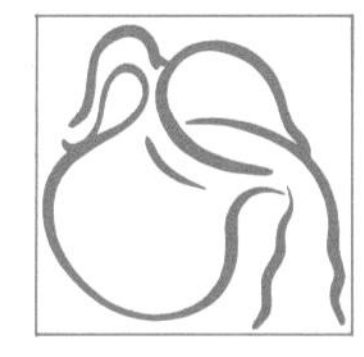

Janet G. Libin—Wellesley Hills, MA
Donation to: Aid for Cancer Research, Natick, MA

Cranberry Relish

My mother made this for many years. It's fabulous.

INGREDIENTS

- **2 cans** *(16 ounces each) jellied cranberry sauce*
- **1 can** *(16 ounce) crushed pineapples, drained*
- **1 package** *(16 ounce) frozen sliced strawberries, thawed and drained*
- **1 package** *(10 ounce) frozen raspberries, thawed and drained*

DIRECTIONS

Mash cranberry sauce with a fork in a bowl. Add pineapples, strawberries, and raspberries. Mix together. Cover and refrigerate overnight or at least 6 hours before serving.
Makes 2 quarts.

❧ *Serve with poultry or beef.*

Dana W. Hagen—Pompano Beach, FL
Donation to: Museum of Art, Inc., Fort Lauderdale, FL

Ham Sauce

This old family recipe is always served with ham on holidays.

INGREDIENTS

- **½ cup** *sugar*
- **3 tablespoons** *dry mustard*
- **1 heaping tablespoon** *flour*
- **1** *egg*
- *Salt*
- **1 cup** *cider vinegar*
- **1 pint** *coffee cream*

DIRECTIONS

Mix ingredients together. Cook in a double boiler, or stir constantly in a saucepan, until thickened. Serve hot.
Makes 1 quart.

Pamela K. Baxter—New York, NY
Donation to: Sloan-Kettering Institute for Cancer Research, New York, NY

Kalamata Olive Sauce

INGREDIENTS

- **10 ounces** *Kalamata olives*
- 2 *shallots, minced*
- 2 *cloves garlic, minced*
- 1 *hot, red chile pepper, seeded and minced*
- **2 tablespoons** *fresh Italian parsley leaves*
- **¼ teaspoon** *dried thyme*
- **⅛ teaspoon** *dried oregano*
- **1 teaspoon** *balsamic vinegar*
- **½ cup** *extra-virgin olive oil*

DIRECTIONS

Rinse, drain, and pit olives. Mince shallots and garlic in food processor with metal blade. Add chile pepper and mince. Add parsley, thyme, oregano, and vinegar, pulsing to blend. With machine on, add olive oil slowly through feed tube. Blend until emulsified. **Makes 2 cups.**

❧ *Toss sauce with pasta; or serve on grilled fish or chicken, and garnish with 1 bunch fresh, minced chives and zest of 1 lemon; or brush sauce on grilled bread and garnish with the minced chives.*

Martha Sacks—Fort Lauderdale, FL
Donation to: Covenant House Florida, Fort Lauderdale, FL

Aunt Millie's Mustard Sauce

"Aunt" Millie was really my grandmother's best friend, and this was her recipe many, many years ago.

INGREDIENTS

- **½ cup** *FRENCH'S® mustard*
- **½ can** *tomato soup, undiluted*
- **½ cup** *cider vinegar*
- **½ cup** *sugar*
- **1 stick** *margarine*
- 3 *egg yolks, beaten*

DIRECTIONS

Combine all ingredients and cook over low heat. Stir until thickened. Serve warm or cold. This will keep for weeks when refrigerated in a sealed container. **Makes 2 cups.**

❧ *Serve with honey-baked ham, fish, and other meats.*

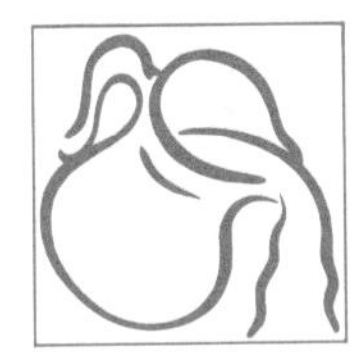

Sharon Tesche—Dallas, TX
Donation to: Family Place, Inc., Dallas, TX

Morilles Sauce

I first had this incredible sauce with a light supper at the Hotel Navigation restaurant in Lausanne-Ouchy, Switzerland. It was served with a beef fillet in a puffed pastry shell. I adapted Helen Corbitt's mushroom sauce recipe to include these fabulous mushrooms. The mushrooms have a strong, smoky flavor. I try to bring in several ounces each time I have the good fortune to visit Switzerland.

INGREDIENTS

1 cup *dried morilles (morels)*
½ cup *milk*
2 tablespoons *butter*
2 tablespoons *flour*
¾ cup *beef or chicken stock*
Salt, to taste
Sherry, to taste
KITCHEN BOUQUET® or other gravy darkener, to taste

DIRECTIONS

Soak morilles 1 hour in milk to cover. (To hasten the process, heat slightly in microwave.) Drain mushrooms. Reserve liquid, including residue, in a separate bowl. Squeeze excess liquid from mushrooms into this bowl. Carefully, pour off half the liquid, including residue. Set aside. Chop mushrooms coarsely. Make a roux with butter and flour. Cook roux 2 minutes and quickly add mushrooms, stirring to coat. Add stock, stirring constantly. Add the soaking liquid to sauce and stir until thickened. Add salt, sherry, and KITCHEN BOUQUET®. **Makes 1 cup.**

❧ *Serve with beef fillet in a puffed pastry.*

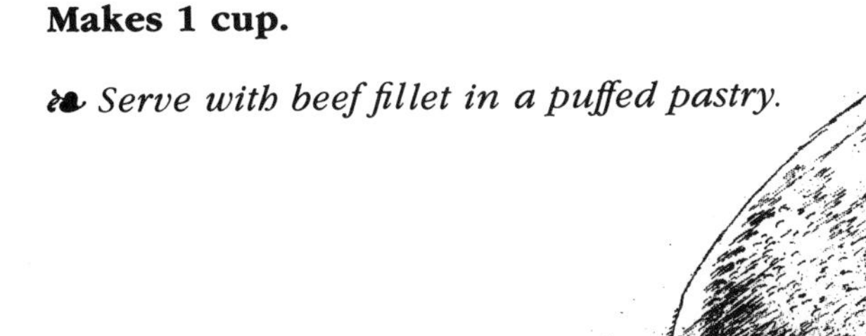

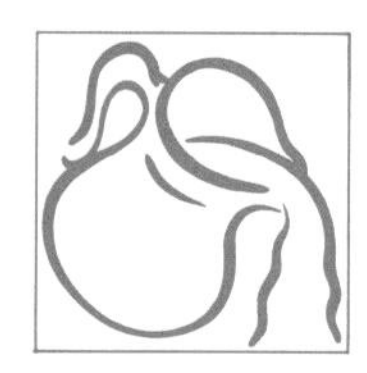

Neiman Marcus—THE NM CAFE Bal Harbour
Donation to: combined charities

Romanov Sauce

Restaurant Manager Mary Ellen Calder swears this velvety sauce enhances any fruit dessert.

INGREDIENTS

2 packages *(8 ounces each) cream cheese*
1/6 cup *milk*
1/2 box *powdered sugar*
1/2 teaspoon *vanilla*
1 cup *heavy cream*

DIRECTIONS

Blend cream cheese and milk until smooth. Add sugar and vanilla, beating until smooth. Add cream and blend well. **Makes 1 pint.**

❧ *Serve with fresh strawberries.*

Mrs. Thomas Wehling—St. Charles, IL
Donation to: Garfield Farm Museum, LaFox, IL

Secret Shrimp Sauce

I received this shrimp sauce recipe from a lady who was in my employ many years ago. She received it from a former employer in North Carolina. It has been kept secret for a long time. This is the first time I have passed it on!

INGREDIENTS

1 cup *mayonnaise*
3 tablespoons *chopped, tender, fresh spinach*
1/2 teaspoon *onion powder*
1 1/2 tablespoons *tarragon white-wine vinegar*
1 tablespoon *chervil*

DIRECTIONS

Mix mayonnaise, spinach, onion powder, and vinegar. Sprinkle chervil on top. **Makes 2 cups.**

❧ *Serve with fresh, cooked shrimp. This makes an especially attractive presentation when regular cocktail sauce is also served.*

Mrs. William M. Carpenter—Los Angeles, CA
Donation to: Children's Hospital of Los Angeles, Los Angeles, CA

Plum Soy

My parents were given this Plum Soy recipe in the late 1930s by their San Francisco lawyer, long active in wine and food societies. He received it from plum orchard ranchers in the Sacramento Valley.

INGREDIENTS

5 pints *dark-purple plums, halved, pitted, and unpeeled*

6 cups *sugar*

2 cups *apple cider vinegar*

1 tablespoon *cinnamon*

1 tablespoon *black pepper*

1 tablespoon *allspice*

1 level tablespoon *of mixed ground cloves and salt*

DIRECTIONS

Cook plums slowly for 4 hours, stirring occasionally. Drain juice, then mix pulp with remaining ingredients. Cook slowly 1 hour until consistency of applesauce. Place in sterilized jars. **Makes 1 pint.**

❧ *Serve on special occasions as a condiment with roast beef or roast duck.*

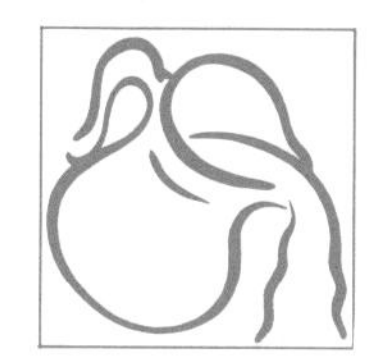

Catherine E. Brackbill—Dallas, TX
Donation to: Dallas Opera, Dallas, TX

Southwest Barbecue Sauce

I embellished a recipe given to me by a dear friend in 1965 in West Texas.

INGREDIENTS

1 *small onion, quartered*

1 *clove garlic*

Juice of ½ lemon

1 cup *thick ketchup*

2 tablespoons *vinegar*

1 teaspoon *dry mustard*

½ teaspoon *basil*

3 tablespoons *brown sugar*

1 teaspoon *salt*

¼ teaspoon *ground pepper*

½ cup *raisins*

⅔ cup *butter, melted*

DIRECTIONS

Blend all ingredients in a blender until raisins are pulverized. Remove and place in saucepan. Simmer on top of stove for about 45 minutes. **Makes 2 cups.**

❧ *Serve with baby-back pork ribs or loin pork chops.*

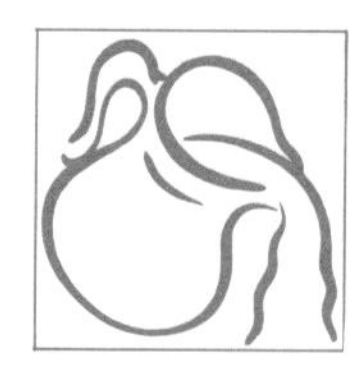

O.B. Williams—Dallas, TX
Donation to: Presbyterian Hospital of Dallas, Dallas, TX

Sauce for Vegetable Terrine

The source of this recipe may have been a cooking magazine ten or more years ago. I've had it on my computer file for six years.

INGREDIENTS

- **2** *medium-sized yellow onions, minced*
- **6 tablespoons** *olive oil*
- **1 can** *(32 ounce) plum tomatoes, drained*
- **⅓ cup** *minced fresh basil (or 1 teaspoon dried thyme)*
- **1 tablespoon** *minced fresh garlic*
- **1 tablespoon** *minced parsley*
- **1 teaspoon** *sugar*
- **1 teaspoon** *salt*
- **¼ teaspoon** *pepper*
- **1 cup** *heavy cream*

DIRECTIONS

Cook onions in olive oil until softened. Add all ingredients, except cream. Simmer 30 minutes. Then, process in food processor with steel blade until puréed. Return to heat and simmer until sauce has the consistency of relish. Reduce cream to one-half over high heat and add to tomato sauce. Heat to boiling, stirring constantly. Pour half of the sauce over vegetable terrine and serve half in a bowl on the side. **Makes 2 cups.**

Marilyn E. Brown—Houston, TX
Donation to: The Salvation Army, Houston, TX

Tomato Sauce for Spaghetti

This is a recipe that I have developed over the years while trying to produce the perfect tomato sauce.

INGREDIENTS

1 *large onion, minced*
1 *green bell pepper, chopped*
1 *clove garlic, minced*
1 *carrot, shredded*
1 *stalk celery, minced*
¼ cup *olive oil*
4 tablespoons *butter*
½ teaspoon *basil*
½ teaspoon *oregano*
½ teaspoon *thyme*
2 teaspoons *sugar*
½ teaspoon *salt*
½ teaspoon *red-pepper flakes, to taste*
Black pepper, to taste
1 cup *sliced fresh mushrooms*
1 pound *ground beef, browned and drained*
½ pound *Italian sausage, browned and drained*
3 cans *(28 ounces each) tomatoes, chopped*
1 can *(6 ounce) tomato paste*
⅓ cup *red wine*

DIRECTIONS

Sauté vegetables in oil and butter until softened. Add remaining ingredients. Bring to boil and simmer, uncovered, 2 to 3 hours until sauce thickens, stirring occasionally. This recipe doubles easily and freezes well. **Makes 2 quarts.**

❧ *Serve over pasta with a tossed green salad and fresh garlic bread.*

CHAPTER SIX

Fish

Don't hesitate—make friends with the fishes. Knowing how to prepare them is one of the most rewarding accomplishments in cooking. (Next to popcorn, it's the best thing ever made in a microwave.) While there are more and more fresh-fish markets opening, almost every up-to-date supermarket now has a fresh-fish section. No other meat offers such good nutrition per ounce with virtually no fat involved at all. InCirclers must certainly realize that. We had a hard time winnowing these from the hundreds of fish recipes sent from every coast, and all the lakes and rivers in-between. If you have any qualms at all about cooking fish, check our *Pure & Simple* tips on page 310.

Mrs. Ramiro Martinez—Dallas, TX
Donation to: Dallas Museum of Art, Dallas, TX

Ceviche Paradiso

This is the house specialty of our villa in Acapulco on Paradise Drive. My husband, its creator, spent thirty years perfecting the recipe, and although the view of the bay from our dining terrace surely enhances the flavor, this dish can be a refreshing light lunch or starter for summer dinners in Dallas, San Diego, or Washington, D.C. Ceviche Paradiso headed the menu at a recent dinner in Acapulco for twenty-two distinguished friends from New Delhi, garnering rave reviews and transcending international boundaries! The key ingredients are the freshest available fish and very ripe, firm tomatoes.

INGREDIENTS

- **2 pounds** *tomatoes, very ripe but firm*
- **2 cups** *chopped onions*
- **2 tablespoons** *minced garlic*
- **2 cups** *ketchup*
- **1 cup** *green olive halves*
- **1 cup** *sliced, pickled jalapeños*
- **1 teaspoon** *black pepper*
- **1 teaspoon** *plus* **1 tablespoon** *salt*
- **½ teaspoon** *oregano*
- **2** *bay leaves*
- **½ cup** *chopped cilantro*
- **6 ounces** *fresh orange juice*
- **2 quarts** *water*
- **2 pounds** *firm, fresh white-fish fillets, cut into ½-inch cubes*
- **4 ounces** *fresh lime juice*
- **1 pound** *cooked cocktail shrimp (optional)*
- **½ cup** *virgin olive oil*
- **2** *ripe avocados, sliced*

DIRECTIONS

Peel and chop tomatoes. Combine in a bowl with onions, garlic, ketchup, olives, jalapeños, pepper, 1 teaspoon salt, oregano, bay leaves, cilantro, and orange juice. Refrigerate the sauce 2 to 3 hours. To prepare fish, boil the water with 1 tablespoon salt. Remove from heat and immediately add fish fillets, slightly cooking for only 30 to 45 seconds. Drain and cool. Combine fish in a bowl with lime juice, marinate 15 minutes, and drain. Combine fish with the very cold sauce. Add cooked shrimp and olive oil. Marinate the ceviche in the refrigerator, covered, 2 to 4 hours before serving. Garnish individual portions with slices of ripe avocado. **Serves 6 to 8.**

Testing Notes: *This also may be used as an appetizer.*

Mrs. Guy Edward Moman—Tuscaloosa, AL
Donation to: University of Alabama Diabetes Research and Education Hospital, Birmingham, AL

Fish Pie

This recipe came from Nancy Cheney, wife of Captain John Cheney of Florida. It is a wonderful pie to have on hand for guests, for it can be made ahead and frozen. You can use any fish—salmon, shrimp, or any combination of fish.

INGREDIENTS

1 pound *of fish fillets*
1 tablespoon *lemon juice*
6 tablespoons *butter or margarine*
1 9-inch *plain pastry pie shell*
1 cup *chopped onions*
½ cup *chopped celery*
1 tablespoon *snipped parsley*
½ teaspoon *salt*
¼ teaspoon *cayenne*
Minced garlic, to taste
Black pepper, to taste
2 tablespoons *flour*
1 cup *heavy cream*
1 cup *grated cheese*
⅓ cup *bread crumbs*

DIRECTIONS

Poach fish in boiling water, to cover, with lemon juice and 1 tablespoon butter until fish flakes easily. Set aside. Bake pie shell 15 minutes at 450°. Sauté onions and celery in 3 tablespoons butter until soft; add parsley, salt, cayenne, garlic, and black pepper. Blend flour into mixture, stirring constantly. Add cream; cook until thickened. Stir in cheese. Remove from heat and add fish. Turn mixture into pie crust. Toss bread crumbs with remaining butter and sprinkle over pie. Bake 30 to 35 minutes at 325°. One pie will **serve 4 to 6** guests, depending upon their taste and what you serve with the pie.

❧ *I usually serve this with a green salad and yeast rolls.*

Robert M. Seale—San Carlos, CA
Donation to: Rose Resnick Center for the Blind & Visually Impaired, San Francisco, CA

Seafood Calypso

This Caribbean dish is rumored to be an aphrodisiac. It is served to the bride and groom on their wedding night. I learned it from a Jamaican housekeeper and substituted beef consommé for butter to make a low-calorie treat.

INGREDIENTS

- ½ **can** *beef consommé with gelatin*
- ¼ **cup** *minced yellow or white onion*
- 1 **tablespoon** *minced garlic*
- 3 **tablespoons** *minced scallion*
- ½ **cup** *peeled, seeded, and chopped tomato*
- ¼ **cup** *dry white vermouth*
- 1 **tablespoon** *Worcestershire sauce*
- 1 **tablespoon** *lemon juice*
- 1 **tablespoon** *chopped parsley*
- ½ **teaspoon** *ground black pepper*
- 1 **teaspoon** *thyme*
- ½ **teaspoon** *sweet basil*
- ¼ **teaspoon** *sage*
- ¼ **teaspoon** *coriander*
- ¼ **teaspoon** *mace*
- ¼ **teaspoon** *cumin*
- ¼ **teaspoon** *turmeric*
- 2 **drops** *TABASCO® sauce*
- 3 *whole bay leaves*
- 12 *raw shrimp, shelled and deveined*
- 12 *raw bay scallops (or 6 large sea scallops, quartered)*
- ¼ **cup** *warm brandy*
- ½ **teaspoon** *Pernod (a French liqueur)*
- 2 **cups** *cooked white rice*

DIRECTIONS

Pour beef consommé into frying pan sprayed with nonstick cooking spray. Sauté onion, garlic, and scallion until cooked down. Add everything else, except shrimp, scallops, brandy, Pernod, and rice. Simmer sauce 20 minutes until tomatoes break down and sauce is semi-thick. Add shrimp and scallops. When shrimp start to turn pink, warm brandy. Pour brandy over frying pan and ignite. When flame is out, add Pernod and stir. Remove bay leaves. Serve over hot rice. **Serves 4.**

❧ *Serve with fresh bread, a dry white wine, and a small green salad or fresh fruit. Melon, orange slices, or papaya are particularly good with this.*

Mrs. Jack M. Chinn—Dallas, TX
Donation to: American Heart Association, Inc., Dallas, TX

Crab Imperial

The owner of a famous restaurant in Washington, D.C., who prepared Crab Imperial especially for us, gave me this recipe before we moved back to Texas.

INGREDIENTS

1 tablespoon *English mustard*
1 tablespoon *salt*
2 teaspoons *white pepper*
2 *eggs, lightly beaten*
1½-2 cups *HELLMAN'S® mayonnaise*
1 *green bell pepper, finely diced*
2 *pimientos, finely diced*
3 pounds *lump crab meat*
Paprika, to taste

DIRECTIONS

Mix mustard, salt, white pepper, eggs, and 1 cup mayonnaise. Add bell pepper and pimientos. Add crab meat and mix lightly. Prepare 8 crab shells or 8 small casseroles. Fill each with crab mixture. Top each with a light coating of mayonnaise and sprinkle with paprika. Bake 15 minutes at 350°. Serve hot or cold. **Serves 8.**

❧ *Serve with fruit salad, fresh asparagus, and pineapple sherbet drenched in champagne.*

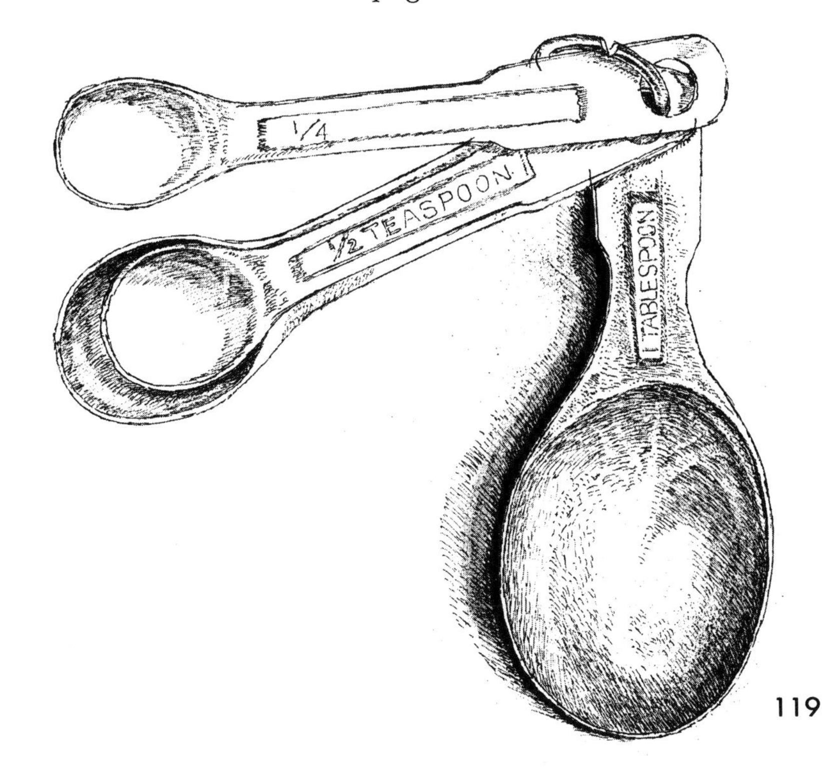

Martha S. Durrett—Simsboro, LA
Donation to: St. Jude's Children's Research Hospital, Memphis, TN

Crawfish Étouffée

INGREDIENTS

½ cup *unsalted butter*
½ cup *flour*
1 *large onion, chopped*
4 *scallions, chopped*
2 *stalks celery with leaves, finely chopped*
1 *bell pepper (red or yellow are sweeter)*
4 *cloves garlic, minced*
2 cups *fish stock, or more if needed*
⅛ teaspoon *thyme*
½ teaspoon *sweet basil*
Salt and freshly ground pepper, to taste
Cayenne, to taste
2 pounds *crawfish tails, peeled and cleaned*

DIRECTIONS

Melt butter in sauté pan. Add flour and cook over low heat, stirring constantly to make a light brown roux. Add onion, scallions, celery, bell pepper, and garlic. Cook vegetables until soft, adding a little fish stock to keep from sticking, if necessary. When vegetables are soft, add thyme, basil, and remainder of stock. Season with salt, pepper, and cayenne. Simmer 20 minutes. Add crawfish and cook 10 minutes. Serve over rice. **Serves 6 to 8.**

Neiman Marcus—THE ZODIAC San Diego
Donation to: combined charities

Flounder with Grapefruit

Not everyone would think to combine grapefruit with fish, but it's one of the most popular and creative dishes at NM.

INGREDIENTS

3½ pounds *flounder fillets*
Salt, to taste
2 tablespoons *butter*
2 tablespoons *olive oil*
1 tablespoon *chopped onion*
1 tablespoon *chopped parsley*
1 cup *American dry white wine*
12 *grapefruit sections*
1 *lime*

DIRECTIONS

Sprinkle flounder with salt. Set aside. In a large ovenproof skillet or pan, melt butter; add olive oil and heat. Add onion, parsley, and wine. Lay flounder on top and simmer 5 to 10 minutes. Place grapefruit sections on top. Place in a 450° oven and bake 15 minutes until top is browned. Serve at once with a wedge of fresh lime in place of the usual lemon. **Serves 4.**

L. R. Herkimer—Dallas, TX
Donation to: Dallas Garden Center, Inc., Dallas, TX

Frog Legs Herkimer

When it was my month to cook for my poker club, this was the recipe I served. And, in 1983 I entered this in the March of Dimes Celebrity Chef Cook-Off and won the award for best entreé.

INGREDIENTS

8 *fairly large frog legs*
2 tablespoons *lemon juice*
Water
Flour
Salt, to taste
Freshly cracked white pepper, to taste
5 tablespoons *salted butter*
2 teaspoons *finely chopped garlic*
2 tablespoons *chopped mixed herbs: tarragon, parsley, and chives*
1 tablespoon *cognac*
2 tablespoons *dry white wine*
2 *lemons, thinly sliced*

DIRECTIONS

Wash frog legs thoroughly in lemon juice and water. Dry on paper towels and dust lightly with flour seasoned with salt and white pepper. Heat butter in skillet until it foams; add garlic. Cook 1 minute. Put in frog legs and shake until golden brown on each side. Add salt, pepper, and mixed herbs. Cook another minute. In a separate little pan, heat cognac and wine. Ignite and pour, flaming, over frog legs. Serve immediately on a hot platter garnished with thin lemon slices. **Serves 4.**

❧ *Serve with fresh spinach or green beans, oven-browned potatoes, and a Caesar salad.*

Testing Notes: *Add cherry tomatoes sautéed in cognac for a more colorful presentation.*

Anton Edelmann—Maître Chef des Cuisines The Savoy, London
Donation to: combined charities

Brochettes de Langoustine Diana (Skewered Langoustinae Diana)

INGREDIENTS

1 pound *medium-sized zucchini*

24-32 *cooked langoustine tails*

2 ounces *olive oil*

7 ounces *noodles, cooked and drained*

½ cup *tomato purée*

Salt, to taste

Freshly ground pepper, to taste

DIRECTIONS

All ingredients must be fresh. Peel 2 zucchini and cut the peel in long strips. Discard the rest of these 2 zucchini. Blanch the strips in boiling, salted water and refresh in ice water. Cut remaining zucchini in long, paper-thin slices. Season them with salt and pepper. Wrap each langoustine in a slice of zucchini and thread 6 to 8 on each skewer. Brush them with 1 ounce of olive oil and grill until golden brown. Toss noodles and remaining zucchini strips in the remaining oil. Season and arrange in the center of each plate. Warm the tomato purée. Position the langoustines on top of the noodles and pour some of the purée around each portion. **Serves 4.**

❧ *To make this meal even more healthful, serve a green salad with lemon dressing.*

Carmen C. de Melgar—Mexico, D.F.
Donation to: Texas Heart Institute, Houston TX

Lobster Salpicon

A delicate dish of Mayan cuisine in the Yucatán Peninsula and Central America. It may also be prepared with venison meat.

INGREDIENTS

½ **teaspoon** *finely chopped onion*

½ *lime*

1 **pound** *of lobster meat, cooked and chilled*

Juice of 2 limes or lemons, to taste

2 **tablespoons** *extra-virgin olive oil*

1 **tablespoon** *chopped, peeled, and seeded tomato*

¾ **cup** *finely sliced lettuce*

1 **tablespoon** *chopped radish*

1 **tablespoon** *chopped fresh cilantro*

1 **teaspoon** *oregano*

½ **teaspoon** *salt*

1 *avocado*

DIRECTIONS

Combine onion and ½ lime in a small bowl. Let them rest 30 minutes. Finely shred lobster meat in a large bowl; add juice of 2 limes and toss. Add olive oil and toss. Add remaining ingredients, except avocado, and toss lightly but well. Before serving, peel and slice avocado and arrange on top. **Serves 2** as a main course.

❧ *Serve with a dry French wine.*

David W. Cowles—Las Vegas, NV
Donation to: Hadassah Hospital, Israel

JJ's Salmon and Béarnaise Sauce with Dill and Capers

My wife, JJ, obtained this recipe from a friend, then adapted the original to suit our family's tastes, which include an inordinate fondness for dill and capers.

INGREDIENTS

1 box *PEPPERIDGE FARM® pastry sheets*

8 *salmon fillets with skin but no scales, cut 2-inches square-by-1-inch-thick*

2 *eggs, beaten*

4 *egg yolks*

Juice of 1 lemon

2 cups *melted butter*

Salt and pepper, to taste

4 tablespoons *capers*

¼ cup *chopped parsley*

1 tablespoon *dried dill weed*

1 tablespoon *tarragon vinegar*

DIRECTIONS

Roll out pastry sheets ⅛-inch-thick. Cut each sheet into 4 squares. Place one salmon fillet, skin side up, on each pastry square. Fold pastry around fillet; brush edges with egg and seal. Place on cookie sheet, seam side down. Brush with beaten egg. Bake 30 minutes at 350° until golden brown. Meanwhile, prepare Béarnaise sauce. Beat egg yolks and lemon juice until well-blended in the top half of a double boiler. Place over bottom half of double boiler and cook slowly over very low heat, never allowing water to come to a boil. Add melted butter slowly, stirring constantly with a wooden spoon. Add salt, pepper, capers, parsley, dill, and vinegar. Stir to blend. Serve salmon immediately after removing from oven, allowing 2 portions per serving. Serve Béarnaise sauce on the side.
Serves 4.

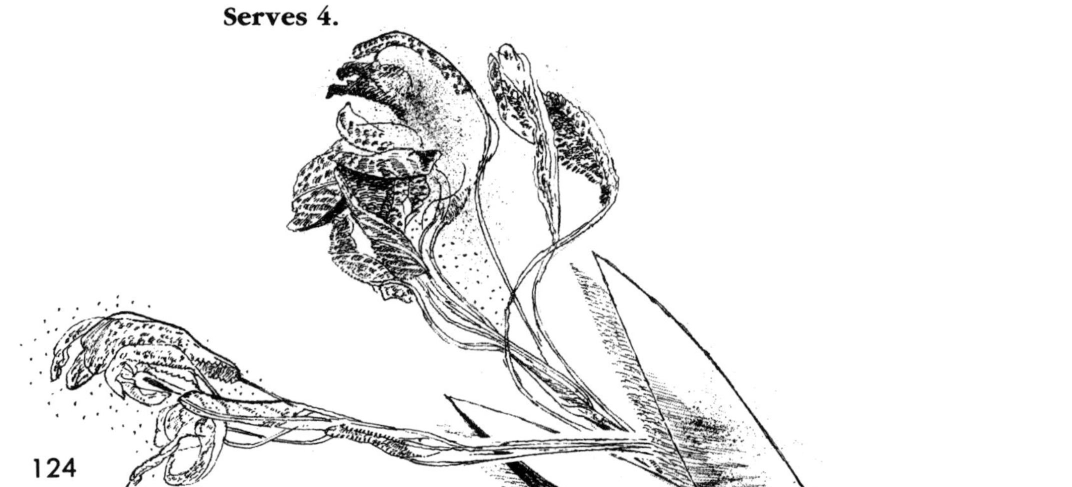

Marion M. Worthington—Houston, TX
Donation to: American Heart Association, Inc., Houston, TX

Saumon en Croûte

Tired of Beef Wellington, I needed a new dish to impress my daughter's boyfriend.

INGREDIENTS

2 pounds *of salmon steak, skinned and boned*

Juice of ½ lemon

1 *bunch fresh spinach*

6 ounces *whole fresh mushrooms*

½ ounce *pink peppercorns, crushed*

Black bean paste

2 *unbaked PEPPERIDGE FARM® puff pastry sheets*

1 *egg, lightly beaten*

DIRECTIONS

Preheat oven to 400°. Spray baking sheet with a nonstick spray and set aside. Wash and dry salmon, cover with lemon juice, and set aside. Wash and spin-dry spinach; discard stems. Separate mushroom caps and stems, setting caps aside. Chop spinach and mushroom stems coarsely. Toss with peppercorns. Spread bean paste on 1 side of each pastry sheet, leaving a 1-inch margin on all sides. Place 1 pastry sheet on baking sheet, bean paste side up. Make a nest in the center with the spinach mixture. Place the salmon on spinach and arrange mushroom caps on top. Cover with remaining pastry sheet, bean side down. Crimp, seal, and trim excess pastry. Use excess strips to decorate. Make slits across the top of the dough and glaze with egg. Bake 20 minutes until golden brown. Serve sliced—hot or cold. **Serves 4 to 6.**

❧ *Serve with braised leeks and green peas.*

Debra Blauwiekel—Geneva, IL
Donation to: Delnor Community Hospital Foundation, Geneva, IL

Savory Salmon Steaks

Adapted from another fish recipe to be fast, easy, and healthful, and taste good to non-fish eaters!

INGREDIENTS

- **3 tablespoons** *Dijon-style mustard*
- **3 tablespoons** *low-sodium soy sauce*
- **3 tablespoons** *dark brown sugar*
- **3 tablespoons** *safflower oil*
- **1 teaspoon** *prepared horseradish*
- **4** *salmon steaks (8 ounces each)*

DIRECTIONS

Combine first 5 ingredients in small bowl. Brush ½ the marinade over fish. Marinate fish up to 6 hours in refrigerator, if desired. Place fish on grill. Grill 5 minutes. Turn and brush with remaining marinade. Grill until fish flake easily. Serve hot or at room temperature. Approximately 460 calories per serving. **Serves 4.**

❧ *Serve with rice and salad.*

Testing Notes: *We suggest you serve tiny, fresh asparagus and a squash soufflé with this dish.*

Neiman Marcus—THE ROTUNDA℠ San Francisco
Donation to: combined charities

Brick's Scallop Piccata

This is a frequent "Memorable Dining" dish on Chef Brick Burleson's Bay Area menu.

INGREDIENTS

1 teaspoon *minced shallot*
2 ounces *butter*
4 ounces *(10 to 20) sea scallops*
1 ounce *white wine*
1 teaspoon *capers*
1 teaspoon *lemon juice*
1 *bunch spinach, cleaned*
Garlic, to taste
3 ounces *pasta, cooked*
Chopped parsley
Sliced lemon

DIRECTIONS

Sauté shallots in 1 ounce butter; add scallops and brown. Deglaze pan with white wine; add capers and lemon juice. Add remaining butter and reduce liquid. Meanwhile, sauté the spinach with a touch of butter and, perhaps, some fresh-ground garlic. Heat the noodles. Arrange on a heated plate. Garnish with chopped parsley and sliced lemon. **Serves 2.**

M. Susan Douglas—Topeka, KS
Donation to: Friends of the Topeka Zoo, Inc., Topeka, KS

Marinated Scallop Kabobs

This is the first seafood recipe that I tried out on my mother-in-law. She is from New York (lots of seafood) and I am from the Midwest where, until recently, there has been little fresh fish. The dinner was a success.

INGREDIENTS

1 pound *sea scallops*
½ cup *salad oil*
¼ cup *cider vinegar*
1 teaspoon *sugar*
1 teaspoon *salt*
¼ cup *fresh basil, or ¼ teaspoon dried*
¼ teaspoon *paprika*
⅛ teaspoon *pepper*
2 tablespoons *chili sauce*
1 teaspoon *prepared mustard*
1 *clove garlic, minced*
2 *large limes*

DIRECTIONS

At least 3 hours before serving, or early in the day, gently rinse scallops in cold water. Pat dry with paper towels. Combine scallops in medium-sized bowl with all ingredients, except limes. Cover and refrigerate. Prepare outdoor grill for barbecuing. Cut each lime into 6 wedges. On 4 long skewers, thread limes and scallops, alternating. Grill over medium-hot coals about 10 minutes, turning often and basting with the marinade. A wonderfully simple **dinner for two.**

❧ *Serve with rice pilaf or fresh pasta.*

Testing Notes: *We prefer this dish served with pasta.*

Bonnie Schiffman—Dallas, TX
Donation to: Dallas SPCA, Dallas, TX

Sherried Scallops

I bought some shell-shaped plates and needed something to serve on them. The scallops at the fish counter looked good, so I tried them. This was one of my more successful experiments.

INGREDIENTS

- **1 pound** *small or medium-sized scallops*
- **¼ cup** *flour*
- **½ teaspoon** *salt*
- **¼ teaspoon** *white pepper*
- *Pinch ground nutmeg*
- **2-3 tablespoons** *butter or margarine*
- **2** *shallots, minced*
- **2** *cloves garlic, pressed*
- **½ cup** *Spanish cream sherry*
- **2 cups** *steamed rice*

DIRECTIONS

Rinse scallops. Pat dry with paper towels. Spread scallops on dish. Sprinkle flour on scallops and roll in flour until all sides are coated. Season with salt, pepper, and nutmeg. Heat butter over medium-high heat. Sauté and stir shallots and garlic 4 minutes until golden. Add scallops to skillet, 1-layer-thick. Sauté 3 minutes on each side. Remove scallops to plate. Set aside. Add cream sherry to skillet. Cook 3 to 4 minutes over high heat, stirring and mixing scrapings from bottom of skillet. Reduce heat to low. Add scallops. Heat 2 minutes. Serve over rice.
Serves 2.

❧ *Serve with a green salad and vegetable, such as asparagus or green beans.*

Testing Notes: *Serve over spinach fettuccine for a more colorful presentation. Add clam juice to skillet while cooking the scallops.*

Mrs. Rachel P. Goldman—Fort Worth, TX
Donation to: Moncrief Radiation Center, Fort Worth, TX

Easy Scampi

Being a working mother and volunteer with various charities, I often find that getting supper on the table is a chore, but this recipe solves the problem because it's quick and delicious.

INGREDIENTS

- **3/4 cup** *unsalted butter*
- **1/2 cup** *finely chopped onion*
- **3-4** *cloves garlic, crushed*
- **4** *parsley sprigs, chopped*
- **1 pound** *medium-sized shrimp, shelled and deveined*
- **1/4 cup** *dry white wine*
- **2 tablespoons** *fresh lemon juice*
- *Salt and freshly ground pepper, to taste*

DIRECTIONS

Melt butter in medium-sized skillet over low heat. Add onion, garlic, and parsley. Sauté 10 minutes until golden. Add shrimp and stir, just until pink. Remove shrimp and place in ovenproof dish. Cover lightly and keep warm. Add wine and lemon juice to skillet. Simmer 2 to 3 minutes. Season with salt and pepper. Pour sauce over shrimp. Garnish with fresh parsley.
Serves 4 to 6.

❧ *Serve with steamed or baked rice and a green salad, or sliced Roma tomatoes and onions with vinaigrette dressing.*

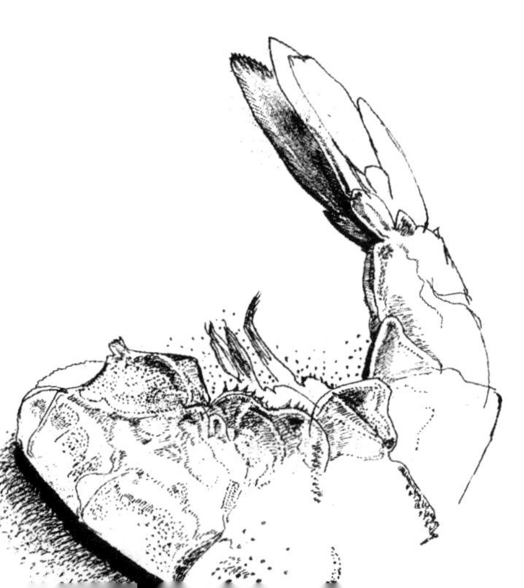

Randy Travis—Nashville, TN
Donation to: Special Olympics Productions, Inc., Washington, D.C.

Lib's Shrimp Picante Mosque

We were more than a little surprised when this country singing star submitted such a citified dish, rather than something more "down home." But then, he obviously appreciates good food, and has in fact, published a cookbook of his own entitled *Randy Travis' Favorite Recipes.*

INGREDIENTS

- **1 cup** *chicken broth*
- **1 teaspoon** *rosemary leaves*
- **1** *medium-sized onion, chopped*
- **6** *green onions with tops, chopped*
- **1 stick** *butter*
- **1 cup** *olive oil*
- **1** *clove garlic, minced*
- *Salt, to taste*
- *Lemon pepper, to taste*
- **2½ pounds** *shrimp, shelled and deveined*
- **3 jars** *(4 ounces each) picante sauce, mild*

DIRECTIONS

Mix all ingredients, except shrimp and picante sauce. Bake 30 minutes at 325° to 350°. Stir in shrimp; bake another 30 minutes. Add picante sauce. Bake 30 minutes more. **Serves 8.**

❧ *Serve with rice and toasted French bread.*

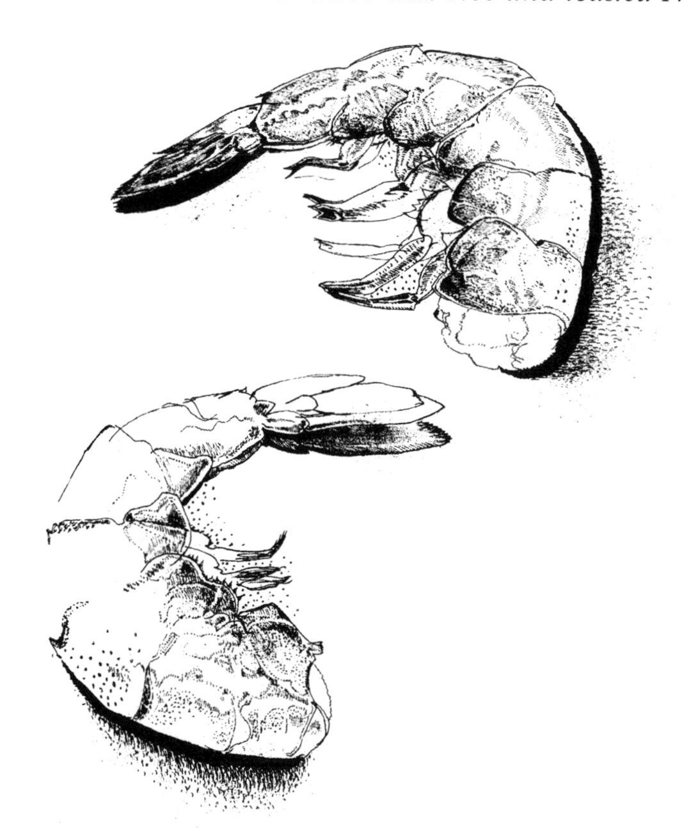

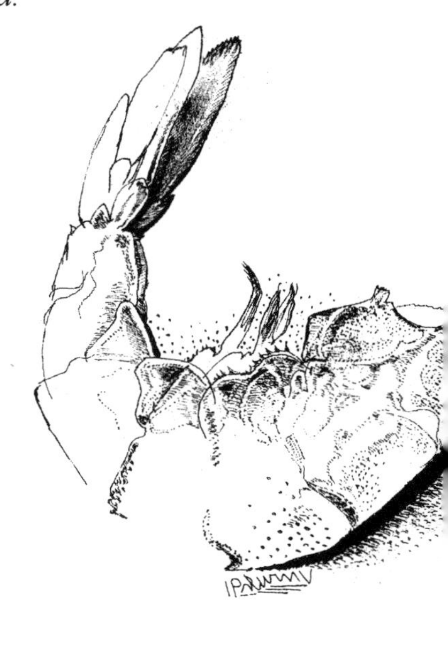

Kam Tin Angela Jhin—Tiburon, CA
Donation to: The Salvation Army, New York, NY

Lover's Shrimp

The red sauce shrimp has always been my specialty, but I needed a dish to serve at a Valentine's Day party. Following the idea of "contrasting," I decided to use a white sauce on the other half of the platter. Now, a complete dish for lovers and all.

INGREDIENTS

Shrimp Marinade:

1 *egg white, slightly beaten*

¼ teaspoon *salt*

1 tablespoon *cornstarch*

1 teaspoon *corn oil*

Red Sauce:

½ teaspoon *salt*

½-1 teaspoon *red pepper*

½ teaspoon *cornstarch*

2 tablespoons *sugar*

3 tablespoons *tomato ketchup*

½ teaspoon *white vinegar*

2 tablespoons *water*

White Sauce:

½ tablespoon *wine*

½ teaspoon *salt*

½ teaspoon *sesame oil*

Shrimp:

1¼ pounds *medium-sized shrimp*

1 tablespoon *salt*

3 cups *cold water*

⅓ pound *green vegetable (spinach or Chinese broccoli)*

1 cup *plus* **2 tablespoons** *oil*

1 *clove garlic, diced*

2 tablespoons *diced green onion*

2 tablespoons *diced ginger*

1 tablespoon *wine*

DIRECTIONS

Stir the ingredients for the shrimp marinade, the red sauce, and the white sauce in separate bowls. Set the bowls aside. Shell, clean, and devein shrimp. Add 1 tablespoon salt to the cold water and soak shrimp 5 minutes. Pat dry. Add shrimp to shrimp marinade. Refrigerate 30 minutes or longer. Fry or boil green vegetable for a few seconds with a little salt and oil. Remove and place vegetable in the center of the platter. Heat a clean wok or frying pan over high heat. Pour in 1 cup oil and heat to 300°. Pour shrimp into warm oil. Remove shrimp when they turn white. Drain oil from wok. Heat 1 tablespoon oil to very hot. Sauté half the garlic with 1 tablespoon, each, of green onion and ginger. Add half the prepared shrimp and stir quickly. Add ½ tablespoon wine and all the white sauce. Mix until well-blended and arrange on one half of the platter. Heat 1 tablespoon oil to very hot and sauté remaining green onion, garlic, and ginger. Add remaining shrimp and wine. Add red sauce. Mix all these ingredients until well-blended and arrange on the other half of the platter. Serve very hot with white or fried rice. **Serves 2.**

Mrs. Bram Goldsmith—Beverly Hills, CA
Donation to: Otis Parsons Art Institute, Los Angeles, CA

Shrimp Creole

This recipe has been handed down in our family.

INGREDIENTS

2 tablespoons *vegetable oil*
4 round tablespoons *flour*
1 *stalk celery, finely chopped*
15 *green onions, minced*
1 *green bell pepper, finely chopped*
1 *small yellow onion, peeled and finely chopped*
2 *cloves garlic, minced*
1 can *(16 ounce) whole Italian-style tomatoes, peeled and drained*
1 can *(8 ounce) tomato sauce*
12 *parsley sprigs, minced*
1 tablespoon *minced olives*
4 tablespoons *dry red wine*
4 *whole basil leaves, crushed*
2 *whole cloves*
6 *whole allspice*
1 teaspoon *cayenne*
¼ teaspoon *mace*
¼ teaspoon *chili powder*
¼ teaspoon *dried basil*
½ teaspoon *dried thyme*
Juice of 1 lemon, strained
2 cups *water*
Salt, to taste
Freshly ground pepper
2 pounds *fresh shrimp, shelled and deveined*

DIRECTIONS

Over medium heat, make a roux with the oil and flour in a large skillet or a 6-to 8-quart Dutch oven. Add and stir vegetables, tomato sauce, and parsley. Thoroughly heat for 5 minutes. Add remaining ingredients, except shrimp. Cook 30 minutes, stirring frequently. Add shrimp and heat until shrimp turn pink.
Serves 6.

❧ *Serve with rice.*

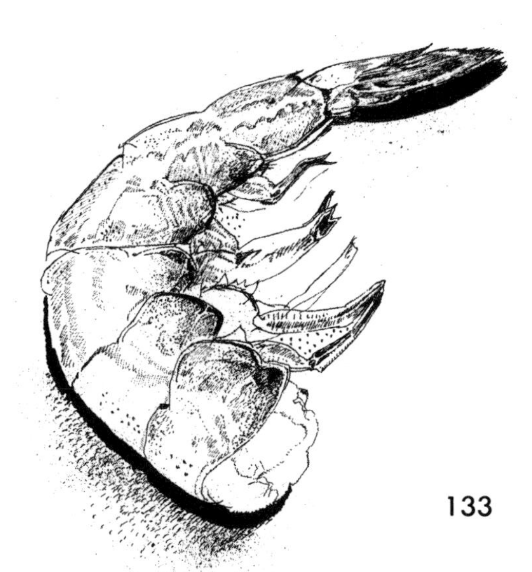

Dr. Fay (Mrs. Dennis L.) Riddle—LaGrange, GA
Donation to: Georgians for Clean Water, Inc., Newnan, GA

New Orleans Barbecued Shrimp

My husband and I are both Tulane graduates, and we love New Orleans, its culture, and, especially, its cuisine. One of our former favorite restaurants served barbecued shrimp. After moving away from New Orleans, we would crave this dish; and at least once a year we would be forced to travel to New Orleans to taste it again. Luckily, about fifteen years ago I saw a recipe with the same title and decided to try it. After making adjustments to the recipe, I can serve something that closely resembles our New Orleans dish. There have been many, many wonderful evenings at the beach (as well as at home) when we have served this dish to family and friends, to the enjoyment of all.

INGREDIENTS

2 sticks *salted butter*
1 cup *vegetable oil*
2 teaspoons *chopped garlic*
1 teaspoon *lemon juice*
4 *bay leaves, crushed*
½ teaspoon *basil*
½ teaspoon *cayenne*
½ teaspoon *oregano*
½ teaspoon *salt*
¾ teaspoon *black pepper*
2 teaspoons *Italian seasoning*
1 tablespoon *paprika*
2 pounds *shrimp in the shell*

DIRECTIONS

Melt butter in a Dutch oven. Except for the shrimp, add remaining ingredients. Cook over medium heat, stirring constantly until the sauce boils. Reduce heat to low; simmer 8 minutes, stirring frequently. Remove Dutch oven from heat. Let sauce stand, uncovered, at least 30 minutes. About 20 minutes before serving, add shrimp, mix thoroughly, and cook over medium heat 6 to 8 minutes until shrimp turn pink. Bake 10 minutes in a preheated 450° oven. Ladle shrimp and sauce into bowls and serve with plenty of crusty French bread for dipping into the sauce. **Serves 6.**

❧ *I usually serve this with French bread and a green salad when we're at the beach where shrimp is plentiful and inexpensive. In town, I add rice, cooked with chopped, green bell peppers, to the menu.*

Neiman Marcus—THE ZODIAC Oakbrook, Chicago
Donation to: combined charities

Stuffed Shrimp with Italian Ham

In Milan, they call it "Gamberi Ripieni con Prosciutto." In Oakbrook, Restaurant Manager Greg Curtis says his customer's pronounce it "delicious."

INGREDIENTS

½ cup *bread crumbs*

1 *clove garlic, minced*

1 teaspoon *minced fresh parsley*

½ teaspoon *oregano*

1 tablespoon *grated Romano cheese*

1 slice *of prosciutto, finely chopped*

3 tablespoons *olive oil*

Salt, to taste

Pinch cayenne

1 pound *fresh jumbo shrimp with shells and tails*

1 cup *cold water*

DIRECTIONS

Mix bread crumbs, garlic, parsley, oregano, cheese, prosciutto, olive oil, salt, and cayenne in a bowl. Do not remove shells or tails from shrimp. Devein, wash, and drain shrimp. Make a slit in shrimp deep enough to flatten shrimp; place shrimp shell side down. Fill each with stuffing. On the bottom of a 14-inch-round baking pan, pour cold water (or enough to coat it). Place shrimp in pan. Bake 25 minutes at 375° until tender. **Serves 3.**

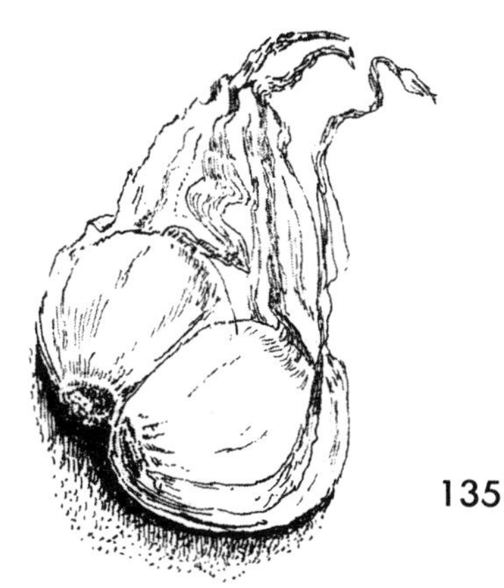

Jo-Ann M. Brown—Bronxville, NY
Donation to: Institute for Research in Behavioral Neuroscience, Inc., New York, NY

Swordfish Supreme

This is an original recipe which I made up because my husband adores swordfish. For a change, he wanted something different than plain-grilled-with-butter-fish, so I experimented with this and that, and came up with this recipe. I surprised him one evening and he deemed it supreme! It's easy, pure, simple, and delicious.

INGREDIENTS

4 *fresh swordfish steaks, each 1½-inches-thick*

1 tablespoon *olive oil*

2-3 *cloves garlic, chopped*

2 tablespoons *fresh or dried dill, chopped*

2 tablespoons *chopped mixed herbs (Herbes de Provence): thyme, basil, and fennel (fresh or dried)*

Salt and pepper (optional)

2 tablespoons *fresh bread crumbs*

Juice from 1 lemon

DIRECTIONS

Preheat broiler. Place steaks in baking dish and coat lightly with olive oil. Sprinkle with garlic, dill, herbs, salt, and pepper. Top with bread crumbs. Squeeze juice of 1 lemon over tops of steak and drizzle remaining olive oil over steaks. Broil, or grill, 5 to 7 minutes until tops are brown and crusty. Do not turn swordfish steaks over when cooking; they will remain moist and succulent. **Serves 4.**

❧ *Serve with boiled new potatoes, endive salad, and French-style green beans.*

Carolyn Farb—Houston, TX
Donation to: Texas Neurofibromatosis Foundation, Dallas, TX

Trota Nel Cuore

My good friend, Archille Arciadiacono, former consul general of Italy, and I occasionally combine our efforts in cooking dinner. This is one of our joint ventures.

INGREDIENTS

4 *trout fillets*
2 tablespoons *heavy or whipping cream*
2 tablespoons *olive oil*
1 *small onion, chopped*
Italian parsley
Salt and pepper
White cooking wine, preferably dry

DIRECTIONS

Combine all ingredients, except wine, and pour over fillets. Place fillets and marinade sauce in plastic bag and refrigerate 1 hour. Place each fillet in some marinade in a heart-shaped piece of aluminum foil. Seal foil pouches by rolling up edges, beginning at both sides, but leave an opening on top of the pouch. Just before placing in the oven, pour a ½ jigger of white wine over each fillet through the opening in the pouch. Totally seal each pouch. Cook 20 minutes on a cooking sheet at 350°. Open silver heart on platter at the table.

❧ *Serve with a bouquet of steamed or grilled vegetables, whole-wheat baguettes, and a sexy chocolate dessert, such as a light chocolate mousse.*

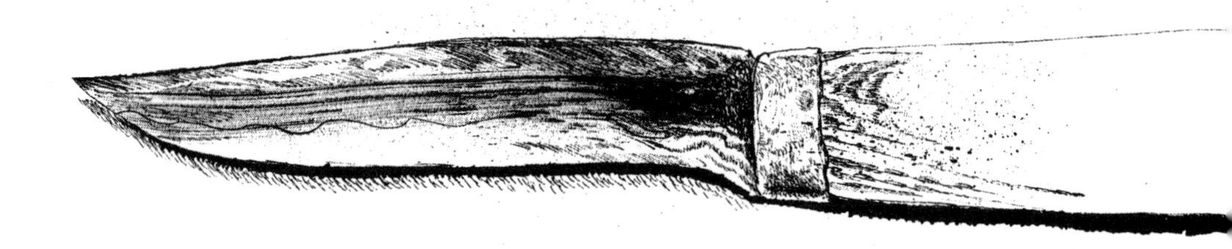

Tuna Loaf with Cucumber Sauce

The creative minds at NM came up with a distinctive way to cook with canned tuna.

INGREDIENTS

2 *eggs*

1½ cups *milk*

1 cup *finely crushed saltine crackers*

1 can *(6 ounce) tuna, drained and flaked*

1½ cups *chopped celery*

⅛ cup *grated onion*

1 teaspoon *plus* **1 tablespoon** *salt*

3 *medium-sized cucumbers, peeled, seeded, and coarsely chopped*

¼ cup *butter or margarine*

¼ cup *all-purpose flour*

1 *grated lemon peel*

1 teaspoon *lemon juice*

3 *egg yolks*

Chopped dill or parsley

DIRECTIONS

Begin preparation 2 hours before serving. Preheat oven to 350°. Generously grease two 9 x 5-inch loaf pans. Lightly beat eggs in a large bowl. Stir in milk and crackers; let stand 5 minutes, stirring occasionally. Add tuna, celery, onion, and 1 teaspoon salt. Spoon mixture into pans. Bake 1 hour until knife inserted in center comes out almost clean. Meanwhile, prepare cucumber sauce. Cook cucumbers until tender-crisp in 3 cups of water for 5 minutes in a 3-quart saucepan over high heat. Drain, reserving liquid. Add enough water to liquid to make 5¼ cups. Stir flour into hot butter in a Dutch oven over medium heat. Gradually stir in liquid and cook, stirring constantly until mixture is thickened. Add 1 tablespoon salt, lemon peel, juice, and cucumber. Cook, stirring, until just boiling. Lightly beat egg yolks in a small bowl with a fork. Stir in small amount of hot cucumber mixture. Pour egg mixture slowly back into sauce, stirring rapidly to prevent lumping. Cook and stir until thickened. Do not boil. Set loaf pans on cooling racks for 15 minutes. Loosen edges of loaves with spatula and invert onto warm platters. Cut each loaf into 8 slices. Spoon ⅓ cup sauce over each serving. Top with dill. **Serves 12.**

CHAPTER SEVEN

Chicken, etc.

Twenty-five chicken recipes plus two for turkey, two for game hens, and one for duck. But, it's chicken that lands in almost every grocery basket every week. And, you are not limited to buying a fryer or a hen these days. You can select only the parts your family likes, so there's no waste at all. Preparation time is reduced, too, because today's chicken comes skinless, in strips, chunks, or ground. The only dilemma is how to cook it. Not to worry. InCirclers come to the rescue with some of the most original chicken ideas ever.

Nancy B. Pettijohn—Newport Beach, CA
Donation to: Hoag Hospital Foundation, Newport Beach, CA

Mexican Chicken

We are very sports-oriented, so I like meals I can prepare ahead of time. A good friend came up with this when I needed something new.

INGREDIENTS

8-10 *chicken breasts, boned*

Flour

2-3 tablespoons *oil*

¼ cup *chopped onions*

1 can *(15 ounce) tomato sauce*

½ cup *water*

2 *bouillon cubes, crushed*

1 can *(4 ounce) diced chiles*

1 can *(4¼ ounce) chopped olives*

2 tablespoons *wine vinegar*

¾ teaspoon *cumin*

¾ teaspoon *garlic salt*

2 cups *grated Monterey jack cheese*

DIRECTIONS

Dip chicken in flour and brown lightly in oil. Remove and place in casserole. Mix remaining ingredients in saucepan and simmer 3 minutes. Pour over chicken. Cover and bake 45 minutes to 1 hour at 350°. Remove cover and sprinkle with grated cheese. Bake 10 minutes. **Serves 8.**

❧ *Serve with rice or noodles, a mixed green salad, and flan.*

Testing Notes: *Serve this with Spanish rice.*

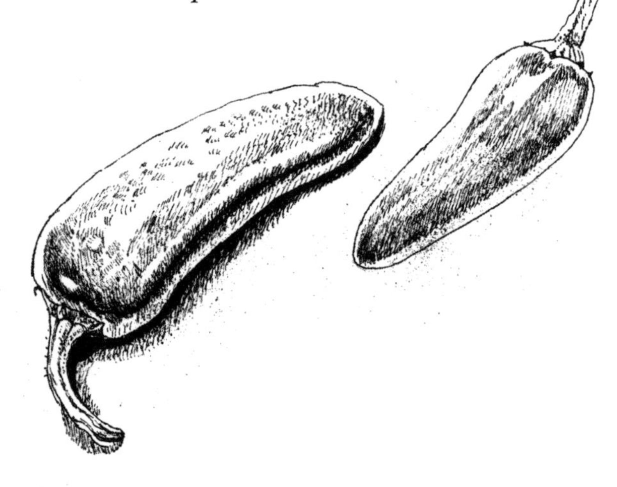

Nancy Brinker—Dallas, TX
Donation to: Susan G. Komen Foundation, Inc., Dallas, TX

Twin Mallets Ranch Chicken

This is a favorite dish at our Twin Mallets Ranch.

INGREDIENTS

4 *chicken breasts, cooked, boned, and shredded*

1 can *(10 1/2 ounce) cream of chicken soup*

1 can *(10 1/2 ounce) cream of mushroom soup*

1 pound *VELVEETA® cheese, cut into chunks*

1 cup *chopped onion*

1/2 cup *chopped celery*

1/2 cup *milk*

12 *corn tortillas, cut or torn into 1-inch pieces*

Shredded sharp Cheddar cheese

Sliced jalapeños (optional)

DIRECTIONS

Mix first 8 ingredients together and pour into a 9 x 13-inch casserole. Top with grated cheese and garnish with jalapeños, if desired. Cover and bake 45 minutes at 350°. Uncover and bake 15 minutes more. (Tastes best if prepared the day before, refrigerated, and brought to room temperature before baking.) **Serves 6 to 8.**

❧ *Serve with tacos, refried beans, fruit salad, and enchiladas.*

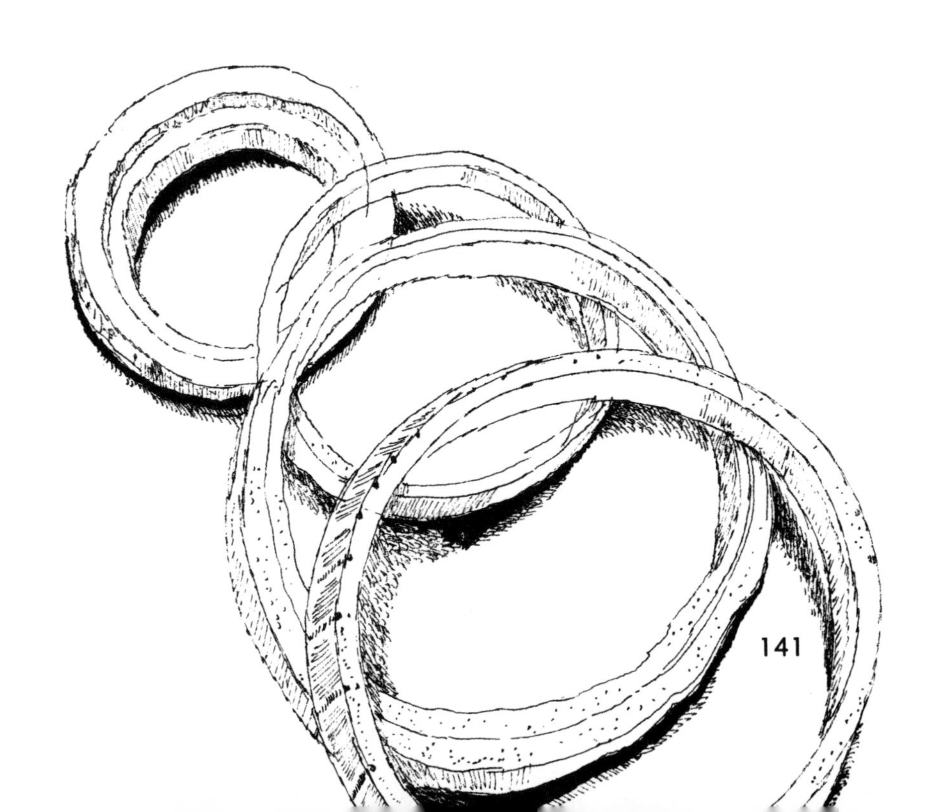

Neiman Marcus—THE ZODIAC Downtown, Dallas
Donation to: combined charities

Chicken with Vegetable Salsa

This dish, created by Chef Maxine Johnson, was a favorite of Zodiac diners even before Southwestern cooking became famous.

INGREDIENTS

Salt and pepper, to taste
4 *chicken breasts (6 ounces each)*
½ cup *flour*
½ cup *oleo, melted*
1 *medium-sized carrot, finely diced*
1 *medium-sized zucchini, finely diced*
1 *medium-sized yellow squash, finely diced*
6 *green onions, finely sliced*
2 cups *small broccoli florets*
½ cup *finely diced red bell pepper*
½ cup *finely diced green bell pepper*
¼ cup *red-wine vinegar*
1 teaspoon *grated lemon peel*
⅛ teaspoon *salt*
6 tablespoons *sugar*
1 cup *oil*

DIRECTIONS

Sprinkle salt and pepper over chicken. Let stand 4 to 5 minutes. Dust chicken in flour, shake off excess flour, and sauté in oleo. Set aside. Blanch, or steam carrot in hot water. Mix carrot and the remaining ingredients well. Add chicken and let set one hour. **Serves 4.**

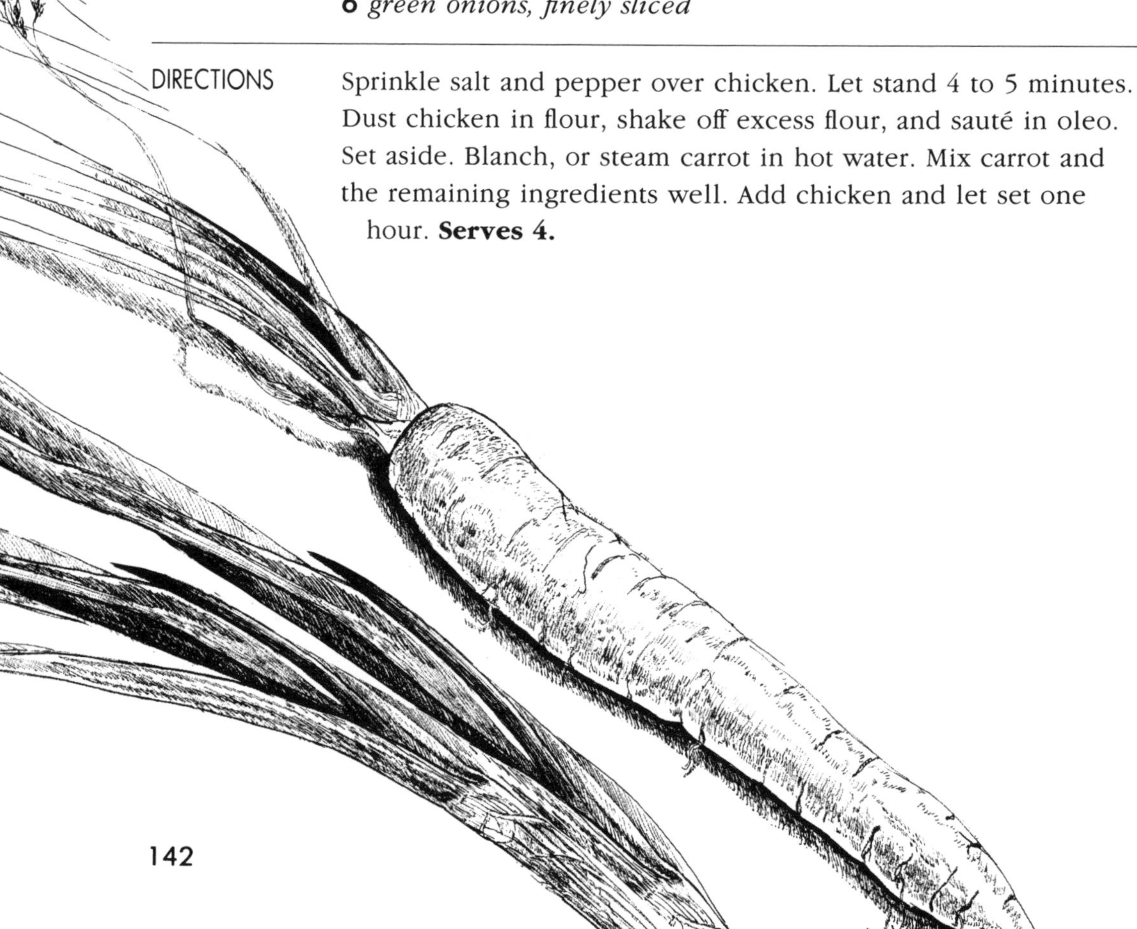

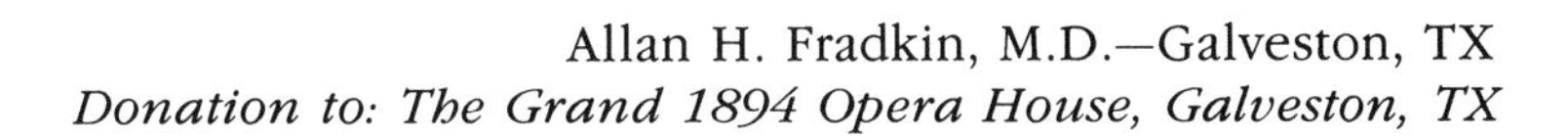

Allan H. Fradkin, M.D.—Galveston, TX
Donation to: The Grand 1894 Opera House, Galveston, TX

Chicken Tamale Pie

This is an original recipe designed for friends who live in Switzerland and crave Mexican food.

INGREDIENTS

- **3** *eggs*
- **1 cup** *sour cream*
- **1 cup** *milk*
- **1 teaspoon** *sugar*
- **1 can** *(7 ounce) green chile salsa*
- **1¾ cups** *yellow corn meal*
- **1½ cups** *all-purpose flour*
- **1 teaspoon** *baking powder*
- **1 teaspoon** *baking soda*
- **1 teaspoon** *salt, or to taste*
- **½ teaspoon** *hot-pepper sauce*
- **1 can** *(12 ounce) GREEN GIANT MEXICORN®, drained*
- **2⅔ cups** *shredded Monterey jack cheese*
- **2 tablespoons** *vegetable oil*
- **2** *medium-sized onions, chopped*
- **5** *cloves garlic, minced*
- **1** *green bell pepper, chopped*
- **2 cans** *(14½ ounces each) whole tomatoes, drained and chopped*
- **1 tablespoon** *dried oregano*
- **1 teaspoon** *cumin*
- **1 teaspoon** *cinnamon*
- **1 tablespoon** *chili powder*
- *Salt and pepper, to taste*
- **2 pounds** *chicken breast, cooked and cut into ½-inch cubes*
- **6 ounces** *shredded Cheddar cheese*

DIRECTIONS

Beat eggs until frothy; stir in sour cream and milk. Add sugar, salsa, corn meal, flour, baking powder, baking soda, salt, and hot-pepper sauce. Stir until combined. Mix in corn and 2 cups Monterey jack cheese. Set aside. Heat oil over moderately-high heat in saucepan. Sauté onions and garlic until soft. Add bell pepper, tomatoes, and seasonings. Cook, uncovered, stirring often, over medium heat until most of liquid evaporates. Set aside. Preheat oven to 350°. Generously butter bottom and sides of a 3-quart glass casserole. Spread corn mixture evenly to a depth of ½-to ¾-inch. Spread chicken to form an even layer. Spoon tomato mixture over chicken. Combine Cheddar cheese and remaining Monterey cheese; sprinkle on top. Bake 1 hour until cheese melts and turns golden brown. Serve immediately. To prepare ahead, completely assemble pie, but do not bake. Cover and freeze, or refrigerate up to 24 hours. Defrost in refrigerator. Bring to room temperature and proceed with baking instructions. **Serves 12 to 14.**

❧ *Serve with black beans, guacamole, and Mexican-style squash.*

Jill Bee—Dallas, TX
Donation to: Special Camps for Special Kids, Dallas, TX

Chicken Chili

This is my own creation.

INGREDIENTS

2 *medium-sized onions, finely chopped*

2 *cloves garlic, finely chopped*

½ cup *canola oil*

2 pounds *chicken, coarsely ground*

4 cans *(8 ounces each) tomato sauce*

4 cups *water*

2 tablespoons *Mexican-style chili powder*

2 tablespoons *ground cumin*

2 teaspoons *granulated sugar*

1 teaspoon *cayenne*

4 teaspoons *paprika*

4 tablespoons *flour*

DIRECTIONS

In a stockpot, sauté onion and garlic in oil until limp. Add chicken and sauté until done. Add remaining ingredients and mix well. Cover and simmer 4 hours, stirring occasionally. **Serves 4.**

❧ *Serve with shredded cheese, diced onions, and jalapeño corn bread.*

Dolly Granatelli—Montecito, CA
Donation to: Institute for Cancer and Blood Research, Beverly Hills, CA

White Chili

I adapted my chili recipe to this when I had a guest to dinner who loved chili, but wouldn't eat beef.

INGREDIENTS

- **1 pound** *large dry white beans*
- **2** *whole chickens (3½ pounds each)*
- **2 quarts** *water*
- **1** *medium-sized whole onion plus* **2** *medium-sized onions, chopped*
- **1** *stalk celery*
- **1** *carrot*
- ½ *bunch parsley*
- **2** *bay leaves*
- **2 tablespoons** *salad oil*
- **3** *cloves garlic, minced*
- **1 can** *(7 ounce) whole green chiles, diced*
- **1 can** *(28 ounce) whole tomatoes, crushed*
- **2 teaspoons** *cumin*
- **1½ teaspoons** *oregano*
- **3 tablespoons** *chili powder*
- **1-2** *jalapeño peppers, minced (optional)*
- *Salt and black pepper, to taste*

DIRECTIONS

Wash beans and soak overnight in water to cover. Drain. Prepare chicken stock by simmering chickens in 2 quarts water to which the whole onion, celery, carrot, parsley, and bay leaves are added. Simmer until meat is tender. Remove chickens and cool. Remove meat and skin from bones; dice meat. Strain broth and skim off fat. Mix beans, chicken broth, and 1 chopped onion. Cook until beans are just tender. Heat oil in skillet; add garlic and remaining chopped onion. Sauté until tender and golden. Add this mixture and remaining ingredients to beans. Simmer 20 minutes. Add chicken and simmer 15 minutes.
Serves 8 to 12.

❧ *Serve a good cole slaw and some corn bread with this.*

Debra A. Wheelan—Dallas, TX
Donation to: Scottish Rite Hospital for Crippled Children, Inc., Dallas, TX

Picante Chicken on Saffron Rice

We were barbecuing chicken at my husband's Uncle Mickey's home which overlooks the Gallatin River in Montana. We were looking for a low-fat, tasty chicken marinade since my husband is a cardiologist. Living most of the year in Dallas, picante sauce is almost a staple. The three of us came up with Picante Chicken after a long day of fly-fishing. It's fast, fun, and really low-fat.

INGREDIENTS

PACE® mild picante sauce
Chicken breasts, boned and skinned
MRS DASH® lemon-herb seasoning
MAHATMA® saffron rice mix

DIRECTIONS

Coat glass baking dish with CRISCO® oil. Spoon picante sauce on the bottom of the dish, covering bottom. Place chicken breasts on sauce. Cover chicken with a thick layer of picante. Sprinkle generously with lemon-herb seasoning. Cover with plastic wrap; cut a slit in center of plastic wrap. You may marinate all day, overnight, or 5 minutes. Microwave on medium-high power 4 to 5 minutes per breast. Prepare rice mix while chicken is cooking. Once cooked, place chicken on barbecue, if desired, for a roasting-in-mountain-air flavor!

❧ *Serve with a tarragon tossed salad with mandarin oranges and toasted almonds; sourdough bread; and limeade pie for dessert.*

Suzanne M. Goodman—Santa Ana, CA
Donation to: University of Washington Foundation, Seattle, WA (Diabetes Research)

Curried Chicken Breasts with Chutney

I experimented and developed this recipe last summer while trying to find a new and simple method of preparing chicken. It has proved to be a success.

INGREDIENTS

6 *whole chicken breasts, halved; with bone (skin is optional)*

Garlic powder

Onion powder

12 teaspoons *curry powder*

3 jars *(8½ ounces each) mango chutney*

1 can *(14½ ounce) chicken broth, fat removed*

DIRECTIONS

Rinse and pat dry the 12 chicken breasts. Place them, bone side up, in a large roasting pan that is suitable for serving. Sprinkle each chicken breast lightly with garlic powder; sprinkle each heavily with onion powder. Rub ½ teaspoon curry powder thoroughly onto each chicken breast. Turn chicken and arrange attractively in pan. Repeat application of garlic, onion, and curry powders. Spread mango chutney evenly over the seasoned chicken. The chicken may be covered and refrigerated until 1 hour before serving. Preheat oven to 325°. Pour ⅓ to ½ can of chicken broth over chicken to dilute chutney. Roast, uncovered, 45 to 60 minutes. Add more broth while cooking, if necessary. When chicken is done, remove pan from oven and set oven control to broil. Spoon liquid from the chutney and chicken broth, including pieces of mango, over the chicken. Return to oven and broil on top rack for 1 to 2 minutes until skin is crisp and chutney glaze darkens. (If skinless breasts are used, the chicken should be broiled until the glaze bubbles and darkens.) This recipe may also be prepared with boneless chicken breasts. In that case, decrease roasting time to 30 to 45 minutes. **Serves 10 to 12.**

❧ *Serve with white rice and a green vegetable.*

June R. Bumpas—Dallas, TX
Donation to: American Heart Association, Inc., Dallas, TX

Chicken Curry Bumpas

I was first introduced to curry spices many, many years ago at the Pine Inn in Carmel. We came into the inn out of a cold, rainy night, and they were serving Mulligatawny Soup. Upon returning home, I started experimenting with curries and this is the result of many trial-and-error endeavors.

INGREDIENTS

4 tablespoons *butter or margarine*

4 tablespoons *flour*

2 cups *milk*

Curry powder, to taste

4 *chicken breasts, cooked and cubed*

2 cups *cooked rice*

DIRECTIONS

Melt margarine or butter in a small flat-bottomed saucepan. Add flour and stir until well-blended. Use a fork to keep sauce smooth. Pour in milk gradually, stirring constantly. Bring to boil and boil 2 minutes. Cook a few more minutes to cook flour thoroughly, stirring well. If needed, thin with a little extra milk. Stir in curry powder, starting with 1 teaspoon; add more if you want a hotter curry. (A little goes a long way!) Add cubed chicken to the curry sauce. Keep warm about 20 minutes until flavors blend. Pour over 2 cups cooked rice before serving. Arrange sambals around curry dish and add these, to taste, to the curry on the dinner plate. **Serves 6 to 8.**

❧ *Sambals for curry: a wonderful chutney; chopped green onion; very thinly sliced banana, which has been marinated in maraschino cherry juice and lime juice; finely chopped mixed nuts; very thinly sliced cucumber, sprinkled with lemon pepper and balsamic vinegar; and anything else you like—just use your imagination!*

Michele Zentil—Pompano Beach, FL
Donation to: American Cancer Society, Inc., Pompano Beach, FL

Chicken Florentine

A friend of mine from San Diego, California, once made a similar recipe for me. I decided to change everything to fresh ingredients, and hence, came up with my own delicious version.

INGREDIENTS

8 *chicken breasts, boned and skinned*

Pinch of salt

Pepper, to taste

2 tablespoons *butter, melted, plus* **6 tablespoons** *butter, unmelted*

1 package *(3 ounce) cream cheese*

1 teaspoon *oregano*

½ teaspoon *lemon juice*

1 *bunch fresh spinach, cooked, drained, and chopped*

½ cup *shredded Swiss cheese*

⅓ -½ cup *grated Parmesan cheese (preferably parmigiano-reggiano)*

DIRECTIONS

Preheat oven to 400°. Pound chicken until thin. Season with salt and pepper; set aside. Mix 2 tablespoons melted butter, cream cheese, oregano, and lemon juice with spinach in large bowl. In center of each breast, spread Swiss cheese and ¼ cup of spinach mixture. Fold chicken to cover stuffing completely. Place in baking dish, seam side down, and place ½ tablespoon butter on each chicken breast. Sprinkle Parmesan cheese on each chicken breast. Add remaining butter and small amount of water to pan. Bake 20 minutes at 400° until browned.
Serves 6 to 8.

❧ *Serve with herbed carrots and wild rice.*

Testing Notes: *Add ¼ cup chopped, roasted red bell peppers for enhanced flavor and presentation. We chose to use 1 tablespoon lemon juice.*

Neiman Marcus—THE ZODIAC St. Louis
Donation to: combined charities

Chicken Versailles

Restaurant Manager Mary Kay Coil says first-timers are always delighted to find the shrimp tucked inside these tender, delicious chicken breasts.

INGREDIENTS

2 *large eggplants, chopped*
½ *onion, chopped*
½ *bell pepper, chopped*
½ **cup** *chopped celery*
Butter
2 teaspoons *chicken base*
1 teaspoon *curry powder*
1 cup *Italian bread crumbs*
4 tablespoons *Parmesan cheese*
Salt and pepper, to taste
6 *chicken breasts, boned*
18-24 *large shrimp, peeled, cleaned, and deveined*

DIRECTIONS

Sauté eggplant, onion, bell pepper, and celery in butter. Add chicken base, curry, bread crumbs, cheese, salt, and pepper; mix well. Place 1 cup of stuffing in each chicken breast. Add 3 or 4 large shrimp. Roll breast closed and secure. Bake 45 minutes at 350°. **Serves 6.**

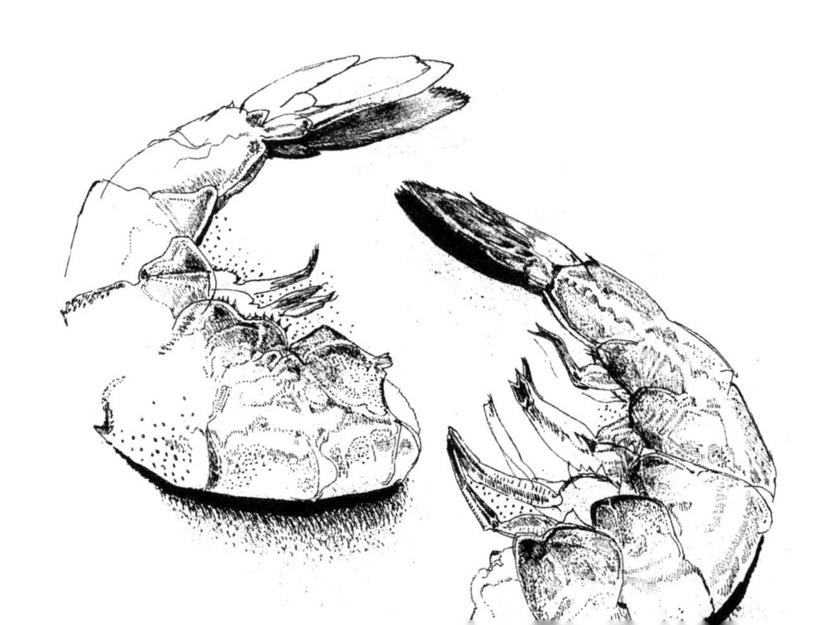

Dorothy B. VanSickle—Dallas, TX
Donation to: American Cancer Society, Inc., Dallas, TX

Oriental Chicken and Noodles

This recipe is from my late grandmother, Mrs. Dessie Gilliam, of Longview, Texas.

INGREDIENTS

Oil for cooking

1 *egg, lightly beaten*

8 ounces *Chinese noodles or vermicelli*

2 pounds *chicken breasts, boned and skinned*

1 tablespoon *dry sherry*

1 tablespoon *soy sauce*

1 ½ teaspoons *cornstarch*

1 ¼ cups *sliced fresh mushrooms*

2 cups *sliced celery*

1 ½ cups *French-style green beans*

1 can *(5 ounce) water chestnuts, drained and sliced*

½ cup *chopped onion*

1 *large clove garlic, finely minced*

½ teaspoon *ginger*

½ teaspoon *red pepper*

DIRECTIONS

Heat 1 tablespoon oil in skillet. Add beaten egg and cook, tilting pan to make a thin omelet. Remove and cut into thin strips. Set aside. Cook noodles in boiling salted water until barely tender. Drain, toss with 1 tablespoon oil, and cover to keep warm. Cut chicken into ½-inch strips, place in bowl, and sprinkle with sherry, soy, and cornstarch. Stir well to coat chicken. Let stand 10 minutes. Combine mushrooms, celery, beans, water chestnuts, onion, garlic, ginger, and red pepper in a bowl. Mix thoroughly. Heat 2 tablespoons oil; add chicken. Cook approximately 5 minutes; brown evenly. Remove chicken; keep warm. Add 3 tablespoons oil to pan and add vegetable mixture; cook until tender. Remove to bowl. Add oil to pan; add noodles. Cook and stir until warm; add chicken and vegetables. Stir until hot. Garnish with omelet strips. **Serves 8 to 10.**

❧ *Serve with green salad and garlic bread.*

Suzanne G. Keith—Houston, TX
Donation to: Save the Whales, Inc., Venice, CA

Sesame Chicken

I was planning an Oriental dinner and asked a friend, who had lived in Tokyo for several years, for a new, authentic recipe that Westerners would like. Sesame Chicken has been a sensation every time I've served it. The leftovers are great, too.

INGREDIENTS

¼ cup *sugar*

1 tablespoon *salt*

½ teaspoon *pepper*

¼ cup *mirin (rice wine vinegar)*

¼ cup *vegetable oil*

¼ cup *dark sesame oil (no substitute!)*

2 *whole chicken breasts*

¼ cup *chopped almonds*

2 tablespoons *sesame seeds*

1 *large head iceberg lettuce, shredded*

2-4 *green onions, tops and bottoms thinly sliced*

¼ cup *shredded coriander, or Italian parsley*

2 ounces *cellophane noodles*

DIRECTIONS

Thoroughly blend the first 6 ingredients and refrigerate. Stew, bone, and shred chicken breasts. Refrigerate. Toast sesame seeds and almonds. Fry cellophane noodles in very hot oil in a deep pan or wok. Fry small amount at a time. Noodles will triple in size and become crisp. Drain on paper towels. Toss everything with the refrigerated dressing. **Serves 8**. This is a very simple dish to expand for 50 people. The cellophane noodles may be cooked a day ahead and sealed in plastic bags. The noodles are a taste treat when crunchy, but are still very good the next day when they become limp and slippery. The chicken will keep several days in the refrigerator.

❧ *Serve with sake or hot tea, fried egg rolls with hot mustard sauce and marmalade thinned with mirin, and fresh plum halves and seedless grapes (or canned nectarines, if fresh fruit isn't available).*

Kathryn Rabinow—Houston, TX
Donation to: Children's Museum, Inc., Houston, TX

Chicken Villa Roma sur mar

Adapted from recipe ideas given to me by dear friends who spent their graduate school days in Italy.

INGREDIENTS

4 *boned chicken breasts, cut into 4-inch-long pieces*

4 *chicken thighs, cut into 4-inch-long pieces*

Olive oil

4-8 *cloves garlic, crushed or minced*

Coarsely ground black peppercorns

1 *large bunch fresh rosemary leaves*

1 can *(2 ounce) anchovies in olive oil, cut into small pieces*

4 *carrots, peeled and cut into "pennies" (optional)*

Balsamic vinegar

DIRECTIONS

Brown chicken in hot olive oil in heavy pot. Add garlic, peppercorns, and rosemary leaves. Stir 5 minutes over low heat. Add anchovies and carrots. If mixture looks oily, drain pan and wipe it with paper towel. Return chicken, et al., to pan and cover with balsamic vinegar. Cook over low-to medium-heat 30 to 35 minutes, stirring every 5 to 10 minutes until balsamic vinegar forms a glaze and chicken is tender. This is delicious served at room temperature. **Serves 4 to 6.**

❧ *Serve with pasta and light tomato sauce and a green salad.*

B. Rhoads Fearn—San Francisco, CA
Donation to: Project Open Hand, San Francisco, CA

Pollo da Pordenone

This dish is named for a small town in northern Italy where we lived in the late 1960s, and has evolved over the years, according to the fresh vegetables available. Years ago when Eugene McCarthy campaigned for president, he was the guest speaker at a dinner in Columbus, Ohio, for which I prepared this dish. That particular evening he had another speaking engagement seventy-five miles away, but we arranged for one of our guests, a former race car driver, to drive him to Columbus. McCarthy arrived with only minutes to spare. He did claim this dish was a vast improvement over the usual hotel banquet food.

INGREDIENTS

4 *chicken breasts, boned, skinned, and cut into bite-sized pieces*

3 tablespoons *vegetable oil*

2 *large onions, thinly sliced*

½ cup *thinly sliced celery*

1 *large red bell pepper, thinly sliced*

1 *large yellow bell pepper, thinly sliced*

1 teaspoon *rosemary*

1 teaspoon *basil*

4 tablespoons *butter*

½ pound *spinach, washed and chopped*

½ pound *mushrooms, washed and sliced*

1 cup *sliced black olives*

½ cup *chicken broth*

2 *large tomatoes, peeled and diced*

3 *cloves garlic, crushed*

Salt and pepper, to taste

2 cups *thinly sliced romaine lettuce*

¾ cup *sliced almonds*

DIRECTIONS

Brown chicken in hot oil and drain on paper towels. Sauté onions, celery, peppers, rosemary, and basil 3 minutes in butter. Add spinach, mushrooms, olives, broth, tomatoes, garlic, salt, and pepper. Bring to boil and simmer 2 minutes. Line a casserole with romaine. Alternate chicken and vegetables in two layers, each. Cover and bake 30 minutes at 350°. Sprinkle almonds over the top. **Serves 4 to 6.**

❧ *Serve with homemade noodles or basmati rice; a salad of pears, Gorgonzola cheese and greens with raspberry vinaigrette; and ginger ice cream with hot chocolate sauce.*

Barbara Wallace—Houston, TX

Donation to: Ronald McDonald House, Houston, TX

Chicken and Fettuccine Casserole

This recipe was given to me by a friend. It is great to make ahead and freeze for unexpected company or a night when you just don't feel like cooking.

INGREDIENTS

- ¼ **cup** *butter*
- ¼ **cup** *flour*
- **1 cup** *milk*
- **1 cup** *chicken broth*
- **1** *large chicken, cooked and boned*
- **5 ounces** *fettuccine, cooked and drained*
- **2 cups** *sour cream*
- **1 package** *(10 ounce) frozen spinach, cooked and drained*
- **1 jar** *(6 ounce) mushrooms*
- **1 can** *(8 ounce) sliced water chestnuts*
- **1 jar** *(4 ounce) pimientos*
- ½ **cup** *chopped onions*
- ½ **cup** *chopped celery*
- ⅓ **cup** *lemon juice*
- **2 teaspoons** *seasoning salt*
- ½ **teaspoon** *cayenne*
- **1 teaspoon** *paprika*
- **1 teaspoon** *salt*
- **1 teaspoon** *pepper*
- **1½ cups** *grated Monterey jack cheese*

DIRECTIONS

Melt butter and flour together, stirring constantly. Add milk and chicken broth. Continue stirring and cook until thickened. Add remaining ingredients, except cheese. Put into buttered casserole and top with cheese. Bake 25 to 30 minutes at 300°. **Serves 6 to 8.**

❧ *I usually serve this with beer bread and a salad.*

Testing Notes: *This is very well suited for a large group or buffet.*

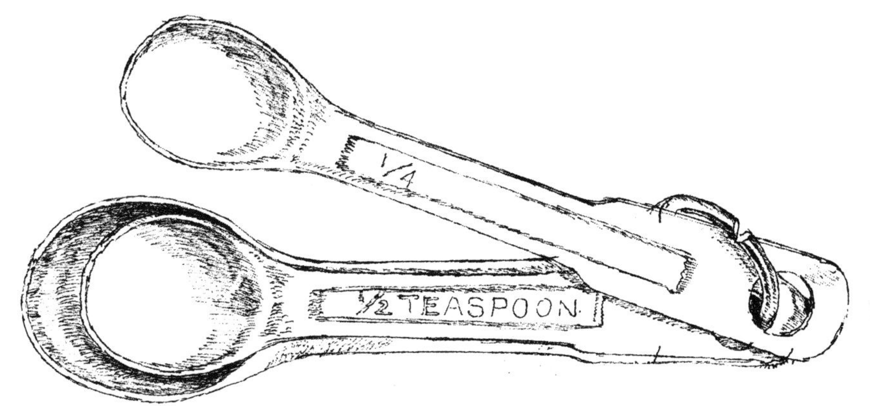

Ruth M. Swanberg—New Canaan, CT
Donation to: New Canaan Nature Center Association, Inc., New Canaan, CT

Portuguese-Style Chicken

Maria, our Portuguese cook in Praia da Luz (Algarve), gave me the ingredients, but not the measurements, for this dish. After some experimenting in the kitchen, my adaptation comes pretty close to her wonderful dish.

INGREDIENTS

- **1** *large onion, sliced*
- **1** *green bell pepper, seeded and sliced into strips*
- **2** *cloves garlic, minced*
- **1/3 cup** *light olive oil*
- **1 can** *(28 ounce) tomatoes, chopped, and liquid reserved*
- **1** *bay leaf*
- **1/4 teaspoon** *dried thyme*
- *Salt and pepper, to taste*
- **3** *parsley sprigs*
- **1/2 bottle** *red wine (not Chianti) or enough to cover chicken*
- **1** *fryer (3-to 3 1/2-pound), cut into serving pieces*

DIRECTIONS

Sauté onion, bell pepper, and garlic in oil in a 4-or 5-quart casserole over moderate heat until softened. Add tomatoes, tomato liquid, seasonings, parsley, wine, and chicken. Cover. Bake 45 minutes to 1 hour. **Serves 3 to 4**. May be made a day ahead and refrigerated. In fact, it's better!

❧ *Serve with white rice or boiled, new potatoes.*

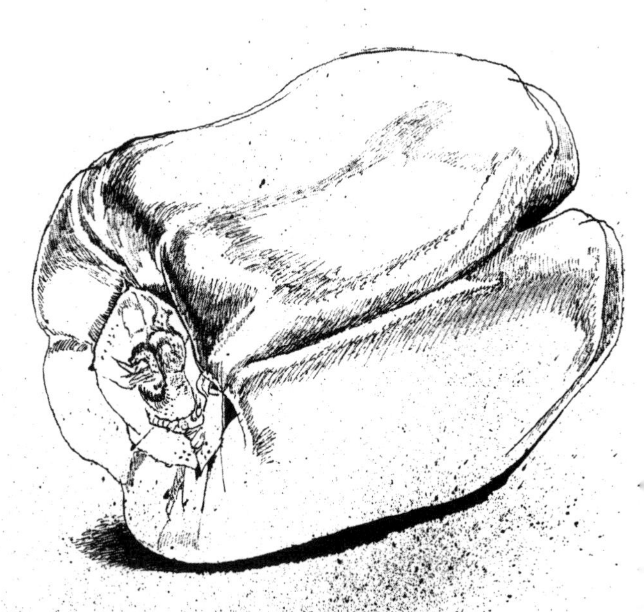

Wayne Hilton, M.D.—Beverly Hills, CA
Donation to: American Heart Association, Inc., Los Angeles, CA

Poulet Hooray

In 1961 I bought a bottle of excellent 1959 French Vouvray wine, which my wife and I sipped with giggling gusto. I canvassed nearly every wine merchant in the city before I finally landed several cases. Eager to share with friends, I created (with advice from my wife) a dish to include some of the wine as an ingredient, in addition to it being an accompaniment. After several variations presented at a number of dinners, my anxious eyes ever-searching to catch rousing signs of approval, I was at last awarded the unanimous "wow" consensus. Hooray! That 1959 vintage is long gone, but I use good Chenin Blanc or Chardonnay wine for equal enjoyment.

INGREDIENTS

- ½ **pound** *large mushrooms, scored*
- *Salt and white pepper*
- *Juice of ½ lemon*
- **4 tablespoons** *unsalted butter*
- **8** *chicken breast halves, boned and skinned*
- **2** *cloves garlic, minced*
- **4** *small white onions, halved*
- **2** *shallots, minced*
- ½ **cup** *white wine (Chenin Blanc or Chardonnay)*
- **2½ tablespoons** *cornstarch*
- ½ **teaspoon** *seasoned salt*
- ½ **cup** *chicken broth*
- **1 cup** *heavy cream*
- **1 can** *(8 ounce) grapes, drained*

DIRECTIONS

Put mushrooms, dash of salt and white pepper, lemon juice, and 1 tablespoon butter into a saucepan. Cover. Bring to boil, reduce heat, and simmer 2 minutes. Remove from heat and set aside. Lightly season chicken with salt and white pepper. Melt remaining butter in heavy skillet. Add chicken breasts and sauté until light brown on each side. Add garlic, onions, shallots, and ¼ cup wine. Cover and simmer 15 minutes. Transfer into ovenproof serving casserole. Cover and set aside. In same skillet, combine remaining wine with 2 to 3 tablespoons of liquid from the mushroom confit. Bring to boil. Stir cornstarch, seasoned salt, ¼ teaspoon white pepper, and chicken broth in a bowl. Add this to the skillet. Bring to boil. Add heavy cream, mushroom confit, and grapes. Stir everything gently. Bring just to boil. Pour over chicken. Cover casserole and bake 20 minutes at 350°. **Serves 4 to 6.**

❧ *Serve with Chenin Blanc or Chardonnay wine.*

Paulette S. Kneeland—Mexico City, Mexico
Donation to: Women's Auxiliary Cancer Fund, ABC Hospital, Mexico City, D.F.

Coq au Vin

During World War II, I came to the United States as a war bride. These recipes were given to me by my aunt in Oran, Algeria, North Africa.

INGREDIENTS

2 *whole chickens (3½ pounds each), cut into serving pieces*

Salt, to taste

Pepper, to taste

1 teaspoon *pulverized thyme*

1 teaspoon *pulverized bay leaves*

¾ pound *salt pork, cut into ¼-inch cubes*

20 *small onions*

½ pound *mushrooms*

5½ ounces *butter*

2 tablespoons *oil*

¼ cup *cognac*

2 bottles *(fifths) red wine (Bourgogne)*

3 *cloves garlic, chopped*

2½ ounces *flour*

DIRECTIONS

Season chicken with salt, pepper, thyme, and bay leaves. Blanch salt pork 5 minutes; drain. Sauté salt pork, onions, and mushrooms in 2 ounces of butter in a heavy skillet. Spoon this garniture into a Dutch oven or any large cooking pan. Lightly sauté chicken in oil in the heavy skillet; drain. Place chicken on the garniture in Dutch oven. Pour cognac in skillet and scrape bottom and sides with wooden spoon. Ignite cognac and pour over chicken. Add red wine to the Dutch oven and bring to boil. Add garlic, lower heat, and simmer 1 hour. Meanwhile, prepare *beurre manié*: beat flour, 1 tablespoon at a time, into remaining butter until well-blended. Set aside. Remove chicken and arrange on a serving platter. Stirring constantly, add *beurre manié*, 1 tablespoon at a time, to the still-hot garniture and sauce in the Dutch oven, heating after each addition. Remove fat from sauce. Drain sauce and reserve. Arrange garniture over the chicken and pour sauce over everything. Surround with pieces of toast. **Serves 8.**

❧ *I serve this dish with buttered noodles, flavored with a touch of garlic, or with rice.*

Linda Goldenberg Mayman—Los Angeles, CA
Donation to: American-Israel Cultural Foundation, Manhattan, NY

Tagine of Chicken with Raisins and Almonds

When faced with the prospect of serving Passover dinner for 40 people, I adapted a Moroccan lamb stew-type recipe for use with chicken breasts. This slightly spicy dish has become such a hit that it is an untraditional Passover tradition in my household. Of course, it is delicious any time of year.

INGREDIENTS

8 *chicken breast halves, boned*
Olive oil
1½ cups *chopped onions*
3 *cloves garlic, finely minced*
1 teaspoon *salt*
1 teaspoon *freshly ground pepper*
1 teaspoon *turmeric*
¼ teaspoon *ground ginger*
¼ teaspoon *cayenne*
½ pound *fresh tomatoes, peeled, seeded, and chopped (or an 8 ounce can, drained and chopped)*
1 cup *water*
1 tablespoon *chopped fresh parsley-cilantro mixture*
1 cup *raisins, soaked in water and drained*
½ cup *whole almonds, blanched*

DIRECTIONS

Place chicken breasts in Dutch oven with ¼ cup oil, onions, garlic, and spices. Toss to coat evenly. Add tomatoes and water. Bring to boil. Reduce heat. Cover and simmer 10 minutes. Add parsley-cilantro mix and raisins. Continue cooking, covered, another 20 to 30 minutes until chicken is tender. Remove chicken and reduce sauce to a thick gravy. Heat enough oil to cover bottom of another skillet. Fry almonds on both sides. Drain them on paper towels; sprinkle over the chicken before serving. The chicken may be made ahead and refrigerated or frozen. **Serves 5 to 6.**

When I serve this for Passover, I serve it with an onion soufflé and a green vegetable. During the rest of the year, I serve this with couscous or brown rice.

Ruth M. McNeal—Columbus, OH
Donation to: The Opera Association of Central Ohio, Columbus, OH

Baked Chicken Supreme

I've had it so many years and have made it millions of times. Our Minister of Music at our church asked me to prepare a dinner for 200 people after a concert. I did and this chicken dish was a huge success.

INGREDIENTS

6 *chicken breasts, halved, boned, and skinned*
2 cups *sour cream*
¼ cup *lemon juice*
4 teaspoons *Worcestershire sauce*
4 teaspoons *celery salt*
2 teaspoons *paprika*
4 cloves *garlic, finely chopped*
2 teaspoons *salt*
½ teaspoon *pepper*
1¾ cups *dry bread crumbs*
½ cup *butter or margarine*
½ cup *shortening*

DIRECTIONS

Wash chicken and wipe dry. Set aside. Combine sour cream, lemon juice, Worcestershire sauce, celery salt, paprika, garlic, salt, and pepper. Add chicken to mixture. Coat well. Refrigerate overnight. Preheat oven to 350°. Remove chicken from sour cream mixture; roll in crumbs, coating evenly. Arrange in single layer in large shallow pan. Melt butter and shortening in small saucepan. Spoon half over chicken. Bake chicken, uncovered, 45 minutes. Spoon rest of butter mixture over chicken. Bake 10 to 15 minutes longer until chicken is tender and browned. Keep warm until ready to serve. This dish also tastes great the next day served cold. **Serves 6.**

❧ *Serve with buttered green pasta sprinkled with Parmesan; sautéed vegetables; and spinach salad with strawberries, nuts, and raisins.*

Susan S. Cohon—Toronto, Ontario, Canada
Donation to: The Variety Village Sports & Fitness Center, Scarborough, Ontario, Canada

Oven-Fried Lemon Marinated Chicken

INGREDIENTS

- **1** *chicken (3 pound), quartered*
- **1 tablespoon** *soy sauce*
- **1½ teaspoons** *salt*
- **¾ teaspoon** *pepper*
- **1** *clove garlic, crushed*
- **¼ cup** *salad oil*
- **½ cup** *lemon juice*
- **2 tablespoons** *grated lemon peel*
- **½ cup** *all-purpose flour*
- **2 teaspoons** *paprika*
- *Lemon slices*
- *Parsley*

DIRECTIONS

Combine chicken with soy sauce, ½ teaspoon salt, ½ teaspoon pepper, garlic, oil, lemon juice, and lemon peel. Refrigerate 1 hour or more. Preheat oven to 350°. Remove chicken from marinade and save marinade. Combine flour, paprika, and remaining salt and pepper in a plastic bag. Add chicken to bag and shake. Arrange, skin side up, in a shallow pan. Drizzle chicken with some of the marinade. Bake in oven 30 minutes, uncovered. Pour remaining marinade over chicken and bake 20 to 30 minutes until done. Garnish with lemon slices and parsley. 450 calories per serving. For low-fat diet, remove skin from chicken and reduce oil. **Serves 4.**

❧ *For a teenager's party, serve with seasoned potato skins, pasta primavera, chocolate chip cake, and banana gelato.*

Herbert L. Goldberg—Dallas, TX
Donation to: Susan G. Komen Foundation, Inc., Dallas, TX

Pot Chicken Simplicity

I make a living selling diamonds, but cooking and running are my true loves. I find these different pastimes most compatible: I compose recipes while running. The following is a result.

INGREDIENTS

4 *chicken breasts with bone, or 6 thighs*

1 *onion, chopped*

6 *cloves garlic, chopped*

1 cup *dry white wine*

2 cups *chopped celery*

1 *red or green bell pepper, chopped*

1 tablespoon *chicken bouillon powder, or 4 cubes*

1 *apple with peeling, finely diced or grated*

3 *ripe tomatoes, chopped (or one 14½-ounce can)*

1 *jalapeño pepper, chopped*

DIRECTIONS

Combine all ingredients in a Dutch oven; cover and simmer slowly 1 hour. Meatballs may be substituted for chicken by simmering all ingredients 15 minutes before adding meatballs. **Serves 4.**

❧ *Serve with plain cooked rice and salad.*

Testing Notes: *We recommend adding 2 cups of water.*

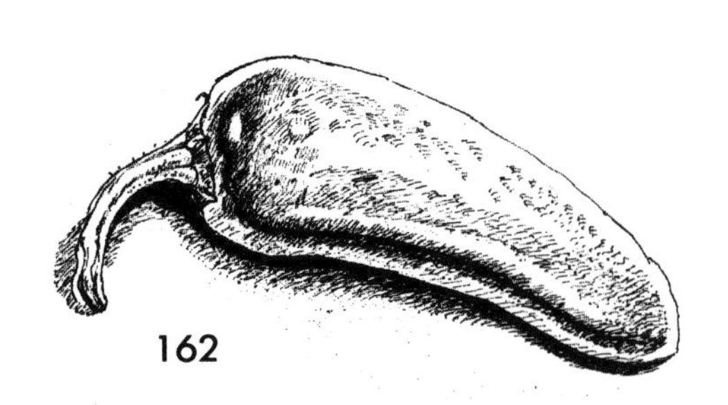

Neiman Marcus—THE ZODIAC Westchester
Donation to: combined charities

Sautéed Chicken with Bacon-Dijon Mustard-Horseradish Sauce

According to William Higinson, who is Assistant Food Service Manager, this "mystery" dish is always well received.

INGREDIENTS

1 *chicken breast (5 ounce)*
Flour
2 ounces *clarified butter*
1 ounce *white wine*
1 teaspoon *Dijon-style mustard*
1 ounce *cooked chopped bacon*
¼-½ teaspoon *grated horseradish*
3-4 ounces *heavy cream*
Salt and white pepper, to taste

DIRECTIONS

Dredge chicken breast in flour. Heat sauté pan and add butter. Heat until hot. Place chicken in pan and cook until done. Add white wine to pan to deglaze. Add mustard, bacon, horseradish, and heavy cream. Reduce by about half, stirring constantly. Season and serve. This dish creates an excellent marriage among all the different flavors present. **Serves 1.**

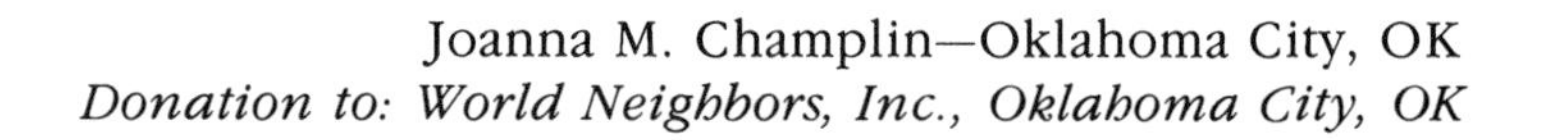

Country Captain

This recipe was brought to my hometown, Enid, Oklahoma, by my uncle's wife, Jewett Treadwell Cotton, from her native city, Memphis, Tennessee. It was an immediate hit, and she graciously shared it with my mother, Jane Champlin, who increased the recipe ten-fold for several large rehearsal dinners that she and my father, Joe Champlin, and my grandmother, Mrs. H. H. Champlin, hosted years ago.

INGREDIENTS

- **6** *pieces chicken*
- *Seasoned flour*
- **2** *large onions, diced*
- **2** *cloves garlic, minced*
- **1** *green bell pepper, diced*
- **1** *sweet-red bell pepper, diced*
- **3 tablespoons** *butter*
- **1 can** *(28 ounce) whole tomatoes*
- **1 teaspoon** *curry powder*
- **1 teaspoon** *thyme*
- **1 teaspoon** *white pepper*
- **1 teaspoon** *salt*
- **1 cup** *long-grain rice*
- **¼ pound** *slivered almonds*
- **2 tablespoons** *currants*

DIRECTIONS

Coat chicken in flour seasoned with salt and pepper. Brown quickly and put aside in a covered dish. Brown onions, garlic, and peppers in 2 tablespoons butter. Add tomatoes, curry, thyme, white pepper, and salt. Cook 5 minutes. Pour over chicken and bake 45 minutes at 400°. Meanwhile, brown almonds in remaining butter. Set aside. Cook rice. Add almonds and currants to cooked rice. Remove chicken from baking dish and add rice mixture to sauce in dish. Blend well. Lay chicken on top of rice and cover. Let stand in warm oven until ready to serve. **Serves 4 to 6.**

José Eber—Los Angeles, CA
Donation to: AIDS Project L.A., Los Angeles, CA

Diet Meat Loaf

José is recognized the world over for his signature ponytail and Panama hat, and for the glamorous hair styles of his celebrity clientele. But, for this recipe, he collaborated with his housekeeper. According to José, it's an ideal "low-fat, low-cholesterol, satisfying dish."

INGREDIENTS

2 *stalks celery, finely chopped*

1 *medium-sized onion, finely chopped*

1 *ripe tomato, finely chopped*

2 pounds *ground turkey breast*

2 *egg whites*

Seasonings, to taste

DIRECTIONS

Add celery, onion, and tomato to the ground turkey meat. Beat egg whites until foamy, but not stiff. Fold into the meat. Combine turkey mixture with seasonings, such as seasoned or plain salt, pepper, and herbs. Place in a PYREX® dish. Using a wet spatula, form meat into a loaf and bake 45 minutes at 350°, uncovered. Cover and bake an additional 30 minutes. Allow meat to cool slightly before cutting. If your diet allows, pour 4 to 6 ounces of PRITIKIN® spaghetti sauce, or any other diet spaghetti sauce, over the meat loaf before baking.
Serves 6 to 8.

❧ *Serve with steamed vegetables and plain rice.*

Testing Notes: *Season with oregano, garlic salt, and white pepper. Serve with steamed, fresh green beans and a mix of steamed yellow and red bell peppers.*

Evy Rappaport—Beverly Hills, CA
Donation to: Museum of Contemporary Art, Los Angeles, CA

Turkey Chili

I have been making this recipe for many years, as it is a family favorite.

INGREDIENTS

1 tablespoon *chili powder*
1 teaspoon *ground oregano*
1 teaspoon *ground basil*
½ teaspoon *crushed red-pepper flakes*
1 tablespoon *ground cumin*
2 *bay leaves*
1 tablespoon *paprika*
2 pounds *ground turkey*
1 *onion, chopped*
¼ cup *Worcestershire sauce*
¼ cup *dry red wine*
1 teaspoon *garlic purée or* **2 cloves**, *mashed*
1 can *(8 ounce) tomato purée*
1 bottle *(8 ounce) ketchup*
Salt, to taste
Chopped onion, to taste
Grated Cheddar cheese, to taste

DIRECTIONS

Combine chili powder, oregano, basil, pepper flakes, cumin, bay leaves, and paprika. Add ground turkey and mix well. Combine turkey mixture with onion. Place in a large saucepan. Add Worcestershire and red wine. Cover and cook over medium heat 1½ hours, stirring often. Add garlic and stir well. Add tomato purée and ketchup. Mix well. Season with salt. Cook over low heat 20 to 30 minutes, stirring occasionally. Serve hot with onion and cheese. **Serves 6 to 8.**

❧ *Turkey chili tastes great in the autumn with salad and bread.*

Testing Notes: *We recommend topping chili with shredded jalapeños, and serving nachos on the side.*

Georgie Bixler—Tallahassee, FL
Donation to: American Heart Association, Inc., Tallahassee, FL

Little Red Hens

It's my original recipe, using my favorite flavors.

INGREDIENTS

- **1 package** *(10 ounce) boil-in-bag frozen white and wild rice*
- **1 package** *(8 ounce) cream cheese*
- **1** *medium-sized onion, chopped*
- **2** *cloves garlic, minced*
- **5 tablespoons** *butter, softened*
- **2 heaping teaspoons** *brine-packed green peppercorns, drained*
- **2 tablespoons** *chopped fresh sage*
- **3 tablespoons** *plus* **1 teaspoon** *chopped fresh parsley*
- **½ cup** *chopped pecans*
- *Salt and freshly ground pepper, to taste*
- **4** *Rock Cornish hens (about 1½ pounds each)*
- **3 tablespoons** *paprika*
- **1 teaspoon** *garlic powder*
- **1 teaspoon** *chopped thyme*
- *Pinch cayenne*
- *Vermouth*
- *Chicken stock*

DIRECTIONS

Cook rice, according to package directions. Place cream cheese in a medium-sized bowl; pour rice over and stir. Sauté onion and garlic in 4 tablespoons butter until wilted . Pour over rice and cream cheese. Add peppercorns, sage, 3 tablespoons parsley, pecans, salt, and pepper. Mix well. Wash Cornish hens and dry well. Stuff birds with dressing, mounding slightly. Rub each bird with remaining softened butter. Mix paprika, garlic powder, remaining parsley, thyme, cayenne, and salt. Rub mixture over birds, covering completely. Place birds in small heavy roasting pan. Pour vermouth and chicken stock into bottom of pan to a depth of about ¼-inch. Bake 50 to 60 minutes at 350° until juices run clear. Remove birds to platter and keep warm. Deglaze pan with vermouth and chicken stock (about ⅓ cup each). Boil down on medium heat until slightly thickened. Place gravy in sauce bowl and serve with birds. **Serves 4.**

❧ *Serve with a green or fruit salad with a very light oil-and-vinegar dressing and Chardonnay wine.*

Nancy R. Engerman—Highland Park, IL
Donation to: American Cancer Society, Inc., National Headquarters, Atlanta, GA

Stuffed Rock Cornish Hens

This is an old family recipe from grandmother's day.

INGREDIENTS

4 *large loaves of stale bread*

6-8 *medium-sized onions, finely chopped*

4 *stalks celery, finely chopped*

½ pound *mushrooms*

4 *eggs, beaten*

Salt, to taste

Pepper, to taste

Cornflakes

½ teaspoon *garlic powder*

4 *large Rock Cornish hens*

Needle and thread, or meat pins

Melted butter

DIRECTIONS

Soak stale bread in water and squeeze dry. Fry onions and celery until browned. Add mushrooms and sauté for a few minutes. Add mixture to bread. Add eggs, salt, and pepper. Mix. Add cornflakes until mixture is thick enough for stuffing. Add garlic powder and set aside. Wash hens and pat dry with paper towels. Salt and pepper inside and outside. Sew, or pin, one end closed. Fill loosely with stuffing and sew up, or pin, other end closed. Baste with melted butter and place on rack in roasting pan, breast side up. Roast about 1 hour and 15 minutes. Baste, occasionally, with melted butter. To serve, remove thread, or pins, and slice each hen in half from front to back. One half per person is usually sufficient for each serving. **Serves 8.**

Diane P. Nelson—Dunlap, IL
Donation to: Lakeview Museum of Arts & Sciences, Peoria, IL

Wild Duck with Orange Sauce

This is my own recipe, made up after years of cooking my husband's ducks. It's great because all the fat and grease are discarded.

INGREDIENTS

1 bunch *celery, chopped*
2 *Bermuda onions, chopped*
2 *apples, chopped*
2 *oranges, chopped*
6 *wild mallard ducks*
Salt and pepper, to taste
1 teaspoon *poultry seasoning*
4 *bay leaves*
4 cups *fresh orange juice*
4 cups *chicken or duck stock*
4 cups *white wine*
GRAND MARNIER® to taste

DIRECTIONS

Chop celery, onions, apples, and oranges. Clean, wash, and dry ducks thoroughly. Pack tightly in roasting pan and cover with water. Bake 2½ hours at 350°. Discard fatty cooking water. Clean, wash, and dry ducks again. Stuff each with celery, onions, apples, and oranges. Pack tightly into clean roasting pan, breast side down. Add spices and cover with juice, stock, and wine. Cover and bake 5 hours at 350°. Ducks will stay tender as long as they are submerged in liquid. When pulled from the pan, the breast meat will fall off the bone. Strain liquid from the roasting pan into a saucepan until saucepan is full. Freeze all remaining liquid from roasting pan for your next duck dinner. Reduce liquid until thickened. (You may also thicken with cornstarch.) Add GRAND MARNIER®, to taste, and serve over ducks and rice. **Serves 8: 1 whole duck per man and ½ duck per woman.**

❧ *Serve with wild rice and spinach soufflé.*

CHAPTER EIGHT

Meats

Dinner equals meat. That's been the attitude of millions of American families for years. But, InCircle cooks see a lot of new options. Beef still reigns as king, although some of the leaner cuts require marinating and slower cooking to make them tender and tasty. We're rediscovering veal, thanks to a European influence. (It has a lot of protein and much less cholesterol.) Pork now calls itself "The Other White Meat®," and lamb is gaining in popularity, due to the adaptation of some exotic Middle Eastern recipes. Many nutritionists advise us to serve meat in five-ounce portions. So, you see, there is no reason to give up the enjoyment of meat for dinner.

Mrs. Wayne C. Morgan—Atlanta, GA
Donation to: Egleston Children's Hospital at Emory University, Atlanta, GA

Christmas Stew

Every Christmas Eve the traditional aroma of this long-simmering stew permeates the house with the spirit of the season, while allowing the cook to abandon the kitchen until dinner.

INGREDIENTS

- **3 pounds** *veal or beef stew meat, cut into 1-inch cubes*
- **1 can** *(28 ounce) tomatoes, undrained*
- **1 cup** *coarsely chopped celery*
- **4** *medium-sized carrots, sliced*
- **3** *medium-sized potatoes, cubed*
- **3** *medium-sized onions, chopped*
- **2 cups** *peas or green beans, fresh or frozen*
- **4 tablespoons** *quick-cooking tapioca*
- **2** *beef or vegetable bouillon cubes*
- **1 teaspoon** *salt (optional)*
- **1 teaspoon** *sugar*
- *Freshly ground black pepper*
- **½ teaspoon** *ground thyme*
- **½ teaspoon** *rosemary leaves*
- **½ teaspoon** *ground marjoram*
- **½ cup** *chopped fresh parsley*
- **½-¾ cup** *red wine*

DIRECTIONS

Combine all ingredients in a 6-quart casserole. Cover and cook 5 to 6 hours at 325°. After 3½ hours, stir well; continue cooking. Remove from oven, let cool for a brief time. **Serves 10 to 12.**

❧ *Serve with French bread and red wine.*

Testing Notes: *Decrease cooking time to 3 to 4 hours.*

Janet Newlan Bower—La Mesa, CA
Donation to: Project Wildlife, San Diego, CA

Homemade Winter Stew

Always one to emphasize vegetables, I adapted this family recipe to my children's needs and tastes.

INGREDIENTS

2 pounds *chuck roast, cut into large bite-sized pieces*

2 *onions, chopped*

4 *carrots, cut diagonally into 2-inch pieces*

4 *stalks celery, cut diagonally into 2-inch pieces*

1 cup *sliced mushrooms*

6 *potatoes, cut into large pieces*

2 *bay laurel leaves*

1 can *(8 ounce) tomato sauce*

1 can *(14½ ounce) beef broth*

1 cup *red Burgundy wine*

5 cups *water*

¼ cup *butter*

½ cup *flour*

DIRECTIONS

Combine meat and vegetables in an electric slow cooker. Add bay leaves, tomato sauce, broth, wine, and water. Cook 6 hours on high; 7 or longer on low. Thirty minutes before serving, melt butter. Add flour and whisk to blend. Add 1½ cups hot broth to roux, then return all to the stew. Stir well. Turn on high for 30 minutes to allow stew to thicken.

Serves 6 to 8.

❧ *Serve with corn bread and honey butter, and a hearty Burgundy.*

Francine Gerson—Dallas, TX
Donation to: Bryan's House, Dallas, TX

Old-Fashioned Belgian Stew (Blanquette de Veau a L'Ancienne)

This a specialty of my country, Belgium.

INGREDIENTS

1 pound *breast of veal, cubed in irregular chunks*

1 pound *shoulder of veal, cubed in irregular chunks*

Sea salt, to taste

Ground pepper

Butter

3 *carrots, peeled and cut into large pieces*

4 *small onions, peeled*

1 *clove garlic, peeled*

1 *sprig of thyme*

1 *bay leaf*

Sprigs of parsley

1-2 *whole cloves*

1 *stalk celery*

1 tablespoon *flour*

1 cup *white wine*

2 cups *cold water*

1 pound *mushrooms*

⅓ cup *crème fraîche, heavy cream, or half-and-half*

2 *egg yolks*

3 tablespoons *chopped parsley*

DIRECTIONS

If you wish, 2 pounds of cubed veal may be used instead of the breast and shoulder of veal. Season meat with salt and pepper. Brown lightly in butter in a large stew pot. Add carrots, onions, garlic, thyme, bay leaf, parsley sprigs, and cloves. Braise briefly, uncovered. Add celery. Sprinkle meat with flour. Mix well with a wooden spoon. Add wine and water. Bring to boil; skim lightly. Cover and cook over low heat 1 hour. Add mushrooms and cook 15 minutes. Beat crème fraîche and egg yolks together; add to the stew, stirring until well-blended. Arrange stew on platter, sprinkle with chopped parsley, and serve. It is very good reheated the next day and it freezes well. **Serves 4.**

❧ *Serve with rice or boiled potatoes.*

Kathryn A. Fiore—Saugus, MA
Donation to: Friends of Breakhart Reservation, Saugus, MA

Kathy Fiore's Chili

Looking for the best chili, I combined various recipes and tastes to form what is now referred to as the best chili in the world!

INGREDIENTS

2 pounds *steak tips, ground beef, or chicken chunks*

¼ pound *bacon, diced*

1 *large onion, chopped*

6 *cloves garlic, minced*

2 teaspoons *salt (optional)*

Black pepper

1 *green bell pepper, chopped*

6 *seeded jalapeño peppers, halved lengthwise*

4 tablespoons *chili powder, or more to taste*

1 tablespoon *whole cumin*

1 tablespoon *oregano*

1 can *(28 ounce) tomatoes, ground*

1 can *(8 ounce) kidney beans, drained*

1 tablespoon *Worcestershire sauce*

1 cup *dry red Burgundy wine*

Chopped onions

Grated cheese

Grated ginger

TABASCO® sauce

DIRECTIONS

Sauté beef, bacon, onions, and garlic. Add salt, black pepper, bell and jalapeño peppers, spices, tomatoes, beans, Worcestershire sauce, and wine. Cook 2 hours. Voila! Serve over spaghetti and top with chopped onions, grated cheese, grated ginger, and TABASCO® sauce. (Optional ingredients: black beans, cinnamon, allspice, and cocoa.) **Serves 6.**

❧ *Serve with ice-cold beer and grilled Italian bread.*

Testing Notes: *Ginger makes this chili different.*

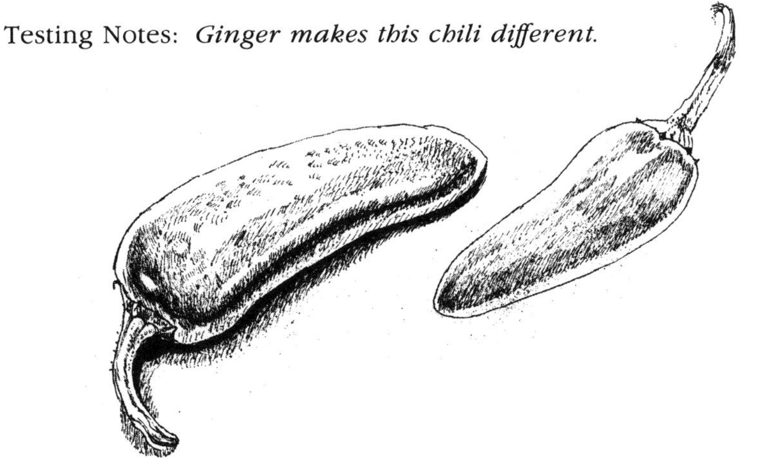

Naomi Denison—W. Bloomfield, MI
Donation to: Children's Leukemia Foundation of Michigan, Southfield, MI

Elegant Roast Tenderloin

Aunt Sadie, who died at the age of 88, was my father's youngest sister. She and I were close. (I was a flower girl at her wedding in 1922!) She and I always exchanged outstanding recipes. This is one she gave me, and each time I serve it, I receive rave reviews.

INGREDIENTS

¼ cup *dry white wine*
¼ cup *brandy*
3 tablespoons *lemon juice*
2 tablespoons *snipped chives*
1½ teaspoons *salt*
¼ teaspoon *freshly ground pepper*
1 teaspoon *Worcestershire sauce*
1 *roast tenderloin (2 pound)*
2 tablespoons *water*
2 tablespoons *margarine*
Mushrooms, halved and sautéed

DIRECTIONS

Combine wine, brandy, lemon juice, chives, salt, pepper, and Worcestershire sauce. Place meat in plastic bag and place in loaf pan. Add marinade and seal. Refrigerate overnight or let stand no more than 2 hours at room temperature. Press bag occasionally. Remove meat from bag and wipe with paper towels. Place on rack in shallow roasting pan and roast 45 to 55 minutes at 425°, basting occasionally with half the marinade. Heat remaining marinade, water, and margarine in a small pan until bubbly. Slice meat, arrange on heated platter and spoon sauce over. Garnish with sautéed mushrooms. **Serves 8.**

❧ *Serve with oven-roasted tiny potatoes, fresh asparagus, and a salad of Bibb lettuce, grapefruit, and hearts of palm.*

Mrs. Leonard Bernstein—Los Angeles, CA
Donation to: World Wildlife Fund, Inc., Washington, D.C.

Meatballs Bourguignonne

This dish is inexpensive to make but looks elegant when served. Ground turkey can be used for those who need to cut down on fat or who do not eat red meat.

INGREDIENTS

1 pound *ground beef or turkey*

1/2 cup *dry bread crumbs*

1/2 cup *milk*

1/4 cup *grated onion*

2 teaspoons *seasoned salt*

Seasoned pepper, to taste

1/4 cup *oil*

3 tablespoons *flour*

2 *beef or chicken bouillon cubes*

2 cups *boiling water*

1 cup *dry red wine*

DIRECTIONS

Combine ground beef, bread crumbs, milk, onion, 1 1/2 teaspoons seasoned salt, and seasoned pepper. Shape into medium-sized meatballs. Brown in hot oil. Remove meatballs to separate plate. Blend flour in the hot oil. Dissolve bouillon cubes in boiling water. Gradually add to flour mixture, stirring constantly. Add wine, seasoned pepper, and remaining seasoned salt. Cook and stir until thick and smooth. Add meatballs. Cover and simmer 30 minutes, stirring occasionally. Serve over buttered noodles. **Serves 4 to 6.**

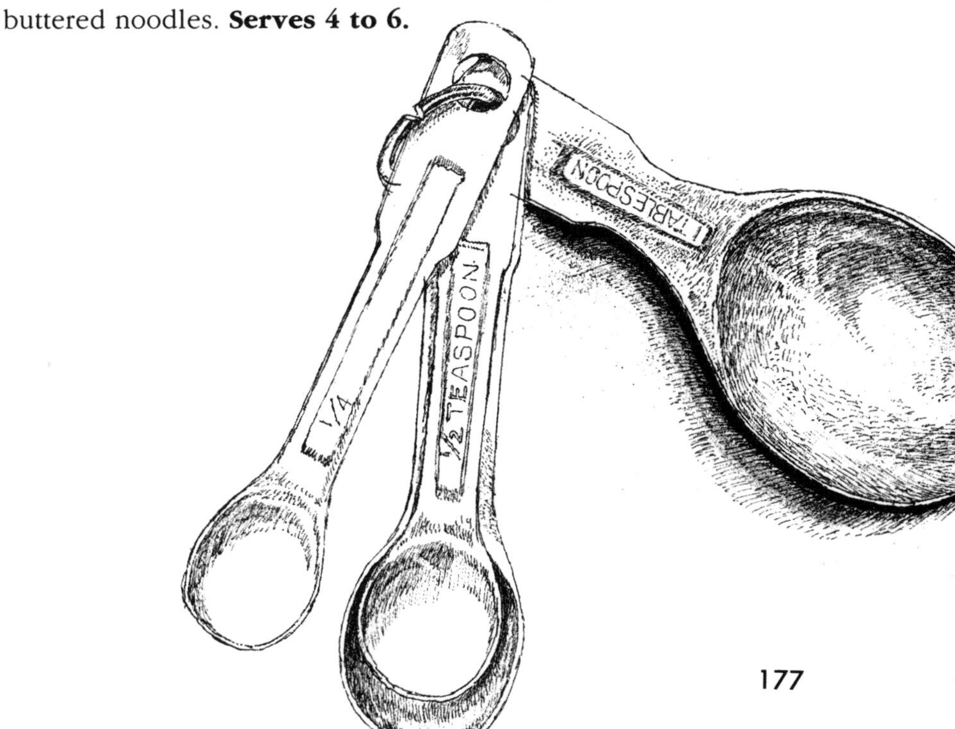

Dixie Unruh—La Jolla, CA
Donation to: Old Globe Theatre, San Diego, CA

Perfect Party Steaks

I've had this recipe about 6 years, and it's a never-fail gourmet presentation and dinner party saver, since it can be prepared the day before.

INGREDIENTS

8 *filet mignon steaks (6 to 8 ounces each), cut 1-inch-thick*

2 *medium-sized cloves garlic, crushed, plus* **½ teaspoon** *crushed garlic*

½ teaspoon *seasoned salt*

¼ teaspoon *seasoned pepper*

1 tablespoon *plus* **½ stick** *unsalted butter*

3 tablespoons *brandy*

4 tablespoons *flour*

2½ teaspoons *tomato paste*

¾-1 cup *dry red wine*

1 cup *chicken broth*

½ cup *beef broth*

¼ teaspoon *Worcestershire sauce*

2½ tablespoons *currant jelly*

½ pound *mushrooms, sliced*

DIRECTIONS

Place steaks on work surface. Make a paste of the 2 garlic cloves, salt, and pepper; rub paste on both sides of steaks. Heat 1 tablespoon butter in large, heavy skillet until very hot. Sauté steaks over moderately-high heat until brown on each side, but still raw in the center. Do not crowd. If butter begins to burn, reduce heat slightly. Place steaks in a casserole. Leave a little space between each steak. Add brandy to skillet. Cook over moderate heat, stirring constantly and scraping bottom of pan. Add ½ stick butter; when melted and foaming, stir in flour. Reduce heat. Cook and stir until mixture is golden. Stir in tomato paste and ½ teaspoon garlic. Mixture will be thick and grainy. Remove pan from heat and whisk in wine and both broths. Bring to boil. Reduce heat; simmer 10 minutes until reduced by one-third, stirring occasionally. Stir in Worcestershire and jelly. When jelly melts, stir in mushrooms. Adjust seasonings. Sauce should be of coating consistency; if too thick, thin with wine. Cool completely. Pour over steaks. Cover and refrigerate overnight. Bring to room temperature. Preheat oven to 400°. Pour sauce into a saucepan and heat just to boiling. Pour sauce over steaks in the casserole. Bake, uncovered, 15 to 20 minutes for medium-rare and 20 to 25 minutes for medium-to medium-well. When serving, spoon sauce from pan over steaks. **Serves 8.**

❧ *Serve with oven-baked potatoes and a fresh green vegetable.*

Ileen Malitz—Weehawken, NJ
Donation to: Starlight Foundation, New York, NY

Stuffed Beef Cabbage Rolls

My mother, Betty Malitz, first learned this from her Russian-born aunt, Rose Aidman. Over the years, my mother updated the recipe and became "famous" for it in Cleveland, Ohio.

INGREDIENTS

1 pound *ground chuck*
2 tablespoons *raw rice*
1 tablespoon *grated onion*
Salt and pepper, to taste
1 can *(15 ounce) HUNT'S® tomato sauce*
1 can *(6 ounce) tomato paste*
Juice of 1 lemon
5 tablespoons *brown sugar, or more to taste*
1 can *(20 ounce) whole tomatoes*
1 *medium or 2 small cabbages*

DIRECTIONS

Combine meat, rice, onions, salt, and pepper. Mix thoroughly and set aside. Mix remaining ingredients, except cabbage, in a roasting pan. Set aside. Core cabbage and bring to boil in a pot of cold water, to cover. Boil 20 minutes until leaves are softened. Drain and shake off water. Separate 20 to 25 leaves. Place on towels on counter. With slightly wet hands, take a walnut-sized portion of meat mixture and roll it between your palms. Place rolled meat on cabbage leaf, tuck in the sides of the leaf and roll the leaf. Place cabbage rolls in roasting pan filled with tomato liquid. Cover and bake 4 hours at 325°. If served immediately, leave in pan. You can freeze the cabbage rolls by cooling and placing in freezer containers. Some people say it's better frozen and used later. The recipe can be doubled, but do not double tomato paste or brown sugar; check to be sure it's to your taste. **Serves 12.**

❧ *Serve with farfel.*

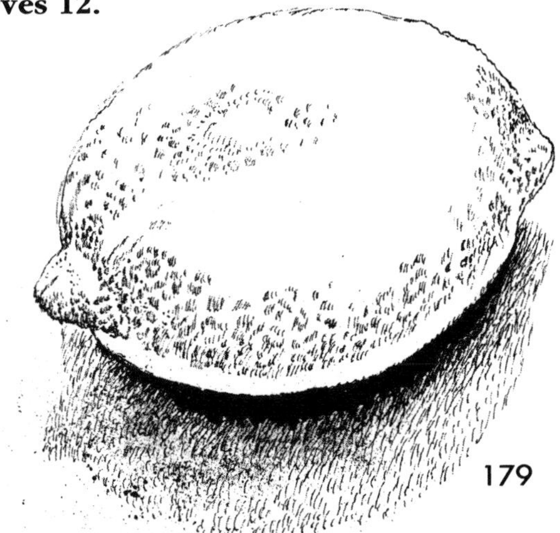

Esther Feder—Suffern, NY
Donation to: American Cancer Society, Inc., New York, NY

Sweet-and-Sour Beef

This family recipe has been used for many years.

INGREDIENTS

1 *beef brisket (4 pound)*
2 *onions, diced*
1 package *sour prunes*
4 *sweet potatoes, peeled and halved*
8 *potatoes, peeled*
1 cup *orange juice*
Juice of ½ lime
Juice of 1 lemon
Salt and pepper, to taste
2 tablespoons *honey*

DIRECTIONS

Sear meat and onion. Add prunes, sweet potatoes, potatoes, orange juice, lime juice, lemon juice, salt, and pepper. Cook 2 hours on low flame (approximately 275°) or until ready. Add honey and cook 10 more minutes. **Serves 8 to 10.**

❧ *Serve with a tossed green salad.*

Ursula Wagenet—Saratoga, CA
Donation to: Lucile Salter Packard Children's Hospital at Stanford, Palo Alto, CA

Wagenet Special

We hosted a Japanese student who prepared shabu-shabu for us. We had some finely sliced, uncooked, eye of beef round left over. What to do with it? This recipe resulted. My friends call it the Wagenet Special.

INGREDIENTS

1 pound *eye of beef round, very thinly sliced*
1 package *(10 ounce) frozen chopped spinach, thawed*
1 package *(10 ounce) frozen chopped broccoli, thawed*
1 pint *regular or light sour cream*
1 package *dry onion soup mix*
Grated cheese

DIRECTIONS

Sear meat quickly in very hot pan. Add vegetables. Stir together and heat. Add sour cream and soup mix. Pour into shallow baking pan. Sprinkle with favorite cheese. Bake 30 minutes at 350°. **Serves 4 to 6.**

❧ *Serve with rice.*

Willie Wilson—Dallas, TX
Donation to: AIDS Research Institute, San Francisco, CA

Cheating Enchiladas

This way I don't have to soften the tortillas in hot oil and fill each one. So, I cheat a little. Pure and simple.

INGREDIENTS

2 pounds *ground meat*

16 ounces *black-eyed pea salsa*

16 ounces *chili*

1 pound *longhorn mild Cheddar cheese*

1 can *(10½ ounce) Cheddar cheese soup*

1 cup *milk*

18 *corn tortillas, quartered*

DIRECTIONS

Note: I use Neiman Marcus' own RED RIVER™ Blackeyed Pea Salsa and RED RIVER™ Chili Fixin's. Brown ground meat in 4-to 5-quart pot or large skillet. Cook redness out of meat. Drain off grease, add salsa and chili to ground meat. Simmer 10 minutes. Blend Cheddar soup, milk, and ½ the longhorn cheese in a saucepan. In casserole, arrange the following in layers: ½ the quartered tortillas; all the meat mix; ½ the cheese sauce; remaining tortillas; and the remaining cheese sauce. Grate remaining longhorn cheese on top. Cover and cook 30 to 35 minutes at 325°. **Serves 8.**

❧ *Serve with tossed green salad or marinated vegetables.*

Mrs. James H. Dudley—Comanche, TX
Donation to: Comanche Public Library, Comanche, TX

Margarita's Fajitas with Pico de Gallo con Alcochofas

Our family raises registered Hereford cattle, and I prefer to serve our ranch beef to guests. This recipe was devised to present beef as a healthful entrée with a Southwestern flair.

INGREDIENTS

4 *ripe avocados, diced*

3 *tomatoes, diced and seeded*

3 tablespoons *chopped fresh cilantro*

Juice of 3 limes

Salt, to taste

1 can *artichoke hearts, diced*

3 *sirloin steaks, all fat removed and thinly sliced diagonally*

3 tablespoons *cumin seeds*

4 tablespoons *ancho chile flakes (or 4 whole dried New Mexico chile peppers)*

Extra-virgin olive oil

2 tablespoons *herb-and-garlic vinegar*

2 tablespoons *white vinegar (90 grain)*

Fajita seasoning, to taste

2 cans *(14½ ounces each) unseasoned tomatoes, diced*

3 *cloves garlic*

Rice to serve 12

8 *tortillas, cut into ⅜-inch-wide strips*

Vegetable oil for frying tortillas

3 *red bell peppers, seeded and sliced vertically*

3 *yellow bell peppers, seeded and sliced vertically*

3 *green bell peppers, seeded and sliced vertically*

3 *sweet onions, sliced vertically*

DIRECTIONS

Combine first 6 ingredients to make the pico de gallo and refrigerate overnight (or several hours). Prepare meat for cooking. Toss with cumin, pepper flakes, 2 tablespoons oil, and both vinegars to lightly coat the meat. (If using whole chiles, seed and scissor into "flakes.") Sprinkle liberally with fajita seasoning, to taste. Place in glass dish and refrigerate overnight. Whiz tomatoes a few seconds with hand-held blender. Place in saucepan with 1 tablespoon olive oil. Press garlic into tomato mixture. Cook over low heat about 30 minutes, stirring as needed until thickened. Cook rice, according to package directions. Fry tortilla strips in very hot oil until crisp. Drain. Using a minimum amount of olive oil, sauté meat in wok in small batches until barely done. Sauté peppers and onions in minimum amount of olive oil until one step past al dente. Add tomato sauce. Return meat to wok and simmer until flavors are combined. Serve immediately. Layer each serving as follows: rice, 5 or more tortilla strips, fajitas, and a crisscross of tortilla strips. Remove the pico de gallo from refrigerator and garnish each plate with a generous portion. To prepare the fajita dish early and hold for serving later, do not combine sauce, meat, and vegetables. Hold at room temperature, or refrigerate if needed, until 10 or 15 minutes before serving. Then, heat everything in a wok, combining as follows: tomato sauce, vegetables, and meat. Allow flavors to blend. **Serves 12.**

❧ *Serve with black beans and praline cheesecake.*

Brenda J. Pangborn—Birmingham, MI
Donation to: Detroit Symphony Orchestra Hall, Inc., Detroit, MI

Braised Lamb Shanks

This is one of the first recipes that I tried when I married thirty years ago. I found a similar one in an old cookbook and adapted it over the years to our taste. It is fairly easy and so delicious. People of all ages seem to love it.

INGREDIENTS

- **8** *large lamb shanks*
- *Flour*
- **¼ cup** *cooking oil*
- **1** *onion, sliced*
- **4** *cloves garlic, minced*
- **1 cup** *ketchup*
- **1 cup** *water*
- **2 tablespoons** *Worcestershire sauce*
- **½ cup** *vinegar*
- **¼ cup** *brown sugar*
- **2 teaspoons** *dry mustard*
- **1 cup** *raisins*

DIRECTIONS

Dust shanks with flour. Heat oil in large roaster on top of stove. Brown shanks well, then drain the fat. Preheat oven to 350°. Scatter onion slices over meat. Combine remaining ingredients in a medium-sized saucepan and heat until dissolved. Pour over shanks and onions. Cover and simmer 2 hours in oven or until meat is tender. Uncover and baste meat. Return to oven, uncovered, and cook 15 minutes. These freeze very well. I leave the shanks in the sauce, cover with plastic wrap, and place in freezer. When frozen, I remove from the casserole, wrap with more plastic and, then, with aluminum foil. **Serves 8.**

❧ *Serve with mashed potatoes and peas for a hearty winter meal.*

Marcy Friedman—Carmichael, CA
Donation to: Crocker Art Museum Foundation, Sacramento, CA

Coriander-Honey Marinated Lamb Rack on a Bed of Spicy Thai Noodles

The lamb recipe was devised for the October 1990 Gourmet Gala in Sacramento. The sweepstakes winners from prior galas were invited to compete again in a "Best of the Best" gala event. My husband and I were again teamed up, and we won the American regional cuisine and the overall sweepstakes. The preparation is so easy that the hotel was able to expand the recipe to serve 500 gala guests.

INGREDIENTS

½ cup *plus* **5 tablespoons** *soy sauce*

7 *cloves garlic, pressed*

3 tablespoons *honey*

1 tablespoon *plus* **1 teaspoon** *coriander seeds, crushed*

1½ tablespoons *grated ginger*

½ teaspoon *cayenne*

2 tablespoons *hoisin sauce*

1 teaspoon *curry powder*

1 teaspoon *turmeric*

⅓ cup *rice vinegar*

2 *racks (2½ pounds each) of lamb*

⅓ cup *finely chopped red bell pepper*

¼ cup *chopped green onions*

¼ cup *finely chopped fresh coriander (cilantro)*

2 tablespoons *chopped roasted peanuts*

2 *eggs, beaten with 2 teaspoons water*

1 tablespoon *Chinese rice wine (or 2 tablespoons sherry)*

3 tablespoons *tomato sauce*

3 tablespoons *lime or lemon juice*

2 tablespoons *light brown sugar*

1 teaspoon *Chinese chili sauce*

Grated peel of 1 lime

½ pound *fresh Chinese noodles*

1 teaspoon *salt*

DIRECTIONS

Prepare a marinade with the first 10 ingredients, but save 3 tablespoons soy sauce and 3 pressed garlic cloves for later. Stir marinade until well-blended. Put lamb racks in shallow, non-aluminum container. Pour marinade over the lamb. Refrigerate 6 hours or overnight, occasionally turning and basting. Prepare bell pepper, green onion, coriander, and peanuts. Do not combine. Set aside. Beat eggs with water. Make thin pancakes with the egg-water mixture in an oiled crêpe pan until all mixture is used. Do not brown pancakes. When cool, stack and cut into thin shreds. Set aside. Preheat oven to 400°. Remove lamb racks from marinade and place in roasting pan.

(Reserve marinade.) Cover bone tips with foil to prevent burning. Roast until pink, about 30 minutes, basting twice with marinade. While lamb racks are roasting, combine, but do not cook, the remaining 3 tablespoons soy sauce and 3 pressed garlic cloves, the rice wine, tomato sauce, lime juice, sugar, chili sauce, and lime peel in a saucepan. Set the pan aside. Cook noodles in boiling water with salt, just until tender. Drain and place in large bowl. Remove lamb racks from oven and slice. Now, heat the wine/tomato sauce just to a low boil. Combine the sauce, peppers, onions, coriander, and shredded pancakes with noodles. Toss well. Sprinkle peanuts on top. For each serving, arrange 2 or 3 ribs on a bed of noodles. Serve at once. **Serves 8 to 12.**

❧ *At the Gala, the plate was garnished with teriyaki-poached shiitake mushrooms served with slivers of sweet red ginger.*

Joan Fanaberia Bloom—Montreal, Quebec, Canada
Donation to: Hope and Cope, Montreal, Quebec, Canada

Oven-Roasted Rack of Lamb with Mustard and Dill

This recipe is such a favorite with family and friends that long ago my children nicknamed it "R of L," as in "Hurray! We're having R of L tonight!"

INGREDIENTS

- ½ **teaspoon** *dried rosemary*
- 1 **clove** *garlic, mashed plus* **2 cloves** *garlic, chopped*
- 1 **tablespoon** *soya sauce*
- ½ **cup** *Dijon-style mustard*
- 4 **tablespoons** *olive oil*
- 4 *racks of lamb*
- ½ **cup** *bread crumbs*
- 1 **tablespoon** *finely chopped dill*

DIRECTIONS

Preheat oven to 375°. Combine rosemary, 1 mashed garlic clove, soya sauce, and mustard. Whisk in oil in slow stream. Whisk until combined and thickened. Brush on lamb, thoroughly coating all sides. Let stand several hours. Roast 15 minutes, fat side down. While roasting, combine bread crumbs, dill, and chopped garlic; set aside. After 15 minutes, turn roast over, brush top and sides with more mustard mixture, and coat top and sides with bread crumb mixture. Return roast to oven, placing pan in the middle of the oven, and broil 5 minutes. Slice into chops and serve. **Serves 6 to 8.**

❧ *Serve with giant potato sticks and snow peas, or green beans with sesame seeds.*

James Villas—Food and Wine Editor, *Town & Country,*
New York, NY
Donation to: combined charities

James Villas' Daube d'Agneau Provençale

This is my variation on *daube de boeuf provençale*, where I use lamb instead of the traditional beef. Leg of lamb tends to be too stringy when braised this long, so be sure to use the lesser cuts of lamb—bones and all. Also, if you want the ragout to have real Mediterranean character, be sure to use both the anchovies and olives.

INGREDIENTS

½ cup *olive oil*

4 pounds *lamb shoulder, trimmed of excess fat and cut into 2-inch cubes*

Flour

3 *medium-sized onions, chopped*

2 *medium-sized carrots, pared and cut into ¼-inch rounds*

2 *cloves garlic, minced*

2 *medium-sized fresh tomatoes or 3 canned Italian-style plum tomatoes, chopped*

5 *anchovy fillets, drained and minced*

½ teaspoon *dried thyme*

½ teaspoon *dried rosemary*

2 *bay leaves*

Salt and freshly ground pepper, to taste

1 cup *pitted black olives, cured in brine*

3 cups *beef bouillon*

DIRECTIONS

Heat half the oil in a large, heavy skillet. In batches, dust the lamb cubes in flour on all sides. Brown well in oil over moderately-high heat. Transfer cubes to an earthenware or enameled casserole. Add remaining oil to skillet, reduce heat, and add onions, carrots, and garlic. Sauté 3 minutes, stirring. Add tomatoes, anchovies, thyme, rosemary, bay leaves, salt, and pepper. Stir well. Cook 5 minutes. Transfer mixture to the casserole, add olives, and turn all ingredients with a heavy spoon. Deglaze skillet with bouillon, scraping the bottom and sides. Add bouillon to the casserole. Cover casserole, place in the refrigerator, and marinate overnight. Return the casserole to room temperature and turn ingredients with a heavy spoon. Preheat oven to 300°. Cover casserole with a heavy lid and braise 3 hours until meat is tender. Remove lid and stir well. Simmer over low heat until sauce thickens. **Serves 8.**

❧ *Serve with simple braised white beans, a romaine, red onion, and orange salad, and perhaps a glazed apple or apricot tart.*

Debra Alper—Chicago, IL
Donation to: American Heart Association, Inc., Chicago, IL

Lamb Couscous

When I graduated college, I lived with my aunt and uncle for a year. My aunt is French and a gourmet cook—never uses recipes, she cooks by taste. This was one of her dishes, and not only is it delicious, it's a beautiful dish for an informal dinner party.

INGREDIENTS

4 tablespoons *olive oil*

4 *medium-sized onions, sliced*

2 pounds *boneless lamb, cut into 1-inch cubes*

Flour

3 tablespoons *fresh minced parsley*

½ teaspoon *salt*

¼ teaspoon *black pepper*

½ teaspoon *ground cumin*

½ teaspoon *coriander*

⅛ teaspoon *saffron threads*

¼ teaspoon *cayenne*

Pinch ground cinnamon

4 cups *chicken broth*

6 *small red potatoes, halved*

3 *carrots, cut into 1-inch pieces*

3 *zucchini, cut into 1-inch pieces*

2 *yellow squash, cut into 1-inch pieces*

1 can *(15 ounce) drained garbanzo beans*

2 *tomatoes, cut into wedges*

1 box *couscous*

Golden raisins

DIRECTIONS

This tastes better when made 1 day in advance. Heat oil in large pot. Add onions, cook until golden, and remove with slotted spoon. Toss lamb with flour; shake off excess. Add lamb to pot and cook until brown all over, adding more oil to pan, if necessary. Add parsley, salt, pepper, cumin, coriander, saffron, cayenne, and cinnamon. Stir in broth; deglaze pot. Add sautéed onions. Simmer 30 minutes. Add potatoes and carrots. Cover and simmer 30 minutes. Add zucchini, yellow squash, and beans. Simmer, uncovered, 40 minutes. Add tomatoes. Simmer until all vegetables are tender. (At this point, you may refrigerate overnight. Bring to room temperature and slowly reheat the next day.) When ready to serve, prepare couscous, according to package directions, substituting chicken broth for water. Stir in raisins. Pass lamb separately. **Serves 10 to 12.**

Joan L. Sheppard—Godfrey, IL
Donation to: Alton Area Animal Aid Association, Godfrey, IL

Goulash Mit Kraut

Our house sits on a bluff overlooking the Mississippi River. This St. Louis recipe, with its rich European peasant flavor, is a favorite of ours on a cold, damp fall night as we watch the barges move slowly up the river on their way north.

INGREDIENTS

- **2 pounds** *sauerkraut*
- **3 tablespoons** *bacon drippings*
- **3** *large onions, diced*
- **3** *cloves garlic, chopped*
- **2 cups** *canned tomatoes, drained and chopped*
- **4 tablespoons** *paprika*
- **3 pounds** *pork tenderloin, cut into 1-inch cubes*
- *Pepper, to taste*
- **2 cans** *(14½ ounces each) beef bouillon*
- *Salt, to taste*
- *Sour cream at room temperature*
- *Dill weed*

DIRECTIONS

Drain and rinse sauerkraut; squeeze dry. Put bacon drippings in large heavy-duty pot; add onions and garlic and sauté until soft. Add tomatoes, paprika, pork, pepper, and sauerkraut. Stir well to blend. Pour in bouillon and stir. Simmer 1½ hours, adding salt the last 30 minutes. When ready to serve, top each bowl of goulash with dollop of sour cream. Garnish with dill weed.

Serves 6.

Neiman Marcus—THE HEDGES℠ Fort Worth
Donation to: combined charities

Momma Mae's Sunday Pork Chops

As you might guess, this is a personal family recipe of Restaurant Manager Wes Glover.

INGREDIENTS

1 cup *flour*
2 teaspoons *coriander*
½ teaspoon *salt*
½ teaspoon *pepper*
2 tablespoons *vanilla*
2 tablespoons *salad oil*
1 teaspoon *cinnamon*
1 teaspoon *lemon juice*
4 *apples with peelings, thinly sliced*
10 *center cut pork chops, split to the bone*

DIRECTIONS

Mix together flour, 1 teaspoon coriander, salt, and pepper. Set aside. Mix vanilla, oil, cinnamon, lemon juice, and remaining coriander. Bathe apple slices in the liquid mixture. Arrange 4 or 5 slices in splits of pork chops. Coat chops with seasoned flour. Fry in skillet over moderate heat just to brown on both sides. Put in ovenproof dish and bake 35 minutes at 350° until done. **Serves 10.**

❧ *Serve with a macaroni-and-green onion casserole and fresh string beans.*

Laura Marie Taylor—Atlanta, GA
Donation to: High Museum of Art, Atlanta, GA

Pork Chops Florentine

This recipe is from an old family friend.

INGREDIENTS

6 *center cut pork chops (10 ounces)*

Seasoned flour

Olive oil

4 tablespoons *butter*

4 tablespoons *flour*

½ teaspoon *salt*

½ teaspoon *pepper*

2 cups *milk*

1 package *(10 ounce) frozen chopped spinach, or fresh spinach, chopped*

3 *egg yolks*

1 cup *grated Swiss cheese*

DIRECTIONS

Dredge chops in seasoned flour and sear both sides over high heat in olive oil until well-browned. Reduce heat, cover and cook 30 minutes, turning chops frequently. Prepare a basic white sauce, using the butter, flour, salt, pepper, and milk. Steam spinach until hot. Drain well. In buttered baking dish, spread spinach on bottom and place chops on top. Beat egg yolks well, stir into white sauce and pour over chops. Sprinkle with cheese. Bake at 350° until sauce bubbles. **Serves 6.**

❧ *I usually serve this with a salad, rolls, and carrots.*

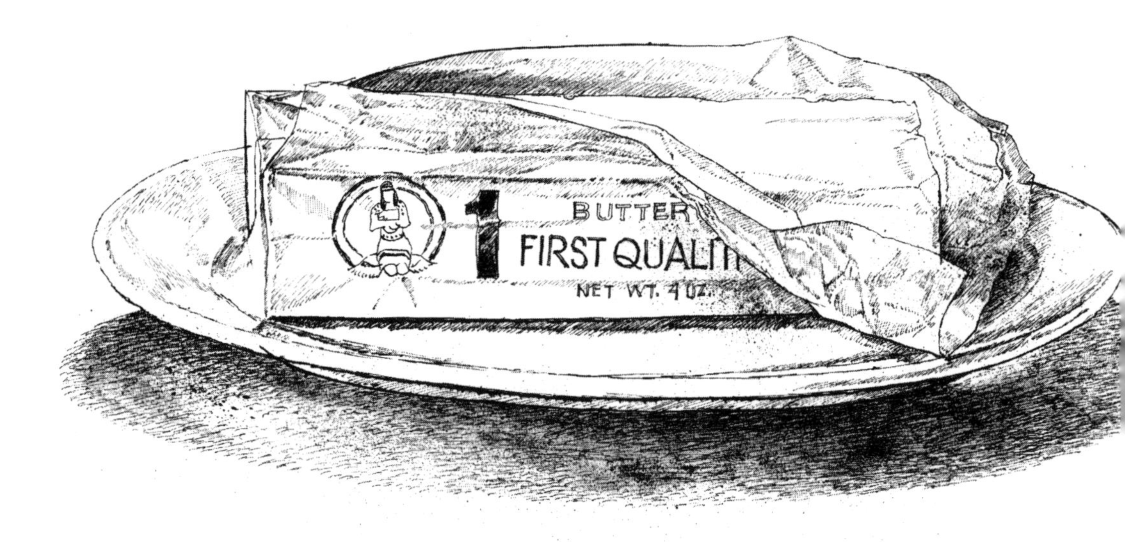

Rebecca S. Leon—Houston, TX

Donation to: Muscular Dystrophy Association, New York, NY

Pork Tenderloin Marinated in Green Peppercorn Mustard

This is my own recipe. I am native Cuban and my Spanish ancestors loved pork.

INGREDIENTS

3-4 *cloves garlic, mashed*

Salt, to taste

Pepper, to taste

1 teaspoon *cumin*

1 teaspoon *oregano*

1 teaspoon *green peppercorn mustard*

2 *pork tenderloin pieces (about 3½ pounds total)*

2 teaspoons *olive oil*

1 *medium-sized onion, sliced*

¼ cup *Marsala wine or red wine*

DIRECTIONS

Make a paste with garlic cloves, salt, pepper, cumin, oregano, and green peppercorn mustard. Spread the paste with your hands over both pieces of meat. Marinate overnight in refrigerator for best results, or at least several hours. Heat olive oil in skillet large enough to contain both pieces of meat. Brown meat on all sides on high heat. Spread onion slices on top and add wine. Cook 45 minutes on top of the stove at moderate-low heat until done. Slice tenderloin into ½-inch-thick pieces, and serve remaining sauce in a separate dish. Leftovers make delicious sandwiches with sliced ham and cheese, or with just lettuce and tomatoes.

❧ *Serve with vegetables or Cuban black beans and rice.*

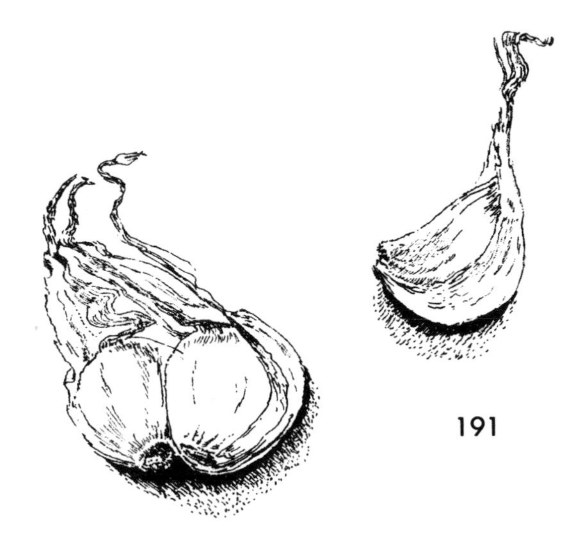

Yaeko W. Westfall—Rockville, MD
Donation to: Ballet Theatre Foundation, Inc., New York, NY

Sweet-and-Sour Pork

My sister gave me this recipe years ago. Since then, it has pleased many people. I especially prepare this dish for a friend's father—a doctor from the West—when he comes to town.

INGREDIENTS

- **1 pound** *loin of pork, cut into 1½-inch cubes*
- **2 tablespoons** *Chinese or Japanese wine or sherry*
- **6 tablespoons** *soy sauce*
- **2 tablespoons** *flour*
- **2 tablespoons** *cornstarch*
- *Oil*
- **3** *green bell peppers, seeded and quartered*
- **1** *onion (4 ounce), quartered*
- **1** *carrot (4 ounce), cut into small wedges and boiled 8 minutes*
- **1** *bamboo shoot (4 ounce), cut into small wedges*
- **2** *pineapple slices, quartered*
- **6 tablespoons** *sugar*
- **2 tablespoons** *vinegar*
- **4 tablespoons** *tomato sauce*
- **½ cup** *water*

DIRECTIONS

Mix pork cubes, 1 tablespoon wine, 2 tablespoons soy sauce, the flour, and 1 tablespoon cornstarch until pork is well coated. Deep-fry pork in oil until crisp and golden brown. Remove pork and set aside. Heat another frying pan, add 5 tablespoons oil, and sauté bell peppers, onion, carrot, bamboo shoot, and pineapples. Meanwhile, mix sugar, vinegar, tomato sauce, and remaining wine and soy sauce in a mixing bowl until well-blended. When vegetables are soft, add sauce and bring to boil. Mix remaining cornstarch with water and add to pan, stirring constantly. Add fried pork and mix well. Serve hot with rice. **Serves 6 to 8.**

❧ *Serve with eggdrop soup and broccoli in bean paste sauce.*

Joan Lunden—New York, NY
Donation to: American Cancer Society, Inc., National Headquarters, Atlanta, GA

Veal Chops

According to the co-host of ABC's *Good Morning, America*, "My mom always joked that some people eat to live, but I live to eat." Apparently, it's an inheritable trait because there is nothing Joan enjoys more than cooking for her family and filling the house with the aroma of one of her favorite family recipes.

INGREDIENTS

4 *veal chops*
2 *eggs, beaten*
½ teaspoon *white pepper*
½ teaspoon *salt*
½ teaspoon *Italian seasoning mixture*
Flour
Safflower oil
¼ cup *tomato sauce*

DIRECTIONS

Tenderize chops on both sides. Beat together eggs, pepper, salt, and Italian seasoning. Set aside. Wet chops and lightly coat with flour. Dip chops into egg mixture and, again, coat with flour. Reserve leftover egg mixture. Brown chops quickly on both sides in oil; place in a non-greased baking dish. Blend tomato sauce and remaining egg mixture together; pour over chops. Bake 45 minutes to 1 hour at 350°. **Serves 4.**

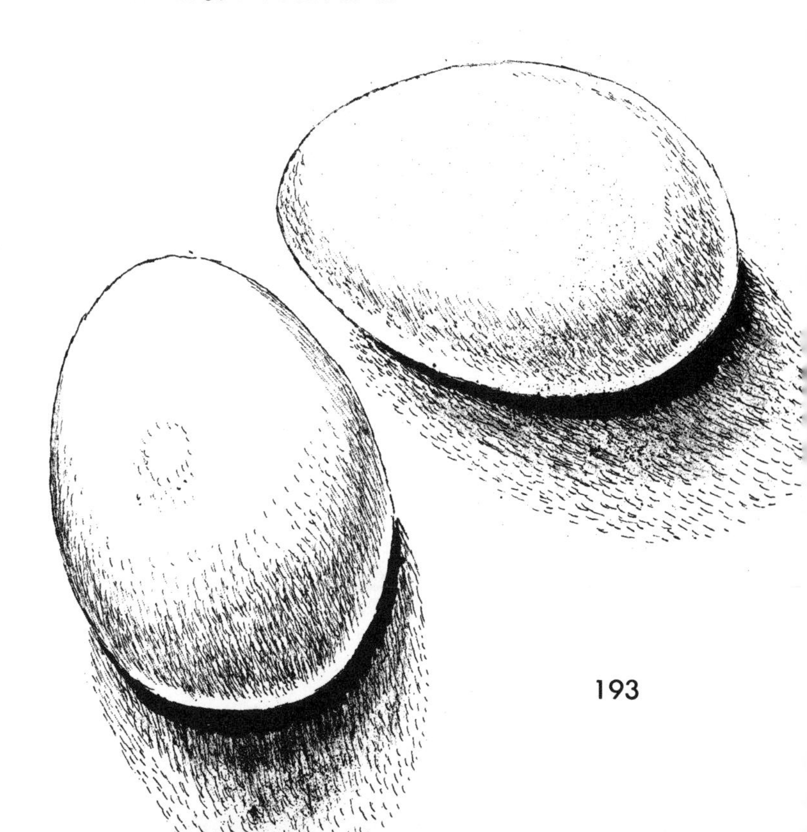

Esther S. Langsam—St. Louis, MO
Donation to: Missouri Chapter of the Lupus Foundation, Inc., St. Louis, MO

Veal Piccata

This was a favorite of a local, well-known cooking columnist. Veal is lean, light, and a good choice for today's health-conscious public.

INGREDIENTS

18 *round veal scallops, cut ¼-inch-thick*

Salt and freshly ground pepper, to taste

Flour

½ cup *margarine*

Juice of 2 lemons

2 tablespoons *chopped parsley*

DIRECTIONS

Place veal scallops between sheets of wax paper and pound as thin as possible, without breaking them. Use the flat side of a meat cleaver. Season with salt and pepper. Dust with flour. Heat 5 tablespoons margarine in a large frying pan over fairly high heat until golden. Quickly brown veal slices, a few at a time, for about 2 minutes on each side. Do not let them touch! Transfer to hot serving platter and keep warm. Add lemon juice and parsley to the pan. Remove from heat. Swirl in remaining margarine, bit by bit, and pour over veal scallops. **Serves 6.**

❧ *Serve with rice cooked in beef or chicken bouillon.*

Carol Garfield—Riverdale, NY
Donation to: North Shore Animal League, Inc., Port Washington, NY

Sicilian Veal Roast

This has been passed down in my brother-in-law's family for generations.

INGREDIENTS

- **1½-2 pounds** *lean boneless veal, pounded ½-inch-thick*
- *Salt and pepper, to taste*
- **¼ pound** *mozzarella cheese, cut into ½-inch cubes*
- **2** *sweet Italian sausages, skinned and chopped*
- **2 teaspoons** *minced Italian parsley*
- **1** *clove garlic, minced*
- **¼ teaspoon** *oregano*
- **3** *hard-cooked eggs, sliced*
- **¼ cup** *olive oil*
- **1** *small onion, sliced*
- **1** *carrot, sliced*
- **2** *bay leaves*
- **¾ cup** *dry white wine*
- **¼ cup** *water*

DIRECTIONS

Preheat oven to 350°. Season veal on both sides with salt and pepper. Combine mozzarella, sausage, parsley, garlic, and oregano. Mix well. Add eggs and mix carefully so slices remain intact. Spread on veal and roll up. Make sure filling does not show, or it will ooze out during cooking. Tie several times with kitchen string, and tie once lengthwise. Rub meat on all sides with salt, pepper, and 1 tablespoon olive oil. Pour remaining olive oil into dish, coating bottom and sides. Dish should not be too big for the veal. Place veal in the dish. Arrange onions, carrots, and bay leaves around the veal. Add ¼ cup wine and ¼ cup water. Cook 1 hour, basting occasionally. Remove meat. Skim fat from pan. In saucepan, add remaining wine, the cooked carrot and onion, and the particles scraped from bottom of pan. Put on stove and cook over high heat, stirring constantly for 3 minutes. Purée this mixture in CUISINART® and drizzle over meat. **Serves 8.**

❧ *Serve with a green salad and garlic-roasted potatoes.*

Ferdinand E. Metz—President, The Culinary Institute of America, New York, NY
Donation to: combined charities

Veau Braise Bavaroise (Bavarian-style Braised Veal)

INGREDIENTS

3 *veal shanks*

12 *strips of lard or 12 slices of bacon*

3 tablespoons *butter*

½ cup *diced carrots*

¼ cup *diced celery*

½ cup *diced onions*

2 *cloves garlic*

1 tablespoon *crushed black pepper*

1 *bay leaf*

½ teaspoon *dry basil*

2 cups *chicken broth*

½ cup *white wine*

DIRECTIONS

Chop bone ends off veal shanks and insert about 4 strips of lard in each, or wrap each with a slice of bacon. Tie with string. Brush shanks with butter, place in pan with carrots, celery, and onions; and brown in oven at 475° or on top of stove for 15 minutes until meat and vegetables are slightly brown. Add spices and simmer a little longer. Deglaze the drippings with some chicken broth and braise the shanks and vegetables in a covered casserole for 1½ hours at 350°. Always maintain about ½-inch of liquid in the roasting pan. Baste frequently. After shanks are cooked, add white wine to the gravy and strain through cheesecloth. Discard vegetables, skim off excess fat, and season gravy with salt and pepper. **Serves 5 to 6.**

❧ *Serve with either savory cabbage, stuffed onions, potatoes or bread dumplings.*

Testing Notes: *Add a tablespoon of brown roux to thicken sauce.*

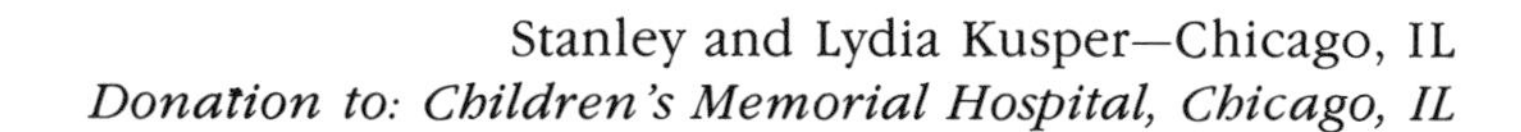
Stanley and Lydia Kusper—Chicago, IL
Donation to: Children's Memorial Hospital, Chicago, IL

Veal Winesap

Eaten at an inn in Maine. The chef would not share the recipe, but at check-out at the inn the next morning, the receptionist, who was the chef's fiancee, indicated that she would be able to persuade him to surrender the recipe.

INGREDIENTS

1 pound *veal scallops, sliced and pounded thin*

2 tablespoons *butter*

3-4 ounces *Chenin Blanc or a sweet white wine you would drink, not an inexpensive substitute*

1 *tart Granny Smith apple, cored, halved, and cut into 1/8 to 1/4-inch slices*

3-4 ounces *of Calvados (apple brandy)*

25-30 *seedless whole green grapes*

1/2 pint *heavy cream*

Salt and white pepper, to taste

DIRECTIONS

Sauté veal lightly on both sides on medium-high heat, being careful not to overcook or brown the butter, as this will discolor the sauce. Remove veal from skillet and keep mildly warm in oven. Deglaze pan with white wine; place apples in skillet. Sauté apples until they are cooked and begin to appear tender. Add Calvados and grapes. Flame brandy; sauté all ingredients 2 or 3 minutes, making certain grapes do not become overly soft. Reduce heat to low and add heavy cream. Continue cooking over low heat to reduce sauce until it thickens to a satisfactory texture. Add salt and pepper. (The sauce texture is determined by the size and frequency of the bubbles. It is up to the chef to decide what texture is best. The texture is in the bubbles.) Remove veal from oven. Either add it to the sauce for a moment, or place it on warmed plates and gently ladle sauce, apples, and grapes over the veal. Garnish with appropriate colors of red and green. **Serves 2.**

❧ *Serve with a small portion of wild rice and a vegetable of choice.*

Linda R. Dunn—Swampscott, MA
Donation to: Dana Farber Cancer Institute, Boston, MA

Veal and Zucchini Sauté

This recipe for two makes any evening feel like "a company night."

INGREDIENTS

¼ cup *flour*

1 *egg*

4-5 tablespoons *butter*

1 *large zucchini, sliced diagonally into ¼-inch-thick pieces*

Salt, to taste

Freshly ground pepper, to taste

4-6 *veal cutlets (½-to ⅔-pound), cut ¼-inch-thick*

1 *large lemon, including juice*

¼ cup, or more, *chicken stock or water*

1 tablespoon *minced parsley*

2 teaspoons *capers (optional)*

DIRECTIONS

Spread flour in a shallow dish. Beat egg in another shallow dish. Heat 2 tablespoons butter in a large skillet over medium heat. Lightly coat zucchini slices with flour, then dip in egg. Sauté zucchini in butter until lightly browned on both sides. Sprinkle with salt and pepper. Place on ovenproof plate in 150° oven. Coat veal cutlets with flour and dip in egg. If necessary, add butter to skillet to make about 2 tablespoons. Sauté 2 to 3 minutes until golden brown. Turn and sprinkle with salt and pepper. Cook other side about 2 minutes until golden brown. Do not overcook. Cut 2 thin slices from the center of the lemon and set aside. Squeeze 2 tablespoons juice from remaining lemon. Pour lemon juice over cooked veal in skillet. Immediately place veal on plate in warm oven. Add 1 tablespoon butter and chicken stock to lemon juice in skillet. Boil and stir to loosen and dissolve any pan drippings. Set skillet aside. Arrange veal and zucchini in alternating rows on 2 warm ovenproof dinner plates. Keep warm in oven until ready to serve. Before serving, boil pan juices until syrupy. Stir in parsley and capers. Pour over veal and zucchini. Garnish with the cut lemon slices. **Serves 2.**

CHAPTER NINE

Pasta

Do the Italians know something we don't? A lot, it would seem. And, of course, they learned it from the Asians after Marco Polo returned from his voyages. Besides being a favorite party fare with endless variations (hot, cold, red sauce or white sauce, meatless or meaty), pasta is fun to eat. And, of course, some of today's most prominent nutritionists believe we should get 60 percent or more of our calories from complex carbohydrates. *Mangé*!

Marlene Hammerman—St. Louis, MO
Donation to: American Heart Association, Inc., St. Louis, MO

Penne with Sun-dried Tomatoes and Walnuts

If you are a sun-dried tomato lover, you will love this combination of pasta, cream cheese, and sun-dried tomatoes.

INGREDIENTS

12 ounces *penne pasta*
4 tablespoons *olive oil*
2/3 cup *chopped green onions, white and green parts*
1/4 cup *chopped walnuts*
1/4 cup *olive oil-packed sun-dried tomatoes, chopped*
2 ounces *feta cheese, crumbled*
1/2 cup *whipping cream*
4 tablespoons *Romano cheese*
Freshly ground white pepper

DIRECTIONS

Cook penne in a large pan of boiling water, according to package directions. Drain pasta well. Heat oil in a large skillet. Sauté green onions and walnuts 5 minutes over medium heat. Add sun-dried tomatoes and sauté 2 minutes. Add pasta and feta cheese. Reduce heat to low; stir gently until cheese melts. Add cream and Romano cheese. Season with white pepper. Stir well. Serve immediately. **Serves 4.**

❧ *Serve with Caesar salad and garlic bread.*

Testing Notes: *Decrease feta cheese to 1 ounce.*

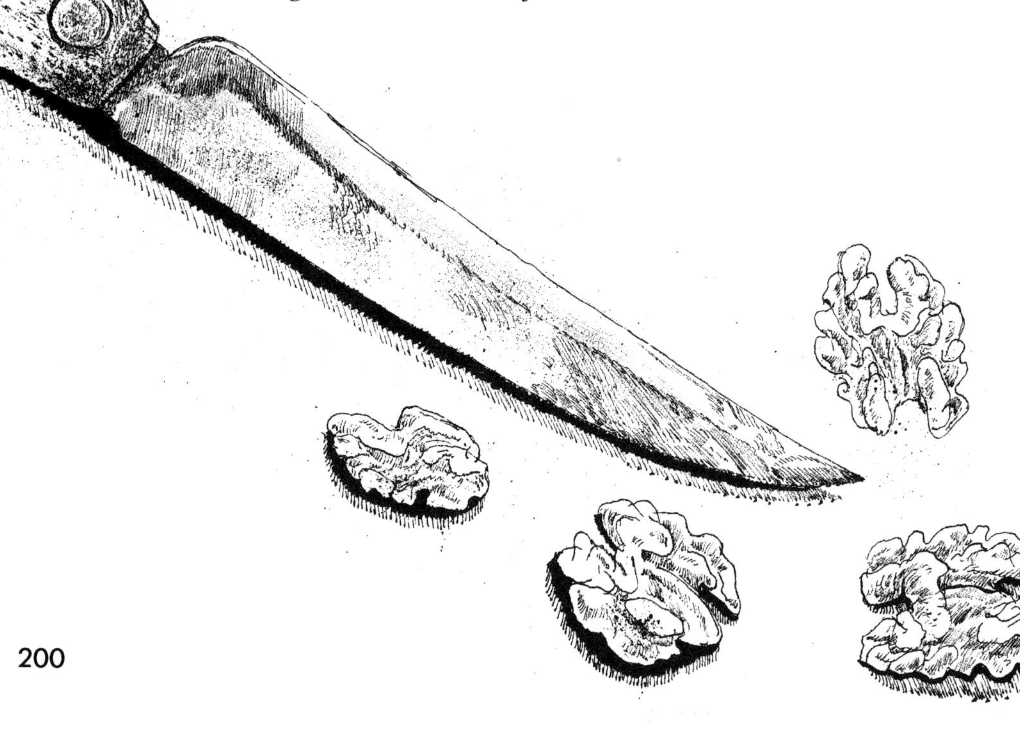

Barbara Breckur—Colleyville, TX
Donation to: United Way of Metropolitan Tarrant County, Fort Worth, TX (Human Services)

Classico Sun-dried Tomato Pasta

It has taken a little trial and error to come up with just the right combination for this original, light pasta, but friends and family tell me they have never experienced a dish they have enjoyed more. This will make your taste buds stand up and cheer!

INGREDIENTS

1 cup *sliced shallots*

1 *large red bell pepper, julienned*

1 *large yellow bell pepper, julienned*

2 cups *raw spinach, cut into thin strips*

2 cans *(14½ ounces each) SWANSON® chicken broth*

2 broth-cans *of water*

¼ cup *pine nuts*

½ teaspoon *plus* **½ cup** *olive oil*

½ cup *finely shredded fresh basil*

¼ cup *olive oil-packed sun-dried tomatoes, drained*

7-9 ounces *angel hair pasta*

¾ cup *finely grated fresh Parmesan cheese*

DIRECTIONS

Prepare shallots, bell peppers, and spinach; set aside. Pour chicken broth and water into a large pot; bring to boil. Do not add salt. Meanwhile, sauté pine nuts until golden brown in ½ teaspoon olive oil; set aside. Heat ½ cup olive oil in a large skillet. Add shallots and peppers. Cook 3 minutes. Add spinach and basil. Cook until tender, but do not overcook. Reduce flame to low heat; add tomatoes. Cook pasta in boiling broth, according to package directions. When cooked, drain all but ½ cup of the liquid. Toss pasta with vegetable mixture and cheese. Garnish with pine nuts. **Serves 4.**

❧ *Serve meatless or with broiled shrimp on the side, a warm crusty bread, a nice Chardonnay, and a sinful dessert.*

Testing Notes: *Use spinach or jalapeño pasta to increase spiciness. Add 1 tablespoon oregano, 1 tablespoon thyme, and 2 cloves minced garlic.*

Mrs. Alfred W. Lasher, Jr.—Houston, TX
Donation to: Freedoms Foundation, Valley Forge, PA

Rigatoni with Gin Sauce

My husband and I enjoyed this at an Italian restaurant in Florida years ago, and I developed this version.

INGREDIENTS

- **1 pound** *rigatoni*
- *Pinch of salt*
- **2 tablespoons** *olive oil*
- **1 jar** *(32 ounce) RAGÚ® Italian cooking sauce*
- **1 can** *(15 ounce) tomato sauce*
- **¼ teaspoon** *McCORMICK'S® Italian seasoning*
- **5 tablespoons** *butter*
- **1-2 teaspoons** *dried basil*
- *Freshly ground white pepper, to taste*
- **1 cup** *cream*
- **8 tablespoons** *gin*

DIRECTIONS

Cook rigatoni al dente in a lot of boiling water with salt and olive oil. Heat Italian cooking sauce, tomato sauce, Italian seasoning, butter, basil, and white pepper. Cook 20 minutes. Remove from heat. Add cream and gin; stir well. Heat almost to boiling. Drain rigatoni, add to the sauce, toss well, and serve immediately. **Serves 6 to 8**, or 12 as an appetizer.

❧ *Serve with a hearty green salad, garlic bread, and a cold tart lemon soufflé.*

Dena K. Horowitz—Dallas, TX
Donation to: Cystic Fibrosis Foundation North Texas, Fort Worth, TX

Munchie Mac & Cheese

I got this recipe from a friend I met on my honeymoon in Maui, Hawaii.

INGREDIENTS

4 tablespoons *butter*
¼ *onion, finely chopped*
2 tablespoons *flour*
Salt, to taste
Pepper, to taste
¼ teaspoon *dry mustard*
1½ cups *milk*
2 cups *grated Cheddar cheese*
1 cup *grated Swiss cheese*
7 ounces *macaroni, cooked*
2 tablespoons *bread crumbs*

DIRECTIONS

Melt butter, stir in onions, and add flour. Stir until smooth. Add salt, pepper, and mustard. Slowly, add milk, Cheddar cheese, and Swiss cheese. Stir until thickened and bubbly. Place macaroni in a 13 x 9-inch glass dish; pour cheese over macaroni. Sprinkle bread crumbs and a little extra cheese on top. Bake 15 minutes at 350°. **Serves 6 to 8.**

❧ *Serve with a green salad and fresh-baked bread.*

Testing Notes: *Increase bread crumbs to 4 tablespoons, and add fresh-ground black pepper, to taste.*

Steven P. Davis—Dallas, TX
Donation to: Alzheimer's Association, Inc., Dallas, TX

Fettuccine Alfredo

My family is from an Italian part of Chicago, and my mother taught me how to cook pasta when I was a young child.

INGREDIENTS

¼ pound *fresh Parmesan cheese*
¼ pound *lightly salted butter*
¼ pound *fresh fettuccine*
1 pint *heavy cream*
Freshly ground pepper
Salt
1 *egg*

DIRECTIONS

Grate Parmesan cheese; set aside. Melt butter; set aside. Boil water and cook pasta 2 to 3 minutes. Strain pasta. Turn heat to low and pour butter and cream into pot. Add pasta and coat noodles thoroughly. Add ground pepper and salt. When mixture is thickened slightly, add raw egg and coat noodles. Add grated cheese, turn off heat, and let cheese melt. Pasta should be eaten immediately, as the Alfredo sauce loses its consistency after 5 to 10 minutes. **Serves 4 to 6.**

❧ *Serve with sliced tomatoes, Italian bread, and Fumé Blanc.*

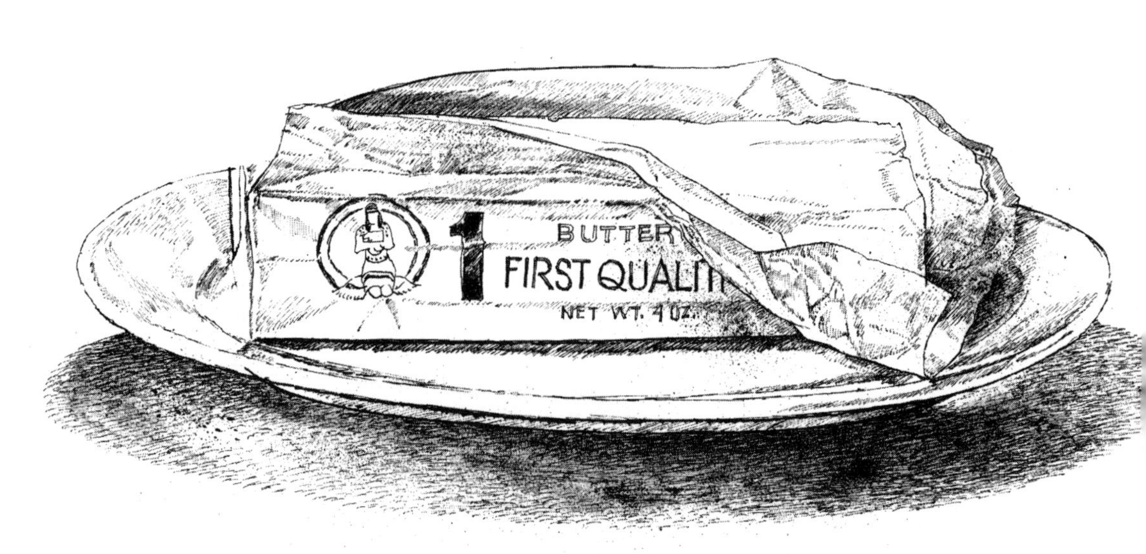

Carol Olson—Cupertino, CA
Donation to: Humane Society of Santa Clara Valley, Santa Clara, CA

Fast and Fabulous Fettuccine

A few years ago, I ordered a similar dish at a small Italian restaurant in San Francisco. A few weeks later, I began craving the wonderful flavor. This recipe is a near-match to the original. (Sometimes, I think it's better!)

INGREDIENTS

- **1 pound** *fettuccine*
- **1** *large onion, thinly sliced*
- **½ pound** *fresh asparagus, cut into ½-inch pieces (or a 10 ounce package of frozen asparagus spears, drained)*
- **1 tablespoon** *butter*
- **8 ounces** *Canadian bacon, sliced (or lean ham, cut into ¼-inch-wide strips)*
- **1¼ cups** *heavy cream*
- **½ cup** *grated Parmesan cheese*
- *Pepper, to taste*

DIRECTIONS

Cook fettuccine, following label directions. Sauté onion and asparagus in butter in medium-sized skillet 4 minutes until onion is softened. Add bacon. Lower heat, cover, and cook 5 minutes until asparagus is tender. If using frozen asparagus, add when adding bacon. Bring cream to a rolling boil in a separate medium-sized saucepan. Boil gently 2 to 3 minutes to reduce slightly. Remove from heat; stir in cheese. Add cream mixture to asparagus mixture. Add pepper. Simmer 2 minutes, stirring once or twice. Drain fettuccine and toss with sauce. **Serves 6 to 8.**

❧ *French bread is really all that is needed, but adding a small salad is nice, too.*

Testing Notes: *This can be served as a cold salad, using tarragon vinaigrette as a dressing.*

Fran Gunner—Bakersfield, CA
Donation to: Friends of Kern County Multiple Sclerosis Patients, Inc., Bakersfield, CA

Andre's Pasta

During his career as a chef, Andre Anastay worked for Greta Garbo. Later in life, he moved to our area to slow down his pace; and we became wonderful friends. He has since passed away, but this recipe he shared with me lives on.

INGREDIENTS

2 pounds *large-shell pasta*
½ pound *butter*
3 *medium-sized zucchini, diced and parboiled*
Salt and pepper, to taste
3 cups *heavy cream*
6 *egg yolks*
¼ pound *mozzarella cheese, diced*
Parmesan cheese, grated

DIRECTIONS

Boil pasta al dente. Melt butter in large pan. Add zucchini, salt, and pepper. Add cooked noodles and stir. Blend cream and egg yolks together in a separate bowl. Add cream mixture and mozzarella cheese to pasta mixture. Cook 5 minutes. Do not boil. Top each serving with a little Parmesan cheese. **Serves 8 to 10.**

❧ *Serve with a green salad and crusty French bread.*

Neiman Marcus—THE ZODIAC Westchester
Donation to: combined charities

Angel Hair Pasta with Goat Cheese and Broccoli

When people ask, "What's cooking today?" chances are it's this frothy pasta by John Rubbo, Restaurant General Manager.

INGREDIENTS

1 pound *pasta*
1 *bunch broccoli*
3 ounces *butter*
11 ounces *goat cheese, cubed*
Grated Parmesan cheese, to taste
1 quart *heavy cream*
¼ cup *chopped fresh basil (optional)*
White pepper, to taste
Salt, to taste

DIRECTIONS

Cook pasta, according to package directions; drain and set aside. Cook broccoli until fork-tender; set aside. Melt the butter and add goat cheese. When goat cheese melts, add Parmesan cheese and heavy cream. Reduce to about half until it has a light consistency. Add basil and season with white pepper and salt. Reheat pasta in boiling salted water. Place pasta and broccoli in a hot sauté pan and toss. Add cheese sauce, heat, and serve. The cheese sauce will not taste like Alfredo sauce; it will have a light, mild goat cheese flavor. **Serves 4 to 6.**

Mrs. Herbert (Joanne) Friedman—Scarsdale, NY
Donation to: Lupus Foundation of America, Connecticut Chapter, West Hartford, CT

Pasta Fagiole

This is my version of a recipe given to me by my son-in-law, who is a wonderful chef. He likes to cook. He says it's a relaxing hobby.

INGREDIENTS

6 ounces *dry, shaped pasta (penne, elbow, etc.)*

1 *head of broccoli, cut into florets*

¼ cup *water*

2-3 tablespoons *olive oil*

4 *cloves garlic, peeled*

1 teaspoon *crushed black pepper*

1 teaspoon *crushed red pepper*

1 teaspoon *oregano*

1 teaspoon *basil*

½ teaspoon *lemon juice*

1 *red bell pepper, seeded and sliced into strips*

1 *green bell pepper, seeded and sliced into strips*

1 *large leek, chopped*

1 tablespoon *balsamic vinegar*

1 can *(16 ounce) red kidney beans*

DIRECTIONS

Cook pasta al dente; drain. At the same time, cook broccoli florets 8 minutes with water in microwave; drain. Pour olive oil into a large skillet and heat. Add garlic, crushed black and red pepper, oregano, basil, and lemon juice. Stir about 30 seconds. Add red and green pepper strips and leek. Cook 5 to 8 minutes until soft. Add broccoli and vinegar; cook 2 minutes. Add red beans and cook 1 minute, stirring constantly. Remove from heat and toss with pasta in a large bowl. **Serves 8 to 10.**

❧ *Serve hot with Romano or Parmesan cheese, a goblet of hearty red wine, and fresh Italian bread.*

JoDale Ales—Baton Rouge, LA
Donation to: Mary Bird Perkins Cancer Center, Baton Rouge, LA

Pasta Giovanni

This is a recipe I created for fun one day.

INGREDIENTS

- **6-8 quarts** *of water*
- **1 tablespoon** *salt*
- **6 tablespoons** *olive oil*
- **1** *whole clove garlic plus* **5** *cloves, minced*
- **1 pound** *fettuccine or angel hair pasta*
- **½ pound** *fresh mushrooms, sliced*
- **¼ cup** *coarsely chopped pecans, walnuts, or toasted slivered almonds*
- **¼ cup** *chopped parsley*
- **1 can** *(2½ ounce) black olives, sliced*
- **1 jar** *(2 ounce) pimientos, sliced*
- *Romano cheese, grated*

DIRECTIONS

Bring water and salt to boil in a large pot. Add 1 tablespoon olive oil and 1 whole garlic clove. (This keeps pasta from sticking and adds flavor.) Add pasta and boil, according to package directions, stirring occasionally. Sauté minced garlic until soft in olive oil over moderately-high heat. Add sliced mushrooms and cook 2 to 3 minutes until soft. Remove from heat and add nuts, parsley, olives, and pimientos. Mix well. Drain pasta and return to pot. Add olive oil mixture and toss pasta. Serve warm with grated Romano cheese sprinkled over top. May be served as a side dish with meat, or as a meatless meal. **Serves 6 to 8.**

❧ *Serve with Brunello (Biondi-Santi) wine, an Italian salad, and a fresh Italian bread.*

Testing Notes: *Decrease minced garlic to 1 tablespoon (approximately 3 cloves). Add salt and pepper, to taste.*

Neiman Marcus—THE RESTAURANTSMPalo Alto
Donation to: combined charities

Pasta Primavera

Restaurant Assistant Manager Ulla Yeager may not be Italian, but she knows her way around delicate pasta dishes.

INGREDIENTS

½ **pound** *egg-and-spinach tortellini*

1 **cup** *fresh assorted vegetables (i.e., asparagus, mushrooms, cherry tomatoes), cut into bite-sized pieces*

½ *bunch fresh basil*

¼ **cup** *pine nuts*

4 *cloves fresh garlic*

¼ **cup** *grated Parmesan cheese*

1 tablespoon *olive oil*

2 cups *heavy cream*

Salt and pepper, to taste

DIRECTIONS

Cook tortellini, according to package directions; set aside. Steam fresh vegetables until al dente; set aside. Combine basil, pine nuts, garlic cloves, Parmesan cheese, and olive oil in food processor or blender. Process until very fine. Heat heavy cream over low heat in saucepan until almost boiling. Add basil purée and mix well. Add tortellini and heat thoroughly. Add vegetables, salt, and pepper. Serve in warm pasta bowls. Garnish with fresh basil, pine nuts, and Parmesan cheese. **Serves 4.**

❧ *Serve with a crusty Italian bread and a glass of wine.*

E.O. Hand—Chicago, IL
Donation to: The Oceanarium, Chicago, IL

Penne Affumicato

A friend in Tuscany, Italy, with whom I often trade recipes, gave this to me.

INGREDIENTS

- **1** *medium-sized yellow onion, chopped*
- **1** *carrot, finely chopped*
- **2** *stalks celery, finely chopped*
- **2** *cloves garlic, minced*
- *Extra-virgin olive oil*
- **1 can** *(14½ ounce) Italian-style tomatoes, drained*
- **1 pound** *cubed pancetta affumicato, or thick-sliced and cubed prosciutto, or chopped smoked ham*
- **1 package** *(16 ounce) penne*
- **1 pound** *mozzarella (di buffalo, if available), cubed*
- *Cream or half-and-half*

DIRECTIONS

Sauté onion, carrot, celery, and garlic in olive oil. Add tomatoes and cook slowly over medium heat. Sauté pancetta affumicato lightly in olive oil until crisp. Cook penne in boiling water—al dente, justo! Put mozzarella cubes in tomato sauce and stir until cheese is stringy. Add small amount of cream. When ready to serve, add sautéed crisp pancetta affumicato to the hot, drained cooked pasta. Then pour sauce over the pasta and meat mixture. Serve at once in oven-heated pasta bowls. **Serves 4.**

❧ *A very good salad with this pasta entrée is fresh romaine, chopped in medium-sized pieces, and a well-blended dressing made of olio extra virgine, pressed garlic, anchovy paste, and wine vinegar.*

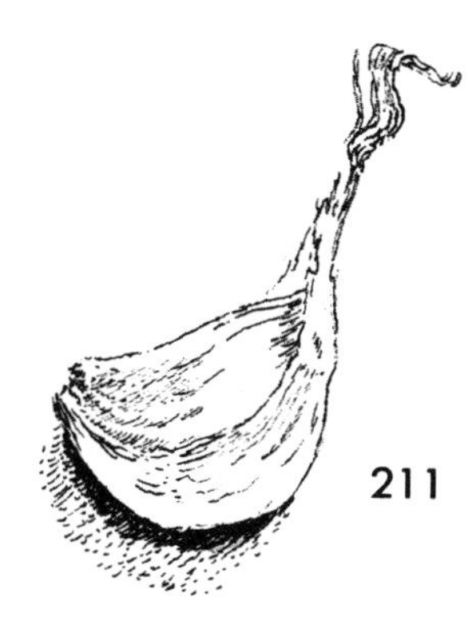

Happy Dumas—Hillsborough, CA
Donation to: Ronald McDonald House, Palo Alto, CA

Tortellini della Nonna Trattoria da Alfredo (Tortellini with Prosciutto and Peas)

I picked up this recipe in Italy while accompanying my husband on a lecture tour, and it's been used by our family ever since. I have never served it without someone asking me for the recipe. When our children were younger, we used to count the little tortellini, one by one, as we put them into their mouths, saying, "Yummy! Yummy! Yummy!" after each bite.

INGREDIENTS

250 *tortellini (about 1 pound, 6 ounces)*

4 quarts *boiling water*

3/4 cup *butter*

1 cup *heavy cream*

5 thin slices *prosciutto, julienned*

1/2 cup *cooked peas*

2 cups *freshly grated Parmesan cheese*

Pepper, to taste

DIRECTIONS

Plunge tortellini into 4 quarts boiling salted water. Cook 7 minutes or until just tender. Drain. Melt butter over moderately-low heat in a deep skillet. Add tortellini and stir to coat in butter. Add heavy cream and prosciutto. Cook mixture until cream thickens slightly. Blend in peas, 1 cup Parmesan cheese, and pepper. Cook and stir until cheese is just melted. Serve pasta immediately with remaining Parmesan cheese and a pepper mill for fresh-ground pepper. **Serves 6.**

Diane C. Eberly—Plano, TX
Donation to: Dallas SPCA, Dallas, TX

Broccoli Lasagna

Many years ago, my great-aunt, Helen, gave this recipe to me. It is a delicious and filling main course that is excellent to serve when company comes, as it may be prepared ahead of time, allowing more time to be spent with guests.

INGREDIENTS

24 ounces *cottage cheese*
2 *eggs*
¼ teaspoon *salt*
¼ teaspoon *garlic salt*
4 tablespoons *snipped parsley*
8 ounces *lasagna, cooked*
2 packages *(10 ounces each) frozen chopped broccoli*
12 ounces *Monterey jack cheese, sliced*
½ cup *grated Parmesan cheese*
12 *bacon slices, lightly fried*

DIRECTIONS

Mix together cottage cheese, eggs, salt, garlic salt, and parsley. In a buttered glass dish, place 2 or 3 layers of the following in the order shown: noodles, cottage cheese mixture, broccoli, Monterey jack cheese, and Parmesan cheese. Top with bacon strips. Bake at 350° until lasagna bubbles. **Serves 6 to 8.**

❧ *Serve with either a green or Caesar salad and garlic bread.*

Testing Notes: *Add fresh garlic and fresh basil. Sauté bacon a little more. Use fresh broccoli.*

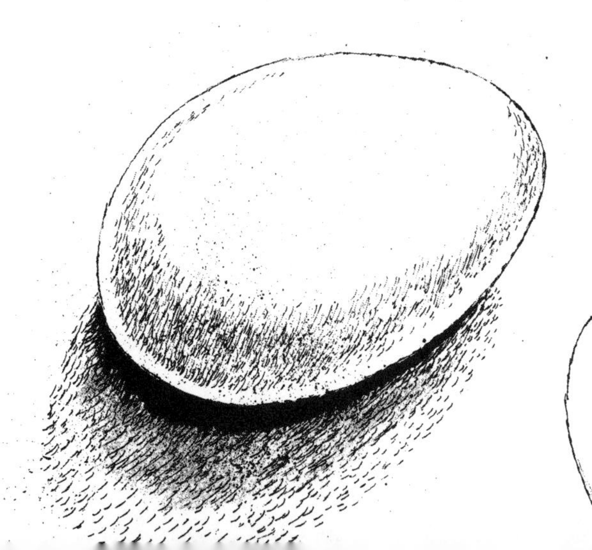

Kelly M. Smith—Andrews, TX
Donation to: The Andrews Adult Literacy Council, Andrews, TX

Vegetable Lasagna

I invented this for my husband and four children, who all love pasta and vegetables, but aren't always in the mood for spicy tomato sauce.

INGREDIENTS

1 cup *zucchini, julienned into 1-inch-long pieces*

1 cup *yellow squash, julienned into 1-inch-long pieces*

1 cup *sliced fresh mushrooms*

½ teaspoon *minced garlic*

6 tablespoons *butter*

1 teaspoon *Italian seasoning*

1¼ teaspoons *salt*

1 cup *carrots, julienned into 1-inch-long pieces and steamed*

1 cup *broccoli florets, separated and steamed*

6 tablespoons *flour*

½ teaspoon *white pepper*

3 cups *milk*

½ cup *Parmesan cheese*

1 package *(16 ounce) lasagna noodles*

1 pound *grated mozzarella cheese*

1 carton *(15 ounce) ricotta cheese*

1 package *(10 ounce) frozen chopped spinach, thawed*

Parsley

DIRECTIONS

Sauté zucchini, yellow squash, mushrooms, and garlic until tender in 2 tablespoons butter. Add Italian seasoning and ¼ teaspoon salt. Stir in carrots and broccoli. Set aside and cool. Melt remaining butter in saucepan. Add flour, pepper, and remaining salt. Cook over medium heat 5 minutes. Stir in milk and cook until thickened. Remove from heat and stir in Parmesan cheese. Set aside. Cook pasta, according to package directions. Rinse in cool water and drain. Grease a 9 x 13-inch dish. Spoon only enough white sauce into dish to barely cover the bottom. Line with 3 noodles. Spoon ½ the vegetable mixture over the noodles, placing it down the center of each noodle. Sprinkle ⅓ of the mozzarella cheese over the vegetable mixture. Cover with another layer of pasta. Spread ½ the ricotta cheese down the center of each noodle. Top with ½ the spinach. Cover with ½ the remaining white sauce. Repeat the layering: 3 noodles; remaining vegetables; ½ remaining mozzarella; 3 noodles; remaining ricotta, spinach, and white sauce. Cover with remaining mozzarella. Sprinkle Parmesan and parsley over top. Bake 45 minutes in a preheated 350° oven. Let stand 15 minutes before serving. **Serves 6 to 8.**

❧ *Serve with crisp green salad and fresh bread.*

Mrs. Janice M. Comis—Westport, CT
Donation to: American Heart Foundation, Inc., Stamford, CT

Seafood Risotto

My mother-in-law comes from northern Italy where they use lots of risotto, which is how I came up with the idea for seafood risotto.

INGREDIENTS

1 tablespoon *oil*

1 teaspoon *minced garlic*

½ cup *white wine*

1 bottle *(8 ounce) clam juice*

½ teaspoon *salt*

¼ teaspoon *ground pepper*

¾ pound *shrimp, shelled and deveined*

½ pound *sea scallops, halved and cut horizontally*

2¼ cups *water*

2 tablespoons *butter or oil*

1 *leek, chopped*

1 cup *arborio rice (short grain)*

Pinch of saffron

2 tablespoons *chopped parsley*

Grated Parmesan cheese (optional)

DIRECTIONS

Heat oil over medium heat in a medium-sized saucepan. Add garlic and sauté 30 seconds; do not brown. Add wine and bring to boil. Add clam juice, salt, and pepper. Return to boil. Stir in shrimp and scallops. Cook, stirring constantly, 3 minutes until shrimp are pink and scallops are opaque. Transfer shrimp and scallops with a slotted spoon to a bowl. Set aside. Add water to the saucepan and bring to simmer. Melt butter (or heat oil) over medium heat in another medium-sized saucepan. Add leek and sauté 3 minutes. Add arborio rice and cook 2 minutes, stirring constantly. Add ½ cup of the simmering liquid and cook 3 minutes, stirring constantly until liquid is absorbed. Continue adding liquid, ½ cup at a time, until all liquid is absorbed, stirring constantly. Add saffron to the last ½ cup liquid before adding it to the rice. Taste rice; if not fully cooked, add ¼ cup more hot water and stir until absorbed. Stir in shrimp, scallops, and parsley. Serve immediately. Pass Parmesan cheese, but if salt intake is restricted, omit the Parmesan cheese. **Serves 4.**

❧ *Serve with a tossed green salad.*

Dawn Fine—Miami, FL
Donation to: Infantry for Project Newborn University of Miami, Jackson Memorial, Miami, FL

Fusilli with Smoked Salmon

I love Mediterranean cooking. My best friend is Italian and we have developed these recipes for our future cookbook.

INGREDIENTS

- **2 tablespoons** *butter*
- **2 tablespoons** *olive oil*
- **2** *Vidalia sweet onions, chopped*
- **4 tablespoons** *cognac*
- **1 cup** *Grade A pasteurized cream (not ultra-pasteurized)*
- **8 ounces** *smoked Scottish salmon, cut into pieces*
- **1 cup** *chopped fresh chives*
- **12 ounces** *fusilli pasta*
- *Capers*

DIRECTIONS

Melt butter with olive oil in large pan. Sauté onions 8 to 10 minutes until translucent in partially covered pan. Add cognac and cook on low 10 to 15 minutes. Add cream and cook on low 10 minutes. Add smoked salmon and chives. Cook on low 5 minutes; set aside. Boil pasta until al dente. Add pasta to sauce. Serve pasta with sprinkles of capers and chopped chives. **Serves 4.**

❧ *Serve with carrot-and-arugala salad and crusty bread.*

Testing Notes: *Limit chopped chives to ½ cup.*

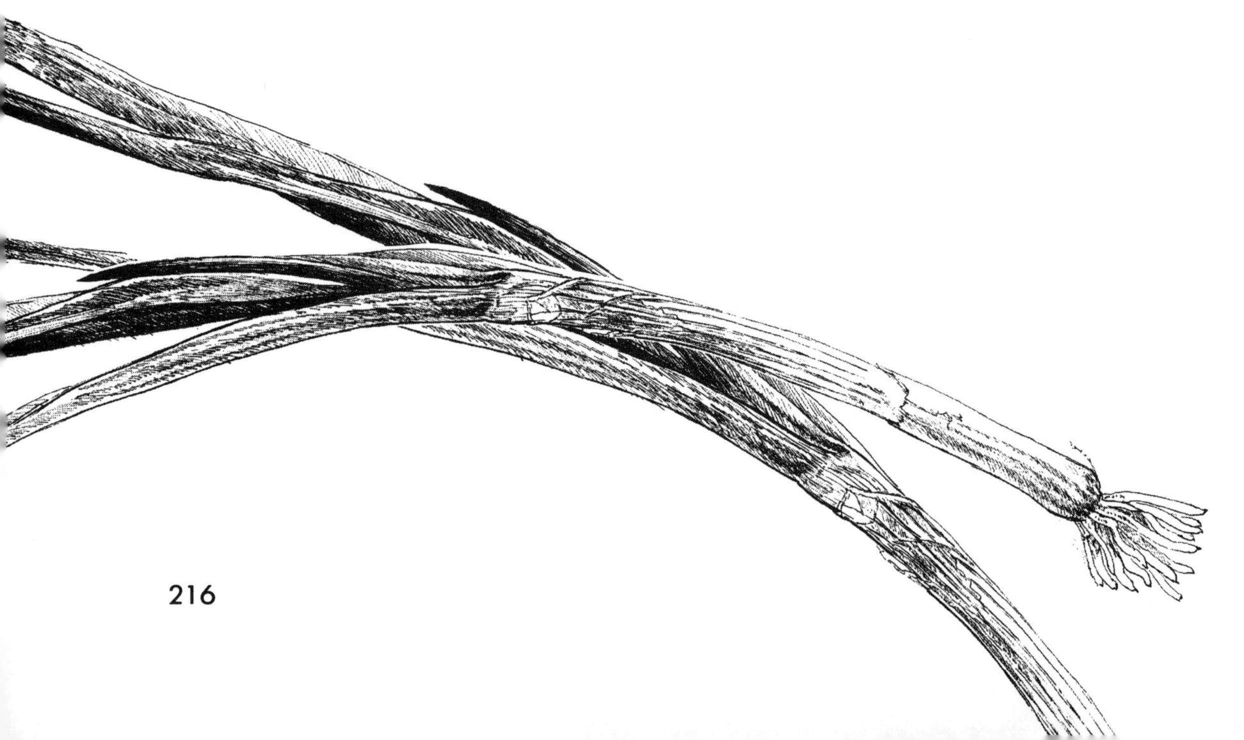

Mrs. Joyce Grunauer—Beverly Hills, CA
Donation to: American Cancer Society, Inc., Los Angeles, CA

Lake Tahoe Seafood Pasta

I originally received and enjoyed this recipe at Lake Tahoe.

INGREDIENTS

1 pound *shelled shrimp (or any seafood)*

6 tablespoons *butter*

½ cup *cognac*

⅓ cup *dry white wine*

3 pounds *tomatoes, peeled and cut into chunks*

¾ cup *cream*

Cayenne

1 teaspoon *Italian seasoning*

Salt

1 pound *spaghetti, cooked and drained*

DIRECTIONS

Sauté shrimp 5 minutes in butter; add cognac and flambé. Add wine and cook 1 minute. Remove shrimp and add tomatoes to sauce. Simmer 20 minutes until tomatoes are broken up. Stir in cream and seasonings. Add shrimp and pour over pasta. **Serves 6 to 8.**

❧ *Serve cake and cookies for dessert.*

Testing Notes: *Use fettuccine instead of spaghetti.*

Neiman Marcus—THE ZODIAC San Diego
Donation to: combined charities

Scampi Primavera with Linguine

Restaurant Manager Steve Heagie put together two favorite Italian pasta ideas for a delectable effect.

INGREDIENTS

- **¼ cup** *olive oil*
- **2 tablespoons** *minced garlic*
- **2 tablespoons** *lemon juice*
- **½ teaspoon** *dry mustard*
- **1 teaspoon** *Worcestershire sauce*
- **½ teaspoon** *dried red-pepper flakes*
- **1 tablespoon** *fresh or dried oregano, minced*
- **1 tablespoon** *fresh or dried basil, minced*
- **1 tablespoon** *fresh or dried tarragon, minced*
- **½ teaspoon** *salt*
- **6 tablespoons** *parsley, chopped*
- **2** *large tomatoes, cut into small pieces*
- **2 pounds** *large shrimp, shelled and deveined*
- **1 pound** *linguine*
- **¾ cup** *butter*
- **10** *asparagus tips*
- **½** *head broccoli, cut into small pieces*
- **1** *yellow bell pepper, cut into small pieces*
- **½ cup** *dry white wine*
- **½ cup** *grated Parmesan cheese*

DIRECTIONS

In a bowl, combine olive oil, garlic, lemon juice, dry mustard, Worcestershire sauce, red-pepper flakes, oregano, basil, tarragon, salt, 4 tablespoons parsley, and chopped tomatoes. Add shrimp to bowl and marinate 10 minutes. Set aside. Cook linguine, according to package directions. Remove shrimp from marinade and sauté shrimp 1 minute in butter. Remove with slotted spoon and keep warm. Add asparagus tips, broccoli, and yellow bell peppers to sauté pan. Sauté 3 minutes. Add marinade, wine, and shrimp to sauté pan. Simmer 5 minutes. Arrange cooked linguine on serving dish; spoon cooked shrimp-and-vegetable mixture on top. Garnish with Parmesan cheese and remaining parsley. **Serves 6.**

Shelly Pedretti—Saddle River, NJ
Donation to: Cancer Research Institute, Inc., New York, NY

Shrimp with Sun-dried Tomatoes and Fettuccine

My assistant and I are constantly exchanging recipes. She came up with this one and I embellished it.

INGREDIENTS

2 *cloves garlic, minced*

½ *bunch parsley, finely chopped*

½ cup *butter*

1 pound *fettuccine*

¼ cup *olive oil*

⅛ pound *olive oil-packed sun-dried tomatoes, including liquid*

1 *large shallot, finely chopped*

1 pound *medium-sized shrimp, shelled and deveined*

¼ cup *chopped fresh basil*

Salt and freshly ground pepper, to taste

DIRECTIONS

Combine 1 clove minced garlic with parsley and butter; set aside. Prepare fettuccine, according to package directions. Drain. Toss fettuccine with garlic-and-parsley butter and keep warm. Place ¼ cup olive oil and liquid from tomatoes into a large skillet. Heat until hot. Add shallot, remaining garlic, and the tomatoes. Stir; add shrimp. Cook until shrimp turns pink. Add basil, salt, and pepper. Serve over cooked fettuccine. **Serves 6 to 8.**

❧ *Serve with an arugula, endive, and radicchio salad; Italian bread; and Santa Margherita white wine.*

Testing Notes: *We sautéed shrimp and, then, added herbs and garlic.*

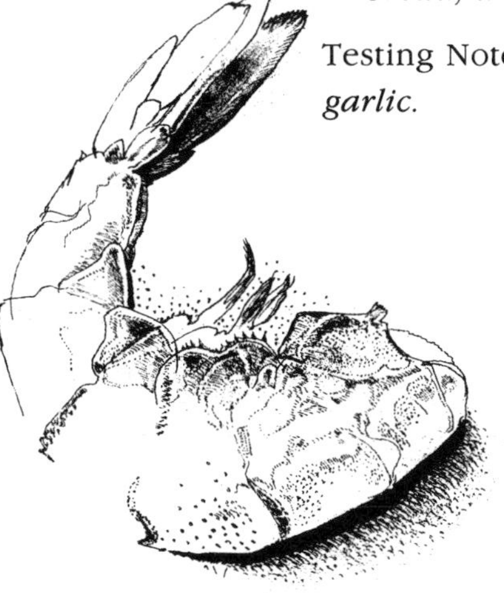

Catherine A. Byles—Dallas, TX
Donation to: Dallas SPCA, Dallas, TX

Chicken Manicotti Florentine

I am always experimenting with low-fat, low-calorie recipes because my husband and I are conscious of our health and try to prolong it.

INGREDIENTS

½ *medium-sized onion, finely chopped*

1 teaspoon *minced fresh garlic*

2 teaspoons *minced fresh basil*

1 teaspoon *Italian herb blend*

1 package *(10 ounce) frozen chopped spinach, thawed and squeezed dry*

6 ounces *chicken breast, cooked and finely chopped*

1 ½ cups *commercial spaghetti sauce*

4 ounces *fresh mushrooms, sliced*

2 tablespoons *white wine*

4 ounces *small-curd cottage cheese*

6 *manicotti shells, cooked*

4 tablespoons *Parmesan cheese*

DIRECTIONS

Spray a large skillet with a nonstick spray. Sauté onion, garlic, basil, and Italian herb blend 2 minutes until opaque. Add spinach and chicken. Cook 2 minutes and blend well. Remove from heat and set aside. Combine spaghetti sauce, mushrooms, and white wine in a small saucepan. Cook 5 minutes. Set aside. Add drained cottage cheese to chicken-spinach mixture. Carefully stuff each manicotti shell and place side by side in a baking dish. Pour sauce over top and sprinkle with Parmesan cheese. Bake 30 minutes at 350°. **Serves 3.**

❧ *Serve with romaine lettuce salad, crusty Italian bread, and Chardonnay wine.*

Testing Notes: *We recommend fresh spinach and a light amount of olive oil.*

Emma DeLucas—Peru, NY
Donation to: Hospice Care of Clinton County, Inc., Plattsburgh, NY

Grandfather's Pasta and Beef

When I was young and living in Sicily, my grandfather often prepared this simple dish. I developed this recipe from my memory of this meal.

INGREDIENTS

2 tablespoons *olive oil*
4 *cloves garlic, chopped*
1 *bunch flat-leaf parsley, chopped*
2 tablespoons *tomato paste*
2 cups *warm water*
1 pound *beef tenderloin, thinly sliced and cut into 2-inch-long pieces*
½ pound *linguine, cooked 5 minutes in boiling salted water*
Salt and pepper, to taste
Pecorino Romano cheese

DIRECTIONS

Heat olive oil with garlic in a large saucepan. Do not brown. Add parsley, tomato paste, and water. Bring to boil over medium heat. Add beef and cook over low heat 40 minutes until beef is tender. Add cooked linguine and heat 7 to 10 minutes. Season with salt and pepper. Serve with sprinkle of grated Pecorino Romano cheese. **Serves 4.**

❧ *Serve with a salad of romaine lettuce and Italian dressing.*

Testing Notes: *Cook ½ pound linguine, according to package directions.*

Emilie A. Morse—Atlanta, GA
Donation to: North Shore Animal League, Inc., Port Washington, NY

Sausage Fettuccine Torte

My fettuccine recipe has been around our family so long that I don't remember where it came from. Both my maternal grandparents were chefs, and with a maiden surname of Guglielmetti, it's not hard to understand why cheese figures so prominently in my cooking.

INGREDIENTS

- **1 pound** *fettuccine, cooked and well drained*
- **2 tablespoons** *butter*
- **1 pound** *Italian sausage (sweet, hot, or combination)*
- **1 tablespoon** *olive oil*
- **1** *medium-sized onion, finely chopped*
- **1** *large green bell pepper, ribs removed and finely chopped*
- **½ cup** *sliced pitted ripe olives*
- **¼ cup** *finely chopped mix of fresh parsley and basil*
- **½ teaspoon** *freshly ground black pepper*
- **3** *eggs, beaten*
- **3** *tomatoes, thinly sliced*
- **½ cup** *grated Gruyère cheese*
- **½ cup** *grated mozzarella cheese*
- **2 tablespoons** *grated Parmesan cheese*

DIRECTIONS

Preheat oven to 375°. Toss hot fettuccine with butter in mixing bowl and cover. Remove sausage casings and finely chop meat. Brown sausage in heated olive oil; pour off fat. Add onion and bell pepper; cook 5 minutes. Combine sausage mixture, olives, parsley-basil mix, pepper, and noodles. Stir in eggs and toss to combine well. Lightly butter and flour a springform pan. Press half the pasta mixture on bottom; layer half the tomatoes over pasta. Sprinkle the Gruyère and mozzarella cheese over the tomatoes. Repeat the layers. Sprinkle Parmesan cheese over the top. Cover with foil and bake 50 minutes until set. To serve, slice in wedges. **Serves 6 to 8.**

CHAPTER TEN

Vegetables

So, broccoli is not on the menu at 1600 Pennsylvania Avenue in Washington, D.C. But, it and its fresh-from-the-garden relatives are more and more popular at InCircler homes. There are a number of satisfactory ways to prepare vegetables. Microwaving is one that is quick and easy and requires only minutes and a spoonful or two of water. Steaming on the stovetop is another way to keep flavor and vitamins intact. And, if you must boil a vegetable, keep the heat low and use as little water as possible. Then, save the remaining water for soup stock.

Mrs. A. D. (Sandra) Crawford—Mineral Wells, TX
Donation to: Keep Mineral Wells Beautiful Campaign, Mineral Wells, TX

Vegetable Soufflé

A friend gave me this recipe about twenty years ago. It became a family favorite, and now my twenty-year-old son insists that I prepare it every time we have a large family gathering. It is a healthy way to get kids to eat vegetables. This casserole is truly pure and simple.

INGREDIENTS

1½ cups *grated sharp Cheddar cheese*

1 can *(4 ounce) chopped green chiles*

2 cans *(16 ounces each) whole green beans, drained*

2 cans *(16 ounces each) whole kernel corn, drained*

Salt and pepper

½ pound *Monterey jack cheese slices*

3 *eggs*

¾ cup *sour cream*

DIRECTIONS

Grease a 3-quart casserole. Layer ingredients in this order: ½ cup Cheddar cheese; ½ can chiles; ½ can green beans; ½ can corn; and salt and pepper. Repeat. Add remaining ½ cup Cheddar cheese on top. Cover this with the slices of Monterey jack cheese. Just before putting in oven, beat eggs and sour cream together; pour over vegetables. Bake 1 hour at 350°. This may be frozen after baking. **Serves 12.**

❧ *Serve with brisket or with turkey and dressing during the holidays.*

Patti Estabrooks—Laguna Beach, CA
Donation to: Hoag Hospital Foundation, Newport Beach, CA
(Sandpipers of Hoag Hospital)

Caponata

This fast and foolproof recipe was passed down to me by my mother, who started the Sandpipers of Hoag Hospital, which is the charity I designated.

INGREDIENTS

- ½ **cup** *olive oil*
- 1 *large eggplant, peeled and cut into ½-inch pieces*
- 2 *large green bell peppers, cut into ½-inch pieces*
- 1 *large red bell pepper, cut into ½-inch pieces*
- 1 *large yellow bell pepper, cut into ½-inch pieces*
- 3 *large onions, diced*
- 3 *cloves garlic, minced*
- 3 **cans** *(14½ ounces each) stewed tomatoes, chopped, including liquid*
- ⅓ **cup** *wine vinegar*
- 3 **tablespoons** *sugar*
- 1 **jar** *(3½ ounce) capers, including liquid*
- 2 **teaspoons** *dried basil*
- ½ **cup** *chopped parsley*
- 1 **can** *(6 ounce) tomato paste*
- 1 **teaspoon** *pepper*
- 1 **teaspoon** *salt*
- 1 **jar** *(5 ounce) pimiento-stuffed olives, rinsed and sliced*

DIRECTIONS

In large pan, combine first 8 ingredients. Cook 30 minutes until tender. Add remaining ingredients and simmer 15 minutes. This dish freezes well. **Serves 8 to 10.**

❧ *Serve warm to complement meat or serve cool with crackers as hors d'oeuvres.*

Testing Notes: *With the addition of shrimp, this may be used as a salad or an omelet filling.*

Barbara Nudelman—Chicago, IL
Donation to: Museum of Contemporary Art, Chicago, IL

Ratatouille Revel

This recipe was developed by a great-aunt.

INGREDIENTS

- ½ **cup** *vegetable oil*
- **2** *large onions, sliced*
- **2** *cloves garlic, minced*
- **2** *green bell peppers, sliced into strips*
- **1 pound** *zucchini, thickly sliced*
- **3 tablespoons** *chopped parsley*
- **1 pound** *eggplant, peeled and sliced*
- **1 tablespoon** *salt*
- **1 teaspoon** *sugar*
- **1 teaspoon** *oregano*
- ¼ **teaspoon** *pepper*
- **1 can** *(14½ ounce) whole tomatoes*
- **8 ounces** *fresh mushrooms, thickly sliced*

DIRECTIONS

Heat oil in large pan or Dutch oven. Sauté onions and garlic 3 to 5 minutes. Add remaining ingredients. Bring to boil and cover. Reduce heat and simmer 15 minutes until tender. Serve warm or cold. **Serves 8 to 10.**

❧ *Serve with any kind of roast.*

Testing Notes: *Add red bell pepper for color and flavor.*

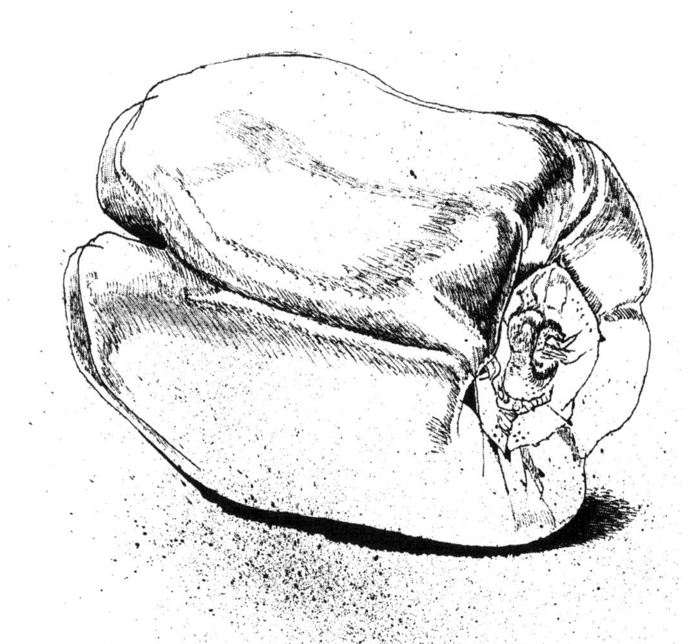

Margaret Kelly—Fort Lauderdale, FL
Donation to: St. Jude's Children's Research Hospital, Memphis, TN

Curried Bananas

We always have bananas on hand. One night I thought we needed a little something to round out our dinner, so we had Curried Bananas.

INGREDIENTS

1 teaspoon *unsalted butter*
Curry powder, to taste
1 *banana*

DIRECTIONS

Melt unsalted butter in a sauté pan. Add a good-quality curry powder, to taste. Stir 1 or 2 minutes until blended. Cut banana in half lengthwise and, then, crosswise. Add banana to curry butter. Turn banana several times to thoroughly coat and gently cook until it is hot, but not mushy. **Serves 1.**

❧ *Serve with ham, pork, or chicken.*

Adele A. Read—Houston, TX
Donation to: Houston Area Parkinsonism Society, Houston, TX

Cuban Black Beans

In Miami in 1969, a Cuban friend gave this recipe to me.

INGREDIENTS

- **1 pound** *black beans*
- **10 cups** *water*
- **1** *large bay leaf*
- **⅔ cup** *plus* **2 tablespoons** *oil olive*
- **1** *large onion, chopped*
- **4** *large cloves garlic, chopped*
- **1** *medium-sized green bell pepper, chopped*
- **3-4 teaspoons** *salt*
- **½ teaspoon** *black pepper*
- **¼ teaspoon** *ground oregano*
- **2 ounces** *red wine*
- **2 tablespoons** *sugar*
- *Cooked white rice*

DIRECTIONS

Rinse beans and soak 2 to 3 hours in water with bay leaf. Cover and boil gently 1 hour in the soaking water. Heat ⅔ cup olive oil in frying pan. (I prefer only ⅓ to ½ cup of oil.) Gently sauté onion, garlic, and bell pepper until tender. Add salt, black pepper, and oregano. Mix well. Add this mixture to beans and cook gently, covered, 1 to 1½ hours. Add wine, sugar, and 2 tablespoons olive oil to beans. Simmer, uncovered, at least 1 hour until beans are soft, but not falling apart, and the liquid is slightly thickened. If not thick enough, remove ½ to ¾ cup of beans, mash, and return to pot. Adjust seasonings. Serve in soup bowls and pass white rice so each person may add as much rice as they desire. **Serves 6 to 8.**

❧ *Serve with grapefruit-and-avocado salad, hard rolls, and beer.*

Patti Imnof—Bellingham, WA
Donation to: Mt. Baker Theater Center, Bellingham, WA

Red German Cabbage

My grandma, Neldia Muenscher, received this recipe from her German mother-in-law, Anna Muenscher, and it's now a fourth-generation recipe in our family in Whatcom County, Washington.

INGREDIENTS

3 *bacon slices, diced*
1 *head red cabbage, finely chopped*
1 *tart apple, peeled, cored, and chopped*
¼ cup *water*
⅓ cup *brown sugar*
⅓ cup *red-wine vinegar*
Salt and pepper, to taste

DIRECTIONS

Sauté bacon. Do not drain. Place bacon, bacon drippings, cabbage, apple, water, brown sugar, and vinegar in large saucepan. Bring to boil. Cover and simmer 45 minutes until tender. Season with salt and pepper. **Serves 6.**

❧ *Serve with roast pork or Thanksgiving turkey dinner.*

Suzanne Russell Wooten—Fort Worth, TX
Donation to: American Heart Association, Inc., Fort Worth, TX

Glorified Cabbage

In the early sixties, my husband and I were newly married and attending Texas Tech. I took a course on how to analyze and change recipes. This recipe made it through the course and has remained a family favorite.

INGREDIENTS

3 tablespoons *butter*
2 tablespoons *flour*
1 teaspoon *salt*
Dash of pepper
1 teaspoon *prepared mustard*
1 1/3 cups *milk*
1 *egg yolk, beaten*
2 cups *shredded cabbage*
1 cup *thinly sliced onion*
1 cup *shredded cheese*
1 cup *toasted bread crumbs*

DIRECTIONS

Melt butter and add flour, salt, pepper, and mustard, stirring constantly until bubbly. Add milk, stirring until thickened. Add egg yolk and cook 1 minute. Layer 1/2 the cabbage, onion, cheese, and cream sauce in a baking dish. Repeat. Top mixture with bread crumbs. Cover and bake 30 minutes at 375°. Uncover and bake 5 minutes. **Serves 4 to 6.**

Serve with baked or broiled chicken, beef, or pork.

Testing Notes: *Shred cabbage and onion finely. Use 1/2 cup onions.*

Joan A. Lee—San Francisco, CA
Donation to: Asian Art Museum Foundation of San Francisco, San Francisco, CA

Chow Mai Fun

This dish is readily available in any Oriental vegetarian restaurant and in the temples in Asia. But, what I have tasted from many places has been, basically, only fried rice sticks with bean sprouts, green beans, and bok choy—that's it! After some experimenting, I improvised my own stir-fry rice stick recipe by adding some extra vegetables and cutting the rice stick portion by half.

INGREDIENTS

- ½ **packet** *rice sticks (available in Oriental markets)*
- **4 tablespoons** *vegetable oil*
- **1 tablespoon** *chopped garlic*
- **1** *carrot, shredded*
- ¼ **pound** *green beans, shredded*
- ½ *yellow, or purple onion, shredded*
- **1** *zucchini, shredded*
- ½ *head white cabbage, shredded*
- **2-3 tablespoons** *light soya sauce*
- ½ **pound** *bean sprouts*

DIRECTIONS

Soak rice sticks in cold water until soft; drain. Heat wok with vegetable oil and sauté garlic. Add all vegetables, except bean sprouts. Stir-fry 10 to 15 minutes. Add rice sticks. Fry 10 more minutes. Season with light soya sauce and, finally, add bean sprouts. Turn off heat and mix well. **Serves 4 to 6.**

❧ *Serve with sliced, fresh chiles with soya sauce.*

Mrs. Marjorie Watkins—Glencoe, IL
Donation to: Northshore Senior Center Alzheimer's Patients, Winnetka, IL (House of Welcome)

Panned Carrots

I made it up for my parents' fiftieth wedding anniversary dinner party. Guests demanded the recipe!

INGREDIENTS

- **3 tablespoons** *oil*
- **4 cups** *coarsely shredded carrots*
- **1 cup** *chopped green bell pepper*
- **1 cup** *chopped onion*
- **1 cup** *chopped parsley*
- **1/2 teaspoon** *salt*
- **1/8 teaspoon** *pepper*
- **1 tablespoon** *tarragon*
- **3 tablespoons** *apple cider vinegar*

DIRECTIONS

Heat oil in heavy skillet. Add carrots, bell pepper, onion, and parsley; season with salt and pepper, stirring constantly. When well-mixed, add tarragon. Cover and cook until tender, but still crisp. Add vinegar; stir and serve. **Serves 6.**

❧ *Serve with roast crown of lamb, leg of lamb, or venison or pork tenderloin.*

P.K. Maguire—Colorado Springs, CO
Donation to: American Heart Association, Inc., Colorado Springs, CO

Apricot Glazed Carrots

This is one of my mom's special dishes.

INGREDIENTS

2 pounds *carrots, cleaned, scraped, and cut on diagonal*

3 tablespoons *butter*

1/3 cup *apricot preserves*

1/4 teaspoon *ground nutmeg*

1/4 teaspoon *salt*

1/2-1 teaspoon *freshly grated orange peel*

2 tablespoons *fresh lemon juice or orange juice*

Parsley sprigs

DIRECTIONS

Steam carrots in salted water 20 minutes until just tender. Drain. Melt butter in saucepan and stir in preserves until blended. Add nutmeg, salt, orange peel, and juice. Toss carrots with fruit mixture until well-coated. Garnish with parsley. Serve at once. **Serves 8.**

❧ *Serve with roast pork, ham, or roast chicken.*

Barbara S. Horowitz—Great Neck, NY
Donation to: The Jewish Museum, New York, NY

Whole Cauliflower and Cheese

This recipe is a low-cholesterol and low-sodium vegetarian idea that I created.

INGREDIENTS

1 *medium-sized cauliflower*

1/4 cup *water*

1/2 cup *grated cheese*

DIRECTIONS

Remove all leaves and wash the cauliflower. Place whole cauliflower in a microwaveable casserole and add 1/4 cup water. Cover and microwave 12 minutes on medium. Remove cover and sprinkle cheese over cauliflower. Microwave, uncovered, 2 minutes on medium. **Serves 6 to 8.**

❧ *Serve with fruit and a green salad.*

Susan Brodarick—St. Louis, MO
Donation to: American Cancer Society, Inc., St. Louis, MO

Celery au Gratin

This recipe comes from my great-grandmother and my grandmother in Mississippi. No holiday dinner is complete without this dish.

INGREDIENTS

4 cups *celery, cut into 1-inch pieces*

½ cup *chopped almonds*

2 tablespoons *melted margarine*

½ cup *milk*

1 can *(10½ ounce) cream of mushroom soup*

½ cup *grated sharp Cheddar cheese*

¾ cup *bread crumbs*

Pimientos (optional)

DIRECTIONS

When cutting celery, reserve some of the green tops for color and flavor. Simmer celery in boiling water 5 minutes. Celery should be firm, not soft. Drain. Sauté almonds in melted margarine. Mix milk with soup in saucepan and heat until bubbles form. Stir in ¼ cup grated cheese. Add celery and almonds. Pour into casserole. Top with bread crumbs and remaining grated cheese. Chopped pimientos may be added for color. Bake 20 minutes at 325°. **Serves 8.**

❧ *Serve with turkey, dressing, and all the traditional holiday favorites.*

Jacqueline Gutman—Key Colony Beach, FL
Donation to: Hospice of Florida Keys, Inc., Key West, FL

Vegetarian Chili

This recipe came from a newspaper article years ago. Quite spicy, low-cholesterol, and great to make ahead.

INGREDIENTS

- **¾ cup** *olive oil*
- **2** *medium-sized zucchini, cut into ½-inch cubes*
- **2** *medium-sized yellow onions, cut into ½-inch cubes*
- **4** *cloves garlic, chopped*
- **2** *large red bell peppers, cut into ¼-inch pieces*
- **1 can** *(35 ounce) Italian-style plum tomatoes, juice included*
- **1½ pounds** *fresh plum tomatoes, cut into 1-inch cubes*
- **2 tablespoons** *chili powder, or to taste*
- **1 tablespoon** *ground cumin*
- **1 tablespoon** *dried basil*
- **1 tablespoon** *dried oregano*
- **2 teaspoons** *freshly ground pepper*
- **1 teaspoon** *salt*
- **1 teaspoon** *fennel seed*
- **½ cup** *chopped Italian parsley*
- **1 cup** *drained dark-red kidney beans*
- **1 cup** *chick-peas, drained*
- **½ cup** *chopped fresh dill*
- **2 tablespoons** *lemon juice*
- *Sour cream*
- *Grated Monterey jack cheese*
- *Sliced scallions*

DIRECTIONS

Heat ½ cup olive oil in large skillet over medium heat. Add zucchini and sauté until tender. Remove to a large casserole or Dutch oven. Lower heat and add remaining olive oil to skillet. Add onions, garlic, and bell peppers; sauté 10 minutes until just wilted. Pour contents of skillet, including the oil, into the casserole. Place casserole over low heat. Add canned tomatoes, juice from canned tomatoes, fresh tomatoes, chili powder, cumin, basil, oregano, pepper, salt, fennel, and parsley. Cook 30 minutes, uncovered, stirring often. Stir in kidney beans, chick-peas, dill, and lemon juice; cook 15 minutes. Stir; adjust seasonings. Garnish with sour cream, Monterey jack cheese, and scallions. **Serves 8.**

❧ *Serve as a main entrée with oyster crackers.*

Testing Notes: *Recommended for someone on a low-calorie diet.*

Mrs. Ted R. (April) Gamble—Carmel Valley, CA
Donation to: Carmel Valley Community Youth Center, Inc., Carmel Valley, CA

Chile Casserole

This was the first meal our new daughter-in-law, Erin, fixed for us in her new home. It is delicious. Most of the work can be prepared ahead, and it appeals to my well-known spicy tastes. We think Erin is a smart cookie!

INGREDIENTS

1 pound *sharp Cheddar cheese*

1 pound *mild Cheddar cheese*

2 cans *(7 ounces each) whole green chiles, deveined seeded, rinsed, and drained*

8 *eggs, beaten*

1 pint *sour cream*

½ pound *Monterey jack cheese, grated*

DIRECTIONS

Grate sharp and mild Cheddar cheeses; keep separate. Grease 2-quart casserole. Layer ingredients in this order: sharp Cheddar on the bottom of casserole, ½ the chiles, the mild Cheddar, and the rest of the chiles. Mix eggs and sour cream; pour over the cheese-and-chile mixture. Bake 45 to 50 minutes at 325°. Add Monterey jack cheese during the last 10 or 12 minutes of cooking time. **Serves 8.**

❧ *Serve with ham for dinner or with sausage patties for brunch.*

Caroline Hite Edens—Dallas, TX
Donation to: American Cancer Society, Inc., Dallas, TX

Corn Casserole

This is an incredibly good dish—good with anything. It has become a real stand-by in our family.

INGREDIENTS

1 can *(16 ounce) cream corn*
1 cup *BISQUICK®*
1 *egg, beaten*
2 tablespoons *salad oil*
½ cup *milk*
1 can *(4 ounce) chopped green chiles*
½ pound *grated Monterey jack cheese*

DIRECTIONS

Blend together corn, BISQUICK®, egg, oil, and milk. Pour ½ the batter into a greased 9 x 10-inch casserole. Sprinkle about ½ the chiles and ½ the cheese on top. Repeat: batter, chiles, cheese. Bake 30 to 35 minutes in a preheated 400° oven. **Serves 6.**

Tina Berman—Framingham, MA
Donation to: AIDS Action Committee of Massachusetts, Inc., Boston, MA

Corn Fritters

INGREDIENTS

3 *egg yolks*
1⅔ cups *cooked corn kernels*
½ teaspoon *salt*
½ teaspoon *pepper*
¼ cup *sifted flour*
3 *egg whites*
6 tablespoons *corn oil*

DIRECTIONS

Beat egg yolks until light. Mix in corn, salt, pepper, and flour. Beat egg whites until stiff peaks form. Fold egg whites into corn mixture. Drop by tablespoons into hot oil. Cook on both sides until golden brown. **Serves 4.**

❧ *Serve with applesauce.*

Testing Notes: *Add diced jalapeño peppers.*

Neiman Marcus—Classic
Donation to: combined charities

Grits Soufflé with Smithfield Ham

One of Bob Jones' recent classics, this recipe won the 1990 Silver Oats Award in a competition sponsored by Quaker Oats Company.

INGREDIENTS

2 cups *milk*
½ cup *grits*
1 teaspoon *salt*
½ teaspoon *baking powder*
½ teaspoon *sugar*
2 tablespoons *melted butter*
3 eggs, *separated*
4 ounces *Smithfield ham, finely chopped*

DIRECTIONS

Scald milk, add grits, and cook until thickened. Add salt, baking powder, sugar, and butter. Beat egg yolks. Add grits and ham to egg yolks. Beat egg whites to a soft peak; fold into the batter. Pour into a well-buttered 1½-quart casserole and bake, uncovered, 25 to 30 minutes at 375°. Serve immediately while hot. **Serves 8.**

Dottie Renfrow—Santa Maria, CA
Donation to: Marian Medical Center Foundation, Santa Maria, CA (Dialysis Treatment)

Wild Rice with Fresh Corn

This is my variation of a dish from Michael's Waterside Restaurant in Santa Barbara, California.

INGREDIENTS

1 cup *wild rice*
2 *shallots, chopped*
2 tablespoons *olive oil*
2¼ cups *chicken stock*
3 *ears fresh corn*
1 *bunch cilantro or flat-leaf parsley, chopped*
Salt and pepper, to taste

DIRECTIONS

Wash and drain rice. Sauté shallots in olive oil in heavy 2-quart saucepan over medium heat until soft. Add wild rice; cook 2 to 3 minutes. Add stock, bring to boil, and cover. Bake 45 minutes at 350°. Check after 30 minutes to see if more stock is needed. Cut kernels from the corncobs. Add corn to rice during the last 10 minutes of cooking. Stir in cilantro. **Serves 6.**

❧ *Serve with a chicken entrée and a fresh fruit dessert.*

Barbara Berdy—New City, NY
Donation to: Rockland Family Shelter, Inc., Spring Valley, NY

Mom's Rice Pilaf

When I was a newlywed, I requested a foolproof recipe from my mom. This is still perfect after twenty-nine years of constant use. Good for company and family dinners.

INGREDIENTS

4 tablespoons *oil*
1 cup *raw rice*
1 can *(14½ ounce) chicken or beef broth*
1 broth-can *of water*
3 *onions, finely chopped*
Salt and pepper, to taste
½ cup *raisins, soaked in cold water and drained*
½ cup *slivered almonds*

DIRECTIONS

Melt 2 tablespoons oil in skillet, add rice, and stir until toasty and crisp. Turn off heat. Add broth and water; stir well. Cover tightly and cook 20 minutes over low flame. Turn off heat and allow to rest 10 minutes. In another pan, sauté onions in remaining oil until very yellow. Add salt and pepper, to taste. Pour onions and their oil, raisins, and almonds into rice mixture. Mix well. Place in serving casserole, sprinkle with additional almonds, and serve. To reheat, dot with butter and place, uncovered, in warm oven. Also, this dish freezes well. **Serves 6.**

❧ *Serve with chicken, veal, or beef. Especially pretty served with plain roast or broiled poultry or meat.*

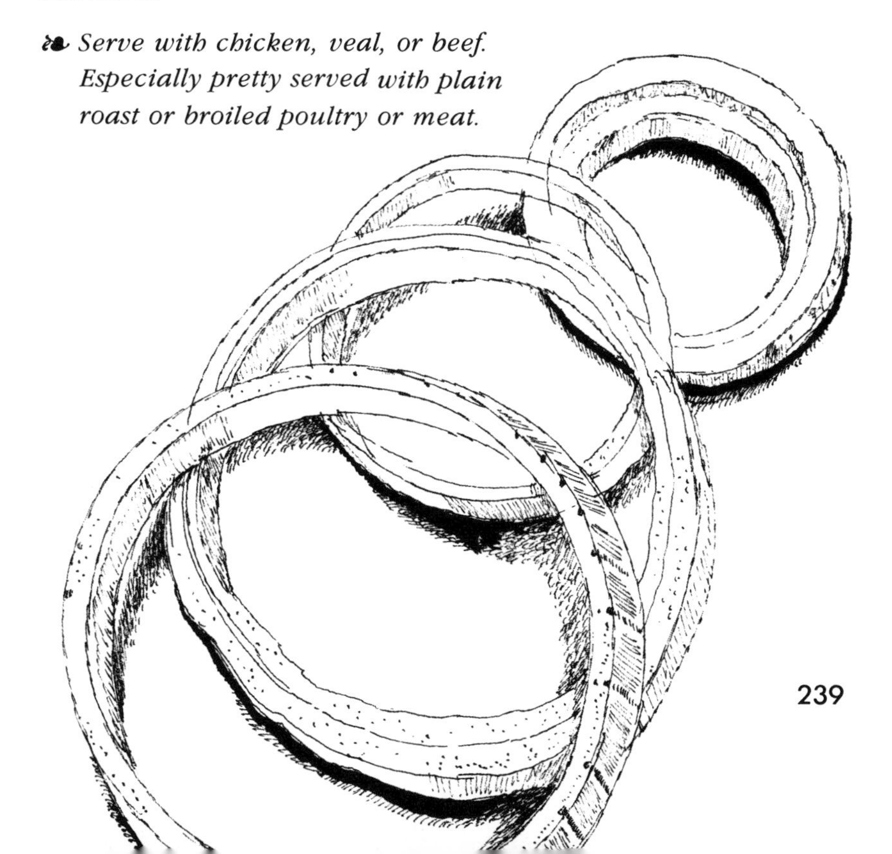

Mrs. Bill (Susan) Roberds—Dallas, TX
Donation to: Dallas Summer Musicals, Inc., Dallas, TX

Lucky Black-Eyed Peas with Rice

This is a combination of several recipes. We have this every New Year's Day to bring good luck in the coming year.

INGREDIENTS

- **2 cups** *dried black-eyed peas*
- **8** *bacon slices, diced*
- **1 cup** *chopped celery*
- **1 cup** *chopped onion*
- **2** *heads garlic, chopped*
- **1 quart** *chicken broth*
- **3 cups** *chopped carrots*
- **1 can** *(14½ ounce) stewed tomatoes, chopped*
- **1 teaspoon** *salt*
- **½ teaspoon** *black pepper*
- **4 tablespoons** *chili powder*
- **2 cups** *rice, cooked*

DIRECTIONS

Wash and sort peas. Cook diced bacon until almost done. Drain, reserving 2 tablespoons of drippings. Sauté celery, onion, and garlic in bacon drippings until tender. Add broth, peas, and carrots. Bring to boil. Cook until peas are almost tender. Add tomatoes and seasonings. Continue cooking until peas are done. Serve over cooked rice. **Serves 6.**

❧ *Serve with tossed green salad and jalapeño corn bread, or with pork roast and sweet potatoes.*

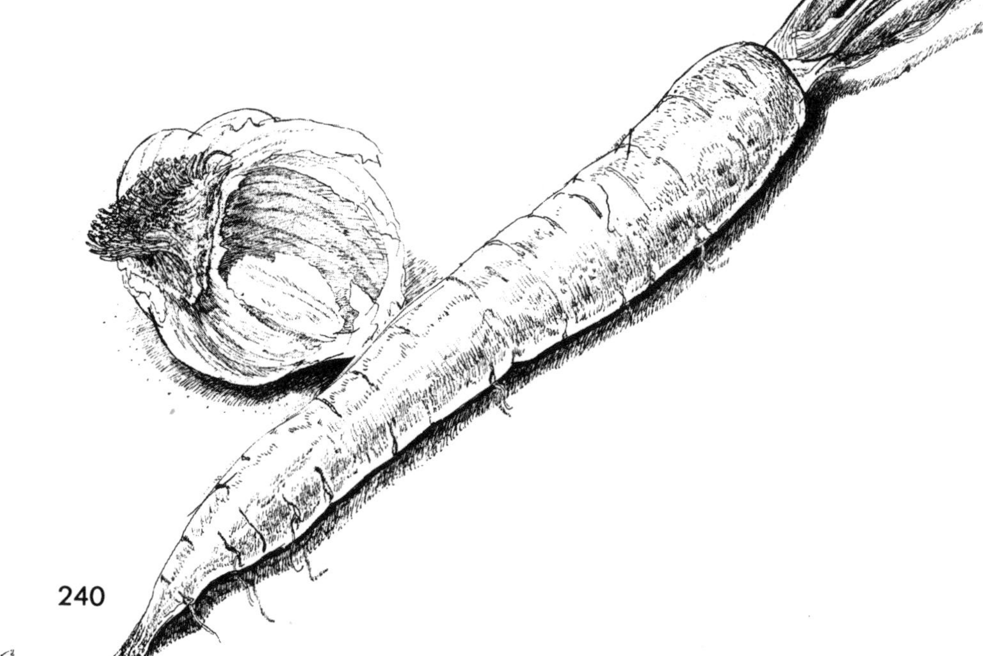

Kaye C. Edwards—San Antonio, TX
Donation to: San Antonio Art Institute, San Antonio, TX

Arabic Rice

This was given to me by a friend after he served it to an enthusiastic group at a cookout.

INGREDIENTS

- ½ **cup** *chopped pecans*
- ½ **cup** *pine nuts*
- ¼ **cup** *slivered almonds*
- ½ **stick** *unsalted butter*
- **1** *medium-sized onion, diced*
- **1 cup** *minced lamb*
- ½ **teaspoon** *powdered ginger*
- ½ **teaspoon** *cinnamon*
- **1 teaspoon** *allspice*
- *Salt and pepper, to taste*
- **1** *small box (1½ ounce) raisins*
- **1 cup** *rice*
- ⅛ **teaspoon** *saffron*

DIRECTIONS

Sauté pecans, pine nuts, and almonds in butter until well-browned. Remove nuts and set aside; reserve butter. Sauté onion in butter until soft. Add minced lamb; sauté until browned. Add ginger, cinnamon, and allspice. Stir until well-blended. Add salt and pepper. Remove from heat; add raisins. In another pan, cook rice, according to package directions, with saffron. When ready to serve, gently fold meat and nut mixtures into the cooked rice. **Serves 6 to 8.**

❧ *Serve with barbecued rack of lamb or grilled chicken.*

Frances L. Chu—Briarcliff Manor, NY
Donation to: Phelps Memorial Hospital Association, North Tarrytown, NY

Stir-Fried Lettuce Pure & Simple

This recipe has been translated from a Chinese cookbook and modified for cooking the pure-and-simple, quick-and-easy way for busy (and lazy) cooks like me.

INGREDIENTS

1 pound *lettuce*
5 tablespoons *peanut oil*
1 *clove garlic, crushed*
1 teaspoon *salt*
5 slices *ginger root*
1 tablespoon *oyster sauce (optional)*

DIRECTIONS

Wash lettuce and drain. Heat peanut oil in pan. Brown crushed garlic; add salt, ginger, and lettuce. Stir-fry 1 minute. Add oyster sauce and serve hot. **Serves 6 to 8.**

❧ *Serve with steamed rice.*

Roslyn Goldstine—Beverly Hills, CA
Donation to: American Cancer Society, Inc., Los Angeles, CA

Cheese Onion Bake

This recipe was given to me at a bridal shower twenty-seven years ago. It was as tasty and simple then as it is now. It has served me well.

INGREDIENTS

3 cups *seasoned croutons*
2 cups *shredded Monterey jack or Cheddar cheese*
1 can *(3 ounce) French-fried onions, crumbled*
2 cups *half-and-half*
4 *eggs*
½ teaspoon *salt (optional)*

DIRECTIONS

Line bottom of small rectangular PYREX® baking dish with seasoned croutons. Sprinkle cheese over croutons. Sprinkle onions over cheese. Beat eggs. Add half-and-half and salt to eggs; blend well. Pour over ingredients in baking dish. Bake 30 to 35 minutes at 350°. Cool and serve. **Serves 6.**

Magda Katz—Los Angeles, CA
Donation to: Magnolia Avenue School Student Body Library Account, Los Angeles, CA

Potato Kugel

This recipe is from my mother, Dina Muller, who learned it from her grandmother in Czechoslovakia. The potatoes must be grated by hand, otherwise the texture is too bland. I always get rave reviews when I serve it.

INGREDIENTS

8 *large white potatoes, grated*
4 *eggs, beaten*
1 ½ teaspoons *salt*
¼ teaspoon *black pepper*
Dash of garlic powder
¼ cup *vegetable oil*

DIRECTIONS

Heat oil in a 13 x 9-inch PYREX® glass dish. Grate potatoes by hand. Fold eggs and the rest of the ingredients into the potatoes. Place mixture on top of heated oil in the glass dish. Bake 1½ hours at 350°. **Serves 12.**

❧ *It's best served with poultry or beef.*

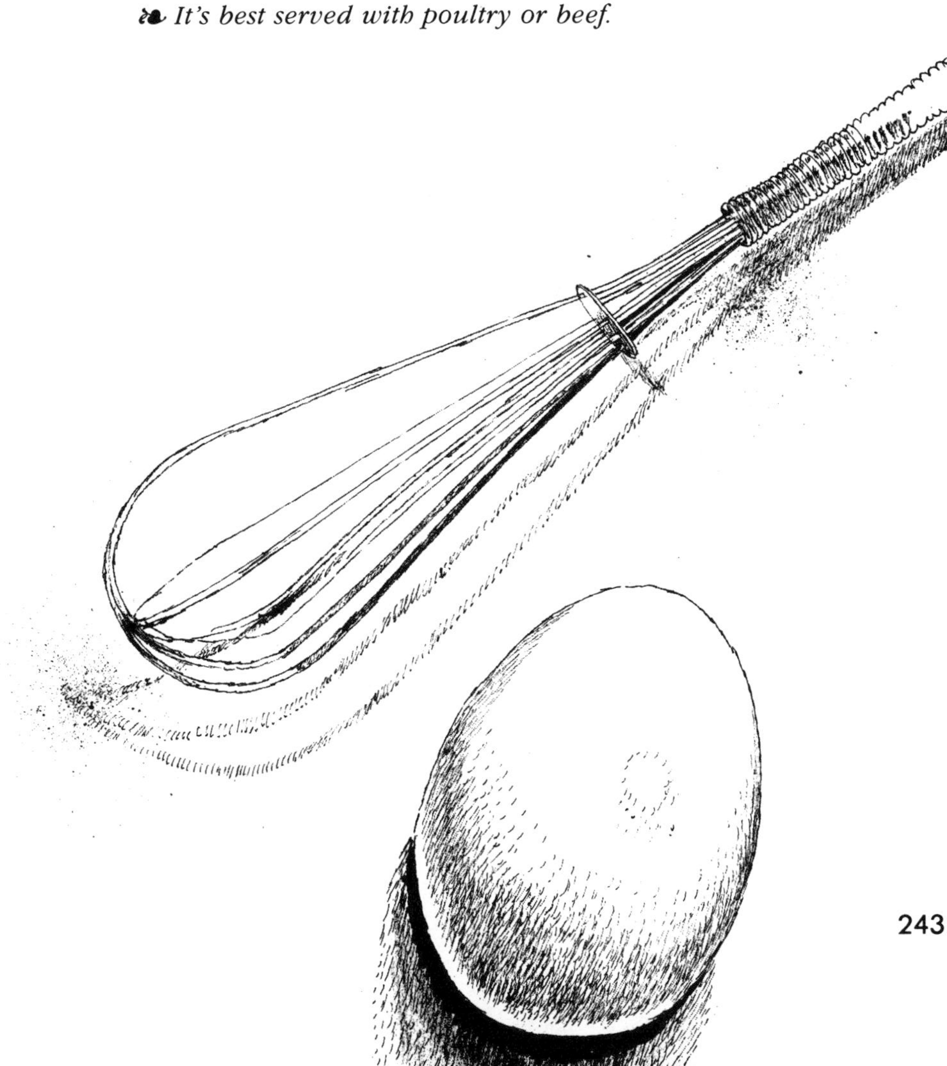

Marilyn Townsend—Foster City, CA
Donation to: Pacific Vision Foundation, San Francisco, CA

Eastern Potatoes

For the past thirteen years, I lived and worked in Saudi Arabia. One of my favorite pastimes was buying fragrant spices from the local souks. After years of experimenting and discussions with my Saudi friends, I have enough recipes to fill a book; but Eastern Potatoes remains a favorite. When I invite six friends for dinner, I make just enough of this recipe to serve 12!

INGREDIENTS

1 teaspoon *whole mustard seed*

3-4 tablespoons *oil*

1 teaspoon *ground ginger (or 2 tablespoons chopped fresh)*

½ teaspoon *turmeric*

2 teaspoons *whole cumin seed*

2 *whole cardamom seeds, crushed*

Pinch of dry, crushed red chile peppers

6 *large potatoes, diced*

1 *large onion, chopped*

1 *box (10 ounce) frozen peas*

1 tablespoon *granulated white sugar*

DIRECTIONS

Fry mustard seed in oil until it turns gray. Cool slightly. Add remaining spices and mix well. If mixture seems dry, add a little more oil. Reheat and stir in potatoes and onions. Fry until potatoes and onions start to turn brown. Add frozen peas and sugar; fry quickly, stirring constantly, until the peas are cooked—about 5 minutes. Serve at once. **Serves 6.**

❧ *Serve with tossed green salad and broiled fish.*

Testing Notes: *This recipe may also be served cold.*

Georgette Mosbacher—Houston, TX
Donation to: Child Help, Inc., Temple, TX

Georgette's Perfect Potatoes

The driving force behind La Prairie cosmetics lives a whirlwind life between business and social commitments in New York, Washington, and Houston. This is what she likes to eat "before going to a charity event where you know you are going to eat late and be tempted by foods you shouldn't eat."

INGREDIENTS

1 *baked potato*
2 tablespoons *low-calorie cottage cheese*
Chopped chives, to taste
Chopped onions, to taste
Salt and pepper, to taste

DIRECTIONS

Cut baked potato lengthwise. Spoon out potato, leaving skin intact. Don't mash potato, leave chunky. Mix potatoes, just enough to blend, with cottage cheese, chives, onions, salt, and pepper. Spoon mixture back into potato skins. Broil 5 minutes and serve. **Serves 1**. To save time, bake 6 Perfect Potatoes; wrap individually in tin foil and freeze. When ready to serve, remove foil and place in preheated 450° oven for 20 minutes. Then, broil 5 minutes. Perfect Potatoes are very low-calorie, nonfat, and very filling.

Testing Notes: *Drain cottage cheese through a sieve so it will not be too watery.*

Albert Kellner—Executive Chef Brenner's Park-Hotel
Baden-Baden, Germany
Donation to: combined charities

Kartoffelpuffer (German Potato Pancake)

INGREDIENTS

2¼ pounds *potatoes*
1 *medium-sized onion*
Salt, to taste
Nutmeg, to taste
3 tablespoons *flour*
2 *eggs*
Vegetable oil

DIRECTIONS

Peel, wash, and wipe potatoes and onions. Pour off some of the potato juice and let juice settle. Add the starch from the bottom of the potato juice to the potatoes. Then, add salt, nutmeg, flour, and eggs. Stir well. Heat vegetable oil. (In Germany we used lard.) Use a spoon to put the potato dough in the frying pan. Press until you get flat little cakes. Fry on both sides until light brown and firm. Serve immediately. **Serves 4.**

❧ *As a complete luncheon, serve with apple purée. As a dessert, serve with Gervais (white cheese) and cranberries and cream. Serve as a supplement to cold meat (poultry, roast beef, etc.) or smoked salmon and caviar.*

Mrs. C. A. Brawner—Dallas, TX
Donation to: American Heart Association, Inc., Dallas, TX

Potato Croquettes

I entered this recipe in the 1949 NM publication called, *A Taste of Texas*; and, of course, I gave the cookbook as shower, graduation, etc., gifts. It was especially successful with the college crowd at the University of Texas.

INGREDIENTS

4 *large or 6 medium-sized potatoes, peeled*
2 tablespoons *hot milk*
2 tablespoons *butter*
2 *egg yolks*
1 teaspoon *grated onion*
½ teaspoon *salt*
¼ teaspoon *pepper*
¼ teaspoon *nutmeg*
1 teaspoon *minced parsley*
Fine cracker crumbs
Beaten egg
Vegetable oil

DIRECTIONS

Cook peeled potatoes in boiling, salted water to cover. Drain and rice the potatoes. There should be 3 to 4 cups. Whip up light with hot milk and butter. Add well-beaten egg yolks, grated onion, seasonings, and parsley. Spread potato mixture in shallow pan. Chill until very cold. Shape into thin finger-length cylinders. Roll in cracker crumbs; roll in beaten egg; roll in cracker crumbs, again. Chill until ready to fry. Fry in 365° deep fat until golden brown. Drain on unglazed paper; keep hot in warming oven. **Makes 3 dozen**. It is simple to convert my 1949 *A Taste of Texas* entry to a heart-healthy dish for the nineties: use EGG BEATERS® instead of eggs, oleo instead of butter, and brown with PAM® instead of deep-frying with oil.

❧ *Serve with any meat dish, green vegetable, and salad.*

Mrs. Niley J. Smith—Cameron, TX
Donation to: American Cancer Society, Inc., Dallas, TX

Meriton Potatoes

This was my sister's recipe. She was a gourmet cook, who enjoyed entertaining and giving dinner parties. I have used this recipe for over forty-five years.

INGREDIENTS

2 *raw eggs*
Salt and pepper, to taste
2 tablespoons *chopped parsley*
1 cup *bread crumbs*
1 quart *mashed potatoes*
1 *large onion, chopped*
1 stick *butter*
2 *hard cooked eggs, chopped*

DIRECTIONS

Stir raw eggs, salt, pepper, 1 tablespoon parsley, and ½ cup bread crumbs into the mashed potatoes. Set aside. Brown onion in 3 tablespoons butter. Add onions and hard-cooked eggs to potatoes. Stir well. Mound the potatoes in a pie plate or baking dish. Make a shallow well in the center of the potatoes with the back of a large spoon. Cover the mound top with remaining bread crumbs and 2 tablespoons butter. Bake 20 minutes at 350° until almost toasted. Remove from oven. Place remaining butter and remaining parsley in the well. Heat in oven until butter is melted. **Serves 10 to 12**. Tastes like stuffed crab.

❧ *Serve with roast beef.*

Neiman Marcus—CLASSIC
Donation to: combined charities

Crusty Potato Balls

All kids love mashed potatoes—they'll beg you to serve this variation again and again!

INGREDIENTS

4 cups *mashed potatoes*
4 tablespoons *minced onion*
2 *egg yolks*
Salt, to taste
Pepper, to taste
2 *egg whites*
1 cup *bread crumbs*

DIRECTIONS

Mix potatoes, onion, and egg yolks. Sprinkle with salt and pepper; shape into balls. Roll these in the egg whites, then in the bread crumbs. Bake 8 to 10 minutes on a cookie sheet at 450°. **Serves 8.**

Mrs. Gerald Klein—Beaumont, TX
Donation to: St. Elizabeth Hospital, Beaumont, TX

Sopa

Years ago, this was given to me by one of our young family members. It is standard fare with my barbecue brisket.

INGREDIENTS

12 *tortillas, halved*
2 *onions, chopped*
2 *cloves garlic, chopped*
4 tablespoons *butter*
1 can *(32 ounce) stewed tomatoes*
2 cans *(4 ounces each) chopped green chiles*
15 ounces *grated longhorn cheese*
½ pint *whipping cream*

DIRECTIONS

Fry and drain tortillas. Set aside. Sauté onions and garlic in butter until soft. Add tomatoes and green chiles; cook 10 minutes. Spray a 3-quart casserole with PAM®, and layer tortillas, sauce, and cheese in that order. Repeat. Let stand a few hours or overnight. Pour whipping cream over the top and bake 45 minutes at 350°. Bake another 15 minutes at 300°. **Serves 8.** For a main course, add turkey or chicken.

❧ *Serve with barbecue or Mexican dishes.*

Mrs. Joan A. Stewart—Houston, TX
Donation to: Houston Grand Opera Association, Inc., Houston, TX

Spinach Alexander

I named this after my daughter, who loves parties. It's perfect for a cocktail party or with dinner as a vegetable.

INGREDIENTS

2 packages *(10 ounces each) frozen chopped spinach*

½ cup *spinach liquid*

5 tablespoons *butter*

2½ tablespoons *flour*

½ cup *finely chopped onion*

½ cup *evaporated milk*

1 teaspoon *black pepper*

8 ounces *jalapeño cheese, cut into small cubes*

1 teaspoon *Worcestershire sauce*

1 teaspoon *red pepper*

4 drops *TABASCO® sauce*

Buttered bread crumbs (optional)

DIRECTIONS

Cook spinach, according to package directions. Drain and reserve liquid. Melt butter in saucepan over low heat. Add flour, stirring until blended and smooth; do not brown. Add reserved spinach liquid, stirring constantly. Cook until smooth and thickened. Add remaining ingredients, except bread crumbs. Stir until cheese melts. Combine with cooked spinach. Serve immediately, or put into a casserole and top with buttered bread crumbs. **Serves 6.** Double recipe if used as a dip.

Testing Notes: *Add crisp, crumbled, cooked bacon.*

Neiman Marcus—CLASSIC
Donation to: combined charities

Gourmet Spinach Ring

Look no further—here is an excellent new way to serve spinach to family or guests.

INGREDIENTS

3 pounds *(2 quarts) raw spinach, chopped*

2 cans *(10½ ounces each) cream of mushroom soup*

4 *eggs, beaten*

Pinch of nutmeg

Salt and pepper, to taste

2 tablespoons *butter*

2 tablespoons *flour*

2 cups *half-and-half, or milk*

2 cups *dry-roasted peanuts*

6 cups *slivered celery, steamed*

Chopped parsley

DIRECTIONS

Finely chop spinach and mix with the soup, eggs, nutmeg, salt, and pepper. Pour into greased 2½-quart ring mold. Bake until firm at 325°. Meanwhile, melt butter in large saucepan. Stir in flour and cook until bubbles form. Pour in the half-and-half and cook until thickened. Add peanuts and celery. Season and sprinkle with chopped parsley. Turn spinach mold onto serving tray and fill center with celery-and-peanut mixture. **Serves 18.**

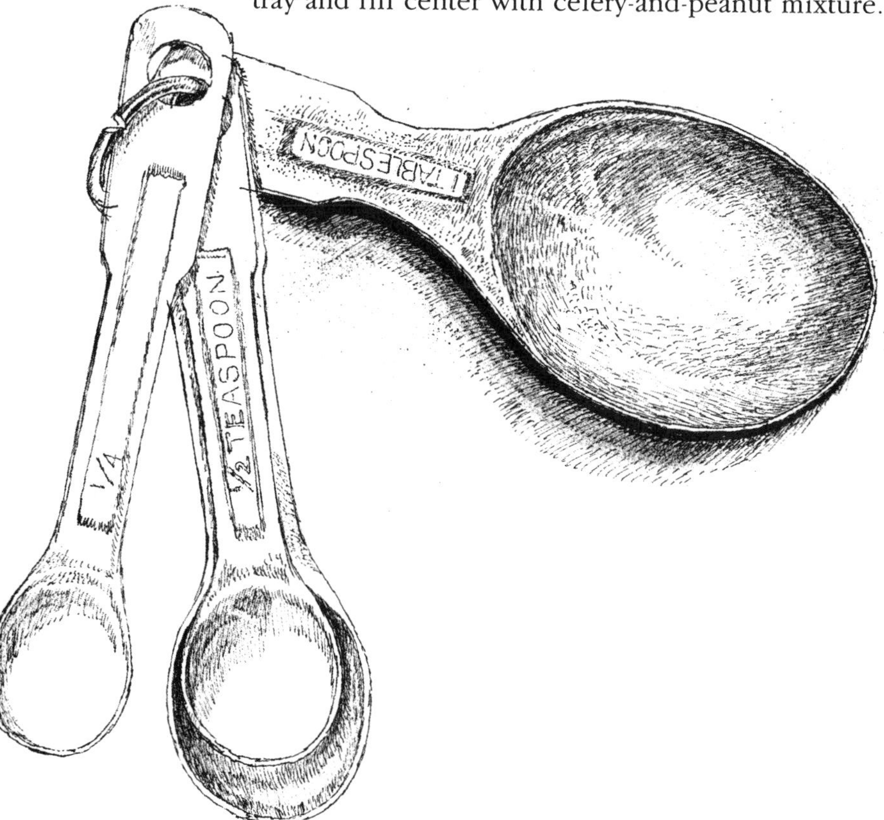

Dr. Helene Seeman Woldenberg—Dallas, TX
Donation to: Zionist Organization of America, Richardson, TX

Creamy Dreamy Spinach

After trying many times to make a tasty spinach dish, I invented this one.

INGREDIENTS

2 packages *(10 ounces each) frozen chopped spinach*

3 tablespoons *butter or margarine*

1 cup *chopped onion*

1 package *(8 ounce) cream cheese*

1 jar *(6 ounce) marinated artichokes, drained and chopped*

½ cup *whipping cream*

1¼ cups *Parmesan cheese*

1 tablespoon *garlic powder*

1 teaspoon *salt*

1 teaspoon *pepper*

DIRECTIONS

Cook and drain spinach. Set aside. Sauté butter and onions in large saucepan until golden brown. Turn heat to medium setting. Add cream cheese in small increments, stirring slowly. Once cream cheese melts, add spinach, artichokes, whipping cream, Parmesan cheese, garlic powder, salt, and pepper. **Serves 4 to 6.**

❧ *Serve with grilled fish or, simply, as a dip for crackers.*

Neiman Marcus—THE ROTUNDA San Francisco
Donation to: combined charities

Spinach Soufflé Terrine

This beautiful soufflé by Assistant Restaurant Manager Diana Parker could be the main course of a social lunch.

INGREDIENTS

- **4 packages** *raw spinach, washed, chopped, and uncooked*
- **1 cup** *grated medium Cheddar cheese*
- **1 cup** *grated Monterey jack or Swiss cheese*
- **2** *scallions finely chopped*
- **4** *eggs separated*
- **¼ cup** *mayonnaise*
- **½ teaspoon** *salt*
- **½ teaspoon** *ground pepper*
- **¼ teaspoon** *cayenne*

DIRECTIONS

Place chopped spinach into colander to drain. Press well with the back of a spoon to squeeze out excess liquid. Spray a 9 x 12-inch glass au gratin pan lightly with a nonstick coating. Finely chop the cheese with a steel blade on the food processor. Beat yolks until frothy. Beat whites until peaks form. Assemble together all ingredients, except the egg whites, in a large mixing bowl. Turn the whites lightly into the mixture. Place mixture in au gratin pan. Bake 45 minutes at 350° until raised and golden. Let rest before cutting.
Serves 10 to 12.

Renée Crown—Wilmette, IL
Donation to: National Multiple Sclerosis Society, Chicago, IL

Mushrooms Florentine

As a mother of seven kids, spending hours in the kitchen was a luxury I never could afford. When I entertained, I wanted simple-to-make, attractive, and of course, delicious dishes. This recipe is wonderful for buffet dinners. In my forty years of marriage, this has never been served to me by another hostess. Perhaps you'll try it.

INGREDIENTS

1 pound *whole fresh mushrooms*

2 packages *(10 ounces each) frozen spinach, thawed*

1 teaspoon *salt*

¼ cup *chopped onion*

¼ cup *melted butter*

1 cup *shredded Cheddar cheese*

Garlic salt

DIRECTIONS

Wash and dry mushrooms. Slice off stems. Sauté stems and caps until browned, browning cap side first. Combine thawed spinach with salt, onion, and melted butter in a bowl. Line a shallow 10-by-1½-inch casserole with the spinach mixture. Sprinkle ½ the cheese and arrange the mushrooms over the spinach. Season with garlic salt. Cover with remaining cheese. Bake 20 minutes at 350° until cheese melts and turns brown. This may be prepared in advance and refrigerated. **Serves 6 to 8.**

Testing Notes: *Sprinkle ¼ cup bread crumbs on top of cheese before baking.*

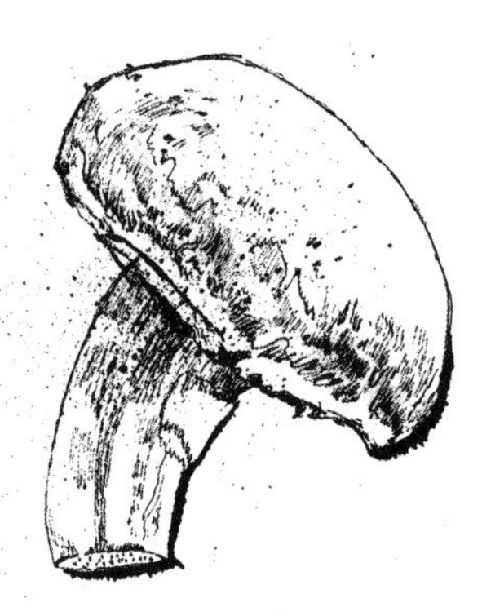

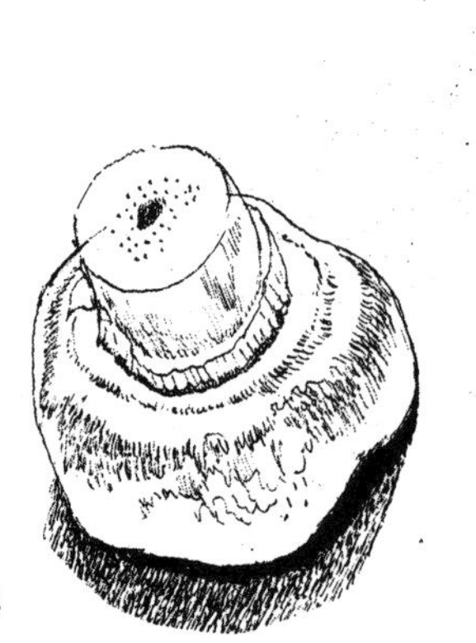

Danna Almon—Richardson, TX
Donation to: Scottish Rite Hospital for Crippled Children, Inc., Dallas, TX

Confetti Squash

We have a large family and there are many family gatherings during the year. These are times of fun and sharing. Everyone brings their latest gourmet dish. The Confetti Squash recipe made its debut long ago. It is a favorite of all and is as traditional as Thanksgiving turkey or Christmas rum pudding.

INGREDIENTS

- **¾ pound** *yellow squash*
- **¾ pound** *zucchini squash*
- **2** *eggs, well-beaten*
- **¾ cup** *plus* **1 cup** *grated cheese*
- **1** *medium-sized onion, grated*
- **1 tablespoon** *sugar*
- **1 teaspoon** *sage*
- **½ teaspoon** *salt*
- **⅛ teaspoon** *pepper*
- **3 tablespoons** *butter or margarine, melted*
- **⅛ teaspoon** *paprika*

DIRECTIONS

Stew squash 10 minutes until tender. Drain and combine with eggs, ¾ cup grated cheese, onion, sugar, sage, salt, pepper, and melted butter. Pour into a 1½-quart baking dish. Sprinkle with 1 cup cheese and the paprika. Bake 25 minutes at 400° until bubbles form and cheese melts. **Serves 6.**

Testing Notes: *Add 1 teaspoon of nutmeg.*

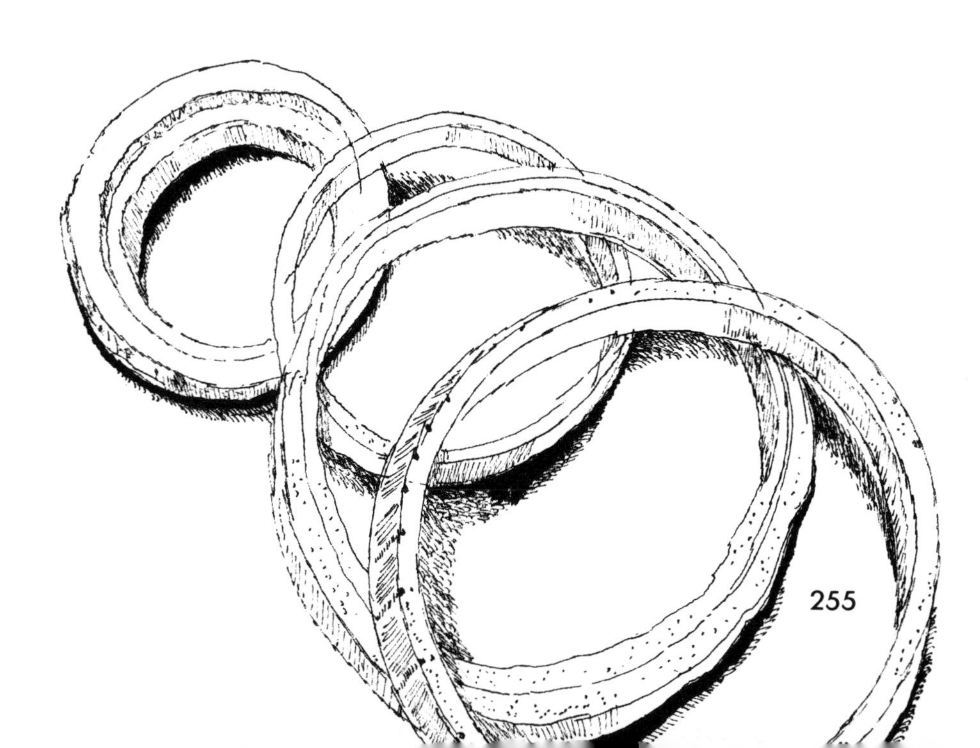

Frances Heyne—Houston, TX
Donation to: Bayou Bend Collection, Houston, TX

Squash-Eggplant Casserole

I collect recipes for squash, and my mother always made eggplant casserole; so this seemed the perfect combination of both. Being from New Mexico, my mother taught me how to introduce green chiles (not hot) into a lot of cooking, and they really add an extra zest.

INGREDIENTS

6 *large yellow squash, sliced*

1 *large eggplant, peeled and sliced*

2 *large garlic pods*

1 tablespoon *minced onion*

1 package *(8 ounce) cream cheese, softened*

2 cans *(4 ounces each) green chiles, drained and chopped*

2 *eggs, slightly beaten*

Salt and pepper, to taste

2 tablespoons *Worcestershire sauce*

Bread crumbs

DIRECTIONS

Boil squash and eggplant until barely tender; drain well. Sauté garlic and onion. Blend cream cheese, chiles, and eggs thoroughly in a bowl. Add garlic, onions, salt, pepper, and Worcestershire sauce until well-blended. Place in buttered 3-quart casserole with bread crumbs on top. Bake 30 minutes at 375°. **Serves 6 to 8.**

❧ *This can be a party dish and will accompany any meat or chicken dish.*

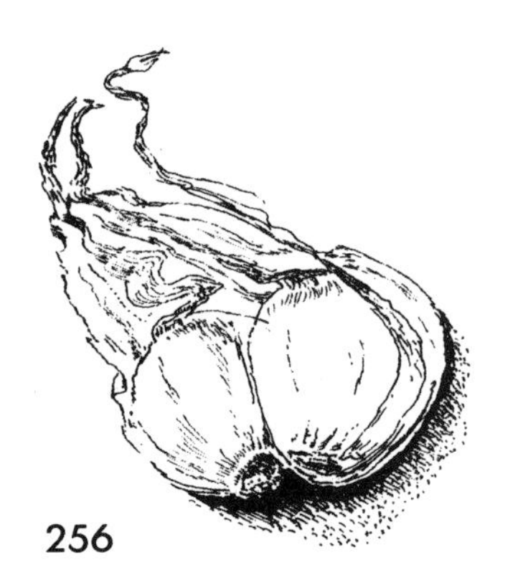

Susan Wilson Walker—Galveston, TX
Donation to: Ducks Unlimited, Inc., Long Grove, IL

Tomatoes Rockefeller

A friend served a similar dish, and I added to it.

INGREDIENTS

- **1 package** *(10 ounce) frozen chopped spinach*
- **½ cup** *seasoned bread crumbs*
- **½ cup** *plain bread crumbs*
- **3** *green onions, chopped*
- **3** *eggs, slightly beaten*
- **½ cup** *melted butter*
- **¼ cup** *grated Parmesan cheese*
- **¼ teaspoon** *Worcestershire sauce*
- **½ teaspoon** *minced garlic*
- **½ teaspoon** *salt*
- **¼ teaspoon** *pepper*
- **½ teaspoon** *thyme*
- **¼ teaspoon** *TABASCO® sauce*
- **6** *thick tomato slices*

DIRECTIONS

Cook spinach, according to package directions, and drain. Add remaining ingredients, except the sliced tomatoes. Mound spinach mixture on tomato slices. Bake 15 minutes at 350°. Spinach mixture freezes well. **Serves 6.**

❧ *Serve with tenderloin, prime rib, or crab casserole.*

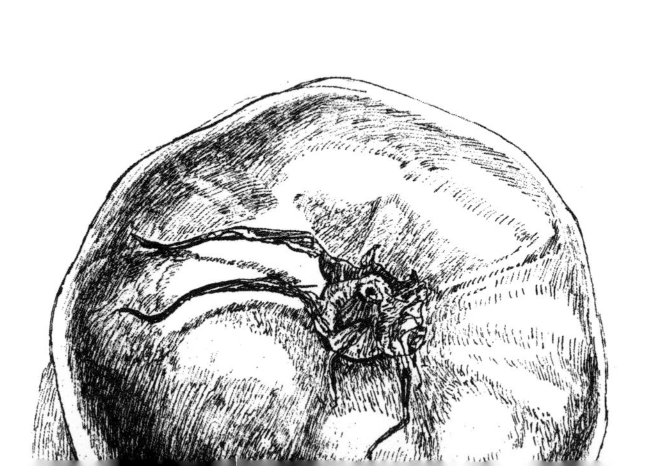

CHAPTER ELEVEN

Breads

Nothing else makes such an impression on guests or family as the breads you bake yourself. And, InCircle bakers seem to know that nothing else is quite as satisfying as the mere making of it. We received old family recipes, new concoctions, and even a lollapalooza of a corn bread recipe from the Governor of Texas' own kitchen. With so many good breads to choose from in bakeries today, we decided to zero in on the quick breads that are best baked at home. Served at breakfast or teatime or coupled with soup or salad, they can be the highlight of a company meal. And, you take the bows.

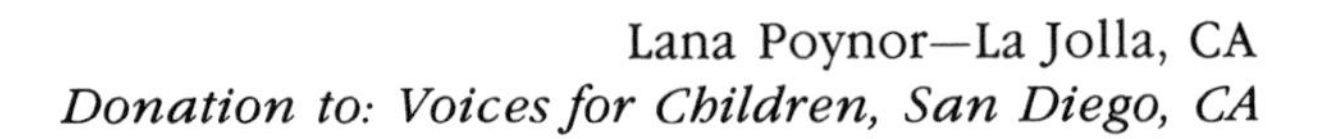
Lana Poynor—La Jolla, CA
Donation to: Voices for Children, San Diego, CA

Perfect Popovers

I remember, as a little girl, going to Neiman Marcus for lunch with my mother and loving the warm popovers they brought with the meal. They always make me think of Neimans and all the fun we have there!

INGREDIENTS

3 *eggs*
1 cup *milk*
3 tablespoons *oil*
1 cup *flour*
½ teaspoon *salt*

DIRECTIONS

Preheat oven to 400°. Beat eggs, milk, and oil together. Sift flour and salt over the egg mixture and beat until smooth. Fill 6 popover cups ¾ full. Bake 30 minutes; reduce heat to 325° and bake 15 minutes. **Makes 6.**

❧ *Serve with strawberry butter.*

Michèle d'Arlin—Los Angeles, CA
Donation to: Children's Cancer Research Institute, San Francisco, CA

Scones

This is our favorite recipe.

INGREDIENTS

6 cups *all-purpose flour*
¾ cup *sugar*
⅓ cup *baking powder*
½ pound *plus* **2 tablespoons** *butter*
2 cups *buttermilk*
1 cup *currants*
1 *egg*

DIRECTIONS

Mix flour, sugar, and baking powder. Cut in all the butter to get a coarse-meal consistency. Combine buttermilk and currants; add this to the flour mixture. Turn out on floured board and pat until it holds together, handling as little as possible. Divide into 6 pieces. Shape into circles and cut each circle into either 4 or 6 wedges. Put an egg in a cup and beat it around with a brush until scrambled. Brush this mixture on top of the scones. Bake 30 minutes at 325°. **Makes 24 to 36.**

❧ *Serve with lemon curd, fresh blueberries, and whipped cream.*

Testing Notes: *Serve with strawberry butter.*

Linda L. Burk, M.D.—Dallas, TX
Donation to: Fight for Sight, Inc., Baltimore, MD,

Rhubarb Coffee Cake

Mother has been making it for years with rhubarb from her garden. She says the sour cream makes it especially good.

INGREDIENTS

- **2 cups** *sugar*
- **½ cup** *plus* **1 tablespoon** *butter*
- **1** *egg*
- **1 teaspoon** *vanilla*
- **1 cup** *sour cream*
- **1 teaspoon** *baking soda*
- **2 cups** *plus* **1 teaspoon** *flour*
- **2 cups** *raw rhubarb or other fruit*
- **1 teaspoon** *cinnamon*

DIRECTIONS

Mix together 1½ cups sugar, ½ cup butter, egg, vanilla, sour cream, baking soda, and 2 cups flour. Batter will be thick. Place a layer of batter, a layer of fruit, and a final layer of batter in a 9 x 12-inch pan. Mix the cinnamon, and the remaining sugar, butter, and flour in a bowl. Sprinkle over the loaf and bake 35 to 40 minutes at 350°.

❧ *Serve with breakfast and coffee or a brunch buffet.*

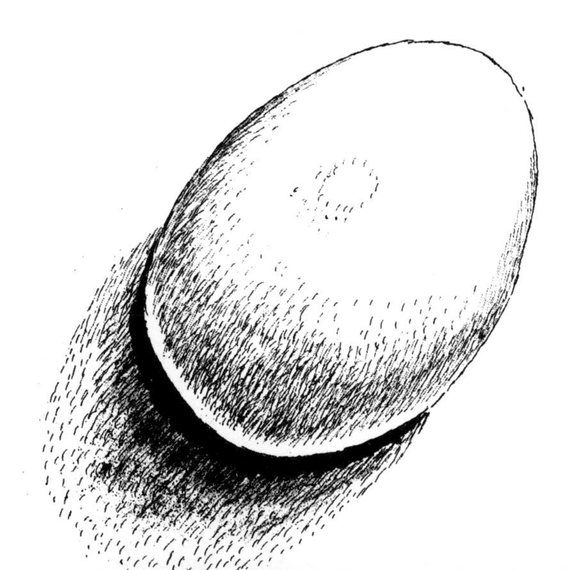

Honey-Pecan Corn Bread Sticks

Truth be known, Bob Jones had this one in his pocket when he first came to Neiman Marcus.

INGREDIENTS

- **⅓ cup** *plus* **1 tablespoon** *firmly packed brown sugar*
- **2 tablespoons** *honey*
- **2 tablespoons** *butter or margarine*
- **¾ cup** *chopped pecans*
- **1 package** *(15 ounce) corn bread mix*

DIRECTIONS

Combine sugar, honey, and butter in small saucepan, stirring occasionally over low heat until it boils and sugar is dissolved. Sprinkle 1 tablespoon nuts into each of 12 average-sized corn-stick forms. Spoon about 2 tablespoons of the hot syrup over the nuts. Prepare corn bread mix, according to package directions, and pour into corn-stick forms. Bake 25 minutes until lightly browned. Immediately invert onto serving platter and serve hot. **Makes 12 corn-sticks.** Or, muffins can be made, using ¾ cup brown sugar, 3 tablespoons each of honey and butter, and 1 cup pecans. Bake in 2½-inch muffin cups. **Makes 16 muffins.**

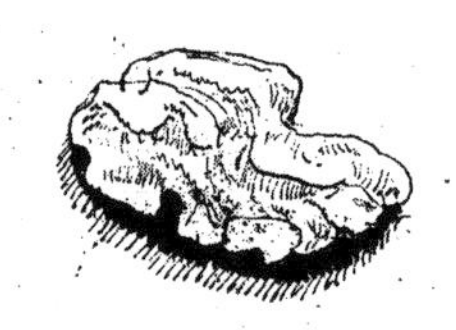

Cherle Venning—S. Barrington, IL
Donation to: Ditka Foundation, Chicago, IL

Na Na's Kolackys

My Na Na would make these every Christmas, and a generation later, I'm carrying on the tradition in her memory. I make these for all my friends during the holidays.

INGREDIENTS

1 pound *butter, softened*

4 cups *flour*

1 package *(8 ounce) cream cheese, softened*

1 package *dry yeast*

Pastry filling (or jam) as desired: apricot, blueberry, poppy, prune, raspberry, etc.

DIRECTIONS

Cut butter into flour in a medium-sized bowl; set aside. Combine cream cheese and yeast by hand in a large bowl until well-mixed. Add flour-and-butter mixture and mix with hands until dough is well blended. Cut dough in half. Shape into 2 rolls, each 1½-inches-wide and about 8-inches-long. Wrap rolls in wax paper; cover with foil. Refrigerate overnight. Cut rolls into ½-inch slices. Arrange slices on ungreased cookie sheet. Indent the center of each slice to allow for filling. Leave a lip around the edge of each slice so filling doesn't overflow. Fill each slice with your choice of pastry filling. Bake 12 to 15 minutes at 400°. When done, Kolackys will be lightly browned on bottoms and lower edges. Cool on cookie sheet. Sprinkle lightly with powdered sugar. Transfer carefully to serving platter. **Makes about 2 dozen.**

Governor Ann Richards—Austin, TX
Donation to: Children's Medical Center of Dallas, Dallas, TX

Jalapeño Cheese Corn Bread

We should have suspected that the Governor was born with a silver jalapeño in her mouth. It goes with the Texas territory and her corn bread recipe wins by a landslide from everyone who's tasted it.

INGREDIENTS

1 ½ cups *corn bread mix*
¾ cup *milk*
1 *egg*
½ *green onion, chopped*
½ cup *creamed corn*
¼ cup *chopped jalapeños*
¾ cup *grated cheese*
Bacon, to taste
Pimientos, to taste
Garlic, to taste
1 tablespoon *sugar*
2 tablespoons *oil*

DIRECTIONS

Mix well. Pour into buttered baking dish and bake 25 minutes at 425° until done. This is a wonderful recipe.

❧ *It is particularly good with chicken or pork, and any vegetable.*

Testing Notes: *You may use sharp Cheddar cheese.*

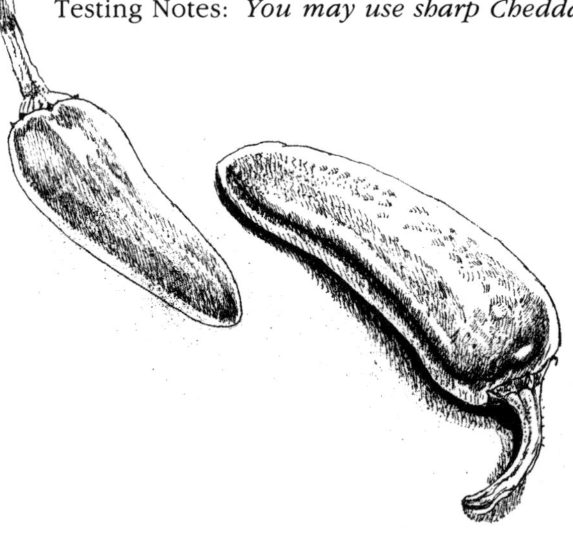

Ms. Janet Shipman—Westford, MA
Donation to: The Children's Hospital League Corp., Boston, MA

Pumpkin Bread

Being a very busy professional, I am always looking for ways to cook and preserve breads so I have them for special events—planned or unplanned. This recipe has evolved over the years and it is great because of its versatility. It's good any time of the day and makes a great gift. It also is a great way for me to use my empty one-pound coffee cans which are not only a perfect size for cooking breads, but are also excellent for storing them.

INGREDIENTS

⅔ cup *butter*
2⅔ cups *sugar*
4 *eggs*
1 can *(16 ounce) pumpkin*
⅔ cup *water*
3⅓ cups *flour*
½ teaspoon *baking powder*
2 teaspoons *baking soda*
1½ teaspoons *salt*
1 teaspoon *cinnamon*
1 teaspoon *ground clove*
1 cup *chopped walnuts*
1 cup *raisins*

DIRECTIONS

Cream butter and sugar until fluffy; add eggs, pumpkin, and water. Sift flour, baking powder, soda, salt, and spices; add to pumpkin mixture. Stir in nuts and raisins. Grease and flour 3 one-pound coffee cans; pour the mixture inside. Bake 1 hour at 350°. For best flavor, bake 2 days before using. Cover cans with plastic coffee can lids to keep bread fresh. Freezes well.

Lovey Kaplan—Beverly Hills, CA
Donation to: Amie Karen Cancer Fund for Children
M. Freedman, Beverly Hills, CA

Roasty-Toasty Cheese and Onion Bread

The first time I tasted this bread was at a friend's house. The recipe was given to her by another friend who, in turn, found this recipe in a newspaper.

INGREDIENTS

2 tablespoons *plus* **1 teaspoon** *corn-oil margarine*

1½ cups *chopped onions*

2 *egg whites*

½ cup *light sour cream*

⅛ teaspoon *freshly ground black pepper*

2 cups *unbleached flour*

1 tablespoon *baking powder*

1 cup *shredded Cheddar cheese (20% fat-free)*

⅔ cup *nonfat milk*

3 tablespoons *minced fresh parsley*

DIRECTIONS

Melt 1 teaspoon margarine in skillet over medium flame. Sauté onions until translucent; allow them to cool slightly. Add egg whites, sour cream, and pepper; mix well and put aside. Combine flour and baking powder in a mixing bowl. Cut in remaining margarine with fork until very crumbly. Stir in ½ cup cheese. Add milk and stir to make soft dough. Pat dough into a 9-inch-square pan which has been sprayed with a nonstick vegetable coating. Spread sour cream mixture on top. Sprinkle remaining cheese and parsley on top. Bake 25 minutes at 425°. Cut bread into squares and serve immediately. **Serves 8 to 10.**

❧ *Serve with a salad during a good football game!*

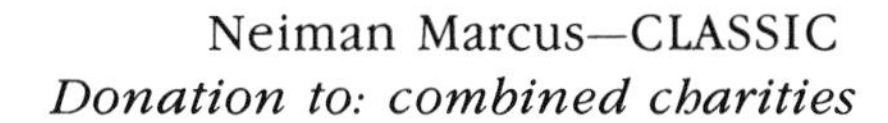

Neiman Marcus—CLASSIC
Donation to: combined charities

Monkey Bread

This was the late Helen Corbitt's hit contribution to the opening of The Mariposa restaurant (now THE NM CAFE), when Neiman Marcus opened at the Houston Galleria in 1967.

INGREDIENTS

1½ *cakes of compressed yeast*
1 cup *scalded milk*
4 tablespoons *sugar*
1 teaspoon *salt*
½ cup *butter, melted plus melted butter for dipping*
3½ cups *flour, sifted*

DIRECTIONS

Preheat oven to 400°. Place yeast and scalded lukewarm milk in a large bowl. When yeast is dissolved, stir in sugar, salt, and ½ cup butter. Add flour and beat well. Cover. Let dough rise to almost double, which will take about an hour. Punch down and roll out on a lightly floured board to ¼-inch thickness. Cut into 2½-inch-long diamond-shaped pieces. Dip each piece in melted butter. Arrange in a 9-inch ring mold until ring mold is half-full. Let dough rise again until doubled. Bake 30 minutes until brown. Dough may be frozen, before baking, for later use.
Serves 12.

Neiman Marcus—THE NM CAFE Galleria, Houston
Donation to: combined charities

Mushroom Spoon Bread

A brunch centered around this tempting dish would make any hostess' reputation.

INGREDIENTS

1½ cups *milk*
1 can *(10½ ounce) cream of mushroom soup*
1 cup *yellow corn meal*
4 *eggs, separated*
2 tablespoons *butter*

DIRECTIONS

Mix milk and soup in a saucepan. Add corn meal and cook slowly, stirring constantly until the consistency of mush. Beat egg yolks; add yolks and butter to saucepan. Beat egg whites until stiff and fold into mixture. Bake 1 hour in a greased casserole in a preheated oven 350°. Spoon bread is ready when the top springs back at the touch of your finger.

Karen Green—Irvine, CA
Donation to: Mother's Against Drunk Driving, Santa Ana, CA

Annie's Banana Bread

When my 17-year-old son was in first grade, his teacher asked him to draw a picture of a bowl of fruit. The teacher asked what the long, black piece was. "Banana," he replied. "But, bananas," she said, "are yellow." "Not in my house!" he answered. All three of my children love the following recipe for banana bread. It is soft and moist to eat, and so simple to make. When the bananas become black on the outside, they are perfect for baking bread.

INGREDIENTS

3 *ripe or overripe bananas (4, if small)*
1 cup *sugar*
1 *egg, room temperature*
1 1/2 cups *all-purpose flour*
1/4 cup *melted butter*
1 teaspoon *baking soda*
1 teaspoon *salt*

DIRECTIONS

Mash bananas in a large mixing bowl. Stir in other ingredients. Lightly grease and flour one 8 x 5-inch loaf pan (or two 8-inch-round cake pans.) Pour batter into pan. Bake in preheated 325° oven until done: 60 to 80 minutes for a single loaf or 45 to 55 minutes for round pans. Test for doneness with a toothpick. Cool in pan 5 minutes; turn out on rack to cool completely. **Yields 1 loaf or 2 rounds.**

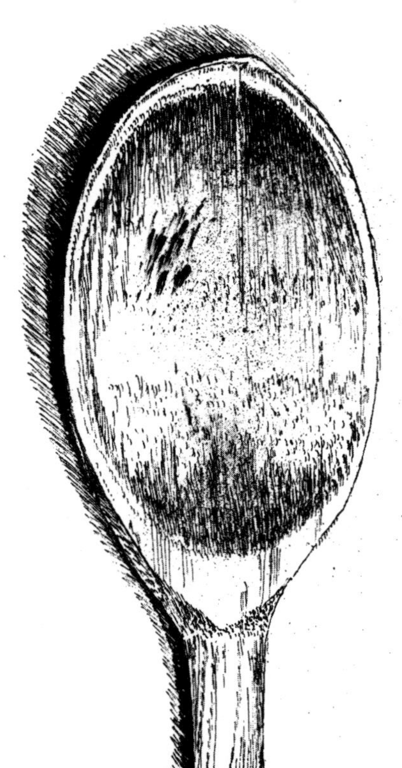

Susan E. Slesinger—Lakewood, CA
Donation to: Community Rehabilitation Industries, Long Beach, CA

Low-Sugar Winter Muffins

I try to restrict my family's intake of sugar. I was experimenting with adapting standard muffin recipes, using ingredients which I had on hand in the store cupboard and freezer, when I hit upon these wonderful muffins. For fun, I make them in a dinosaur muffin pan for my 7-year-old.

INGREDIENTS

- **3/4 cup** *all-purpose flour*
- **3/4 cup** *whole-wheat pastry flour*
- **3 tablespoons** *dark brown sugar*
- **2 teaspoons** *baking powder*
- **1/8 teaspoon** *ground clove*
- **1/2 teaspoon** *cinnamon*
- **1/4 teaspoon** *salt*
- **1** *large egg*
- **1/2 cup** *frozen apple juice concentrate, thawed and undiluted*
- **6 tablespoons** *margarine, melted*
- **4 ounces** *mixed dried fruit, diced*

DIRECTIONS

Preheat oven to 375°. Line 8 muffin cups with paper liners. Mix flours, sugar, baking powder, cloves, cinnamon, and salt in a large bowl. In a small bowl, whisk together egg, apple juice concentrate, and margarine until well-blended. Fold this mixture into the dry ingredients until just blended. Stir in the mixed dried fruit until just blended. Divide mixture into muffin cups and bake 15 to 20 minutes until lightly browned. Cool muffins on a rack before removing them from pan.

❧ *Serve with skim-milk ricotta cheese or yogurt, and herb tea or cappuccino.*

Mrs. Joel T. Broyhill—Arlington, VA
Donation to: Wolf Trap Foundation for the Performing Arts, Vienna, VA

Mimi's Bran Muffins

My mother learned this from her Amish mother.

INGREDIENTS

2 cups *boiling water*
6 cups *all-bran cereal*
1 cup *oil*
4 *eggs, beaten*
3 cups *sugar*
1 quart *buttermilk*
5 cups *all-purpose flour*
5 teaspoons *baking soda*
2 teaspoons *salt*
24 ounces *apple butter*
2 cups *chopped walnuts (optional)*
2 cups *raisins (optional)*

DIRECTIONS

Pour boiling water over 2 cups of bran. Add oil. Mix and set aside. Mix together beaten eggs, sugar, buttermilk, and the remaining bran—in that order. Sift flour with soda and salt. Combine bran mixtures with flour mixture. Stir in apple butter, walnuts, and raisins. Bake in greased muffin tins 15 to 20 minutes at 400°. Mixture keeps 6 weeks in refrigerator. Muffins freeze well. **Makes 6 dozen.**

❧ *Serve with a hearty breakfast or brunch.*

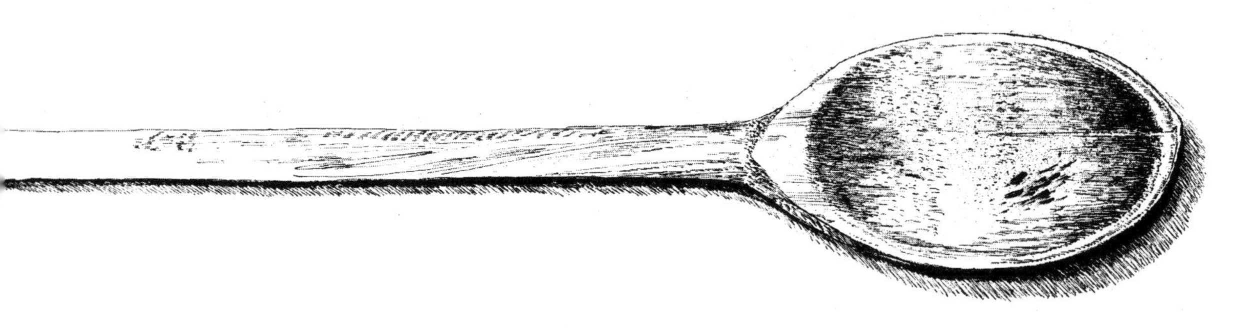

CHAPTER TWELVE

Desserts

No eleven-calorie gelatin here. It's obvious InCirclers subscribe to the European approach: dessert should be for special occasions and uncompromised in richness. We had to lock the kitchen doors while we tested these. Don't miss one recipe that's the epitome of *Pure & Simple*—homemade peach ice cream—a family favorite of former first lady, Lady Bird Johnson. Chocoholics take note: there are at least a half-dozen new ideas for you, including one just called Glop.

Mrs. Frank J. Bush, Jr.—St. Louis, MO
Donation to: American Cancer Society, Inc., St. Louis, MO

Blackberry Cake with Seven-Minute Frosting

This is from my grandmother. The frosting was named before electric beaters, so, if you use an electric mixer, beat only 4 minutes.

INGREDIENTS

- **½ cup** *butter*
- **2 cups** *sugar*
- **3** *egg yolks*
- **1½ cups** *cake flour*
- **½ teaspoon** *salt*
- **1 teaspoon** *baking powder*
- **1 teaspoon** *nutmeg*
- **1 teaspoon** *cinnamon*
- **1 teaspoon** *allspice*
- **3 tablespoons** *sour cream*
- **5 egg** *whites*
- **1 cup** *fresh blackberries (if canned, drain berries)*
- **2 teaspoons** *vanilla*
- **½ teaspoon** *cream of tartar*
- **2 tablespoons** *light corn syrup*
- **3 tablespoons** *water*

DIRECTIONS

Cream butter and 1 cup sugar; add egg yolks and beat. Sift flour, ¼ teaspoon salt, baking powder, nutmeg, cinnamon, and allspice. Add to creamed mixture along with sour cream. Beat 3 egg whites until very stiff. Fold egg whites, blackberries, and 1 teaspoon vanilla into batter. Pour batter into 2 prepared 9x9-inch cake pans. Bake 25 to 30 minutes in 350° oven. Cool on racks. Combine remaining sugar, egg whites, salt, and vanilla with the cream of tartar, corn syrup, and water. Place in top of double boiler. Set aside. Fill bottom half of a double boiler with water and bring to a boil. Remove from flame. Immediately set top of double boiler over the bottom half; beat ingredients 4 minutes. Spread icing between the layers, on the top, and on the sides of cake. **Makes one 2-layer cake.**

Testing Notes: *Add cream of tartar to egg whites and beat until very stiff. Gently fold in egg whites and blackberries.*

Sue Willhoit—Carlsbad, NM
Donation to: Carlsbad Association for Retarded Citizens Farm, Inc., Carlsbad, NM

Chocolate Cake

You will toss out all your other chocolate dessert recipes after tasting this one—it is exquisite. I serve this at every party I have. Everyone loves it.

INGREDIENTS

4 sticks *oleo*
4 *eggs*
2 cups *granulated sugar*
½ cup *plus* **⅓ cup** *cocoa*
1½ cups *flour*
1 tablespoon *plus* **1 teaspoon** *vanilla*
¼ teaspoon *salt*
2 cups *chopped nuts*
½ cup *evaporated milk*
1 box *powdered sugar*
1 jar *(7 ounce) marshmallow creme*

DIRECTIONS

Mix 2 sticks oleo, eggs, granulated sugar, ½ cup cocoa, flour, 1 tablespoon vanilla, salt, and 1 cup chopped nuts. Blend well. Bake 30 to 35 minutes at 350° in a greased cookie sheet. Meanwhile, stir and cook evaporated milk and the remaining butter and cocoa. Cook about 1 minute. Combine powdered sugar, 1 teaspoon vanilla, and remaining nuts in a bowl. Add milk mixture. Mix well. (I use the food processor.) Set frosting aside. Remove cake from oven and cool 10 minutes. Spread marshmallow creme over the cake. Spread the frosting over the marshmallow creme. **Serves 10 to 12.**

Testing Notes: *We suggest baking it in a 9 x 13-inch pan instead of on a cookie sheet.*

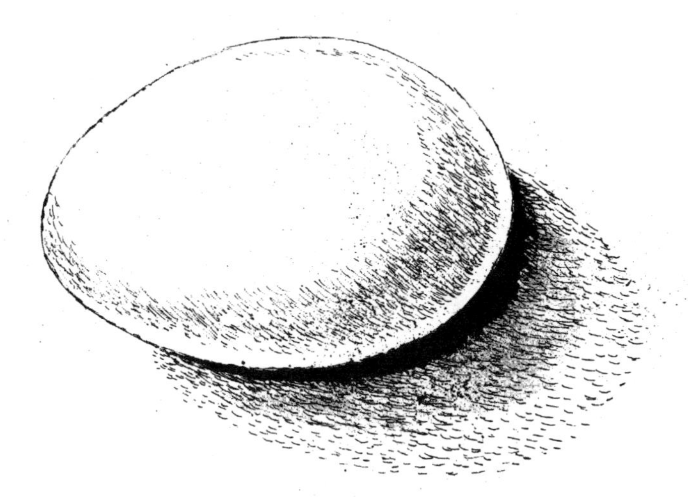

Selene (Mrs. Marvin) Ganek—Glencoe, IL
Donation to: Highland Park Hospital Foundation, Highland Park, IL (Social Services)

Chocolate Chip Bundt®

The quintessential chocolate chip abounds in this delicious cake recipe from my early days as a baker. It's simple to prepare, looks beautiful, and freezes well.

INGREDIENTS

- **3/4 cup** *unsalted butter*
- **3/4 cup** *granulated sugar*
- **1 cup** *light brown sugar, firmly packed*
- **3** *eggs*
- **1 1/2 teaspoons** *vanilla extract*
- **1 1/2 cups** *semisweet chocolate chips*
- **1 1/2 teaspoons** *baking soda*
- **1 1/2 cups** *sour cream*
- **3 cups** *sifted cake flour*
- *Confectioners' sugar*

DIRECTIONS

Heat oven to 350°. Grease and lightly flour a 10-to 12-cup BUNDT® pan. Cream butter with both sugars until light and fluffy. Add eggs, one at a time, beating thoroughly after each addition. Add vanilla and chocolate chips. Beat just until blended. Dissolve baking soda into sour cream and add, alternately, with flour, beginning and ending with flour. Pour into prepared pan and bake 1 hour. Test with cake tester or toothpick. Cake should be golden brown, dry on top, and shrink from sides of pan when done. Cool on wire rack 30 minutes. Invert to finish cooling. Sprinkle generously with confectioners' sugar before serving. **Serves 10 to 12.**

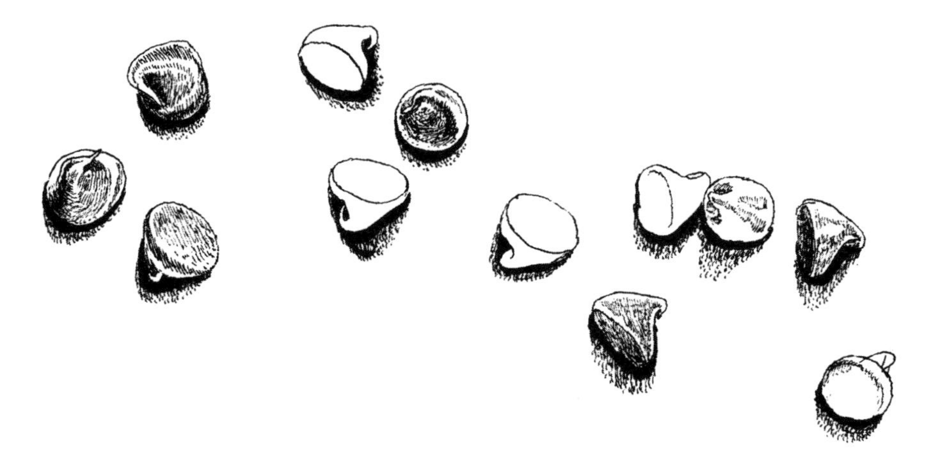

Dorothy Faye Holt Kimsey—Midland, TX
Donation to: Cook-Fort Worth Children's Medical Center, Fort Worth, TX

Hummingbird Cake

This old recipe goes back before my mother's time. We had it every Christmas.

INGREDIENTS

3 cups *all-purpose flour*
2 cups *sugar*
1 teaspoon *baking soda*
1 teaspoon *salt*
1 teaspoon *ground cinnamon*
3 *eggs, beaten*
1 cup *vegetable oil*
2½ teaspoons *vanilla*
1 can *(8 ounce) crushed pineapple, undrained*
2 *ripe bananas, chopped*
1½ cups *chopped pecans*
1 package *(8 ounce) cream cheese, softened*
½ cup *butter, softened*
1 package *(16 ounce) powdered sugar, sifted*

DIRECTIONS

Combine flour, sugar, soda, salt, and cinnamon in large bowl. Add eggs and oil, stirring until dry ingredients are moist. Do not beat. Stir in 1½ teaspoons vanilla, pineapple, bananas, and 1 cup pecans. Spoon batter into 3 greased and floured 9-inch pans. Bake 25 to 30 minutes at 350°. Use toothpick to test. Cool in pan for at least 10 minutes. Remove from pan and cool completely. Combine cream cheese and butter, beating until smooth. Add powdered sugar and remaining vanilla; beat until light. Spread frosting between layers, on the top, and on the sides of cake. Sprinkle ½ cup chopped pecans on top. **Makes one 3-layer cake.**

Edna Marie Allen—Shreveport, LA
Donation to: Shreveport Symphony Society, Shreveport, LA

Individual Nut Cakes

Every Christmas my late husband's mother's cook made a delicious Nut Cake for us, but Bill rarely allowed me to serve it to guests because he loved it so much. One year, I asked his mother for the recipe for a Christmas party I was having, but she flatly refused! So, I concocted my own version of the recipe, baked and served them in small red, green, silver, and gold foil cupcake wrappers; and they were a big hit with Bill and all our friends. For years, I've baked them as gifts. Please note, this is not a fruit cake.

INGREDIENTS

1½ boxes *(22 ounces, approximately) white raisins*

Bourbon whiskey

2 cups *sugar*

6 *eggs yolks*

2 cups *butter*

4 cups *flour*

1 teaspoon *baking powder*

4 cups *pecans, coarsely chopped*

6 *egg whites*

DIRECTIONS

Examine raisins carefully; discard any dark ones and discard stems from the good ones. Pour bourbon over raisins, just to cover. Let soak overnight. Next day, cream sugar and egg yolks well. Melt butter and cool; add to sugar and yolks. Sift flour before measuring, then sift with baking powder. Add to creamed mixture. Add raisins and 3½ cups of bourbon. Shake pecans in a paper bag containing a small amount of flour. Add floured pecans to batter. Whip egg whites stiff and fold into batter until well-blended. Pour batter into small, fluted paper muffin liners, filling a little more than half full. Bake 20 to 25 minutes at 325°. Cool well and store in tightly covered tins. With a teaspoon, drip extra bourbon on each cake every 2 or 3 days. This is not necessary, but the cake tastes that much better. **Makes 60 individual cakes.**

Cathy Taylor Reppenhagen—East Greenbush, NY
Donation to: Schenectady Civic Playhouse Theater, Schenectady, NY

Knobly Apple Cake

This recipe came from my great-grandmother, whom I knew. It is an old farm recipe from Chenango County, New York. Five years ago, I entered the dessert in a small apple festival and won second prize. My children found great humor in the fact I won a $25 gift certificate and the dish I purchased to put it in cost $45. They also found humor in the fact that even though I don't often cook, I would enter a cooking contest. However, my grandmother was very proud of my ribbon because she was the one who actually gave me the recipe in a book twenty-four years ago.

INGREDIENTS

1/4 cup *shortening*
1 cup *sugar*
1 *egg*
3 cups *peeled and diced apples*
1/4 cup *chopped walnuts*
1 teaspoon *vanilla*
1 cup *flour*
1/2 teaspoon *cinnamon*
1/2 teaspoon *baking powder*
1/2 teaspoon *baking soda*
1/2 teaspoon *salt*
1/2 teaspoon *nutmeg*

DIRECTIONS

Cream shortening, sugar, and egg together. Add all other ingredients. Place in an 8-inch greased pan. Bake 45 minutes at 350°. **Makes one 8-inch layer cake.**

❧ *Serve hot or cold with ice cream on top, or serve plain.*

Testing Notes: *Add 1/4 cup coconut and 1/4 cup finely chopped raisins for a heartier cake.*

Amy Davenport—Dallas, TX
Donation to: American Diabetes Association, Dallas, TX

Mom's Almond Pound Cake

"Pound Cake" could be the Davenports' middle name, for it is a favorite of ours. In fact, we have three or four recipes that cannot be surpassed, which have been passed down through several generations. I remember one day when we were young, Mom decided to come up with the ultimate cake; and after combining and testing ingredients from our favorite cake recipes, she came up with this original. It tastes divine and is pure and simple!

INGREDIENTS

2 sticks *butter*

2½ cups *sugar*

6 *eggs*

3 cups *cake flour (sift before measuring)*

1 cup *sour cream*

⅛ teaspoon *baking soda*

1½ tablespoons *almond extract*

½ teaspoon *salt*

Powdered sugar

DIRECTIONS

Preheat oven to 325°. Grease and flour tube pan (or 2 loaf pans). Cream butter and sugar thoroughly. Add eggs, one at a time, beating thoroughly after each addition. Add flour, alternately, with ¾ cup sour cream. Dissolve baking soda in ¼ cup sour cream; add to batter and blend well. Add extract and salt. Stir. Bake in pan for 1 hour and 5 minutes. Cool 20 minutes and remove from pan. Sift powdered sugar over warm cake. **Serves 10 to 12.**

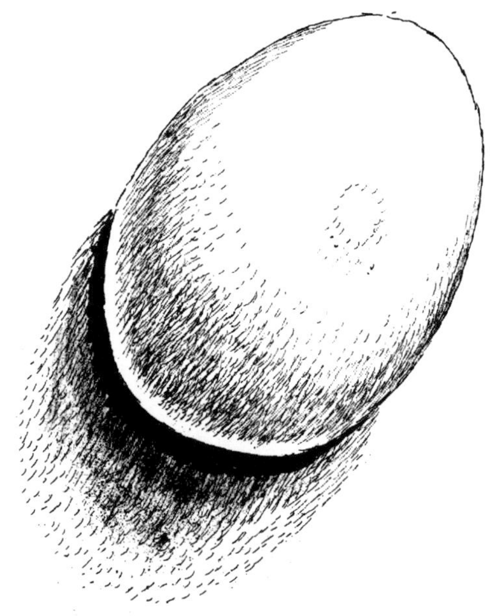

Jo Terrill West—Wichita Falls, TX
Donation to: Alzheimer's Association, Inc., Chicago, IL

Prune Cake

This was my mother's (Mabel Terrill's) recipe. She was a good cook—I'm not—but this is so easy even I can make it! When I take it to someone who hasn't had it before, sometimes I call it a spice cake since some people are turned off by prunes—especially in a cake. It stays good and moist for days.

INGREDIENTS

2 cups *sugar*
1 cup *WESSON® oil*
3 *eggs*
1 cup *cooked prunes*
1 cup *nuts*
2 cups *flour*
½ teaspoon *salt*
1 teaspoon *baking soda*
1 teaspoon *cinnamon*
1 teaspoon *allspice*
1 teaspoon *nutmeg*
1 teaspoon *cloves*
1 cup *buttermilk*

DIRECTIONS

Mix together sugar and oil. Add eggs, prunes, and nuts. Sift together remaining dry ingredients. Mix flour mixture into prune mixture, alternately, with buttermilk. Pour into greased and floured BUNDT® cake pan. Bake about 1 hour at 350°. **Serves 10 to 12.**

❧ *It's great as a snack or as dessert with coffee.*

Testing Notes: *This may also be served as a breakfast bread, as well as a dessert with a whipped cream topping.*

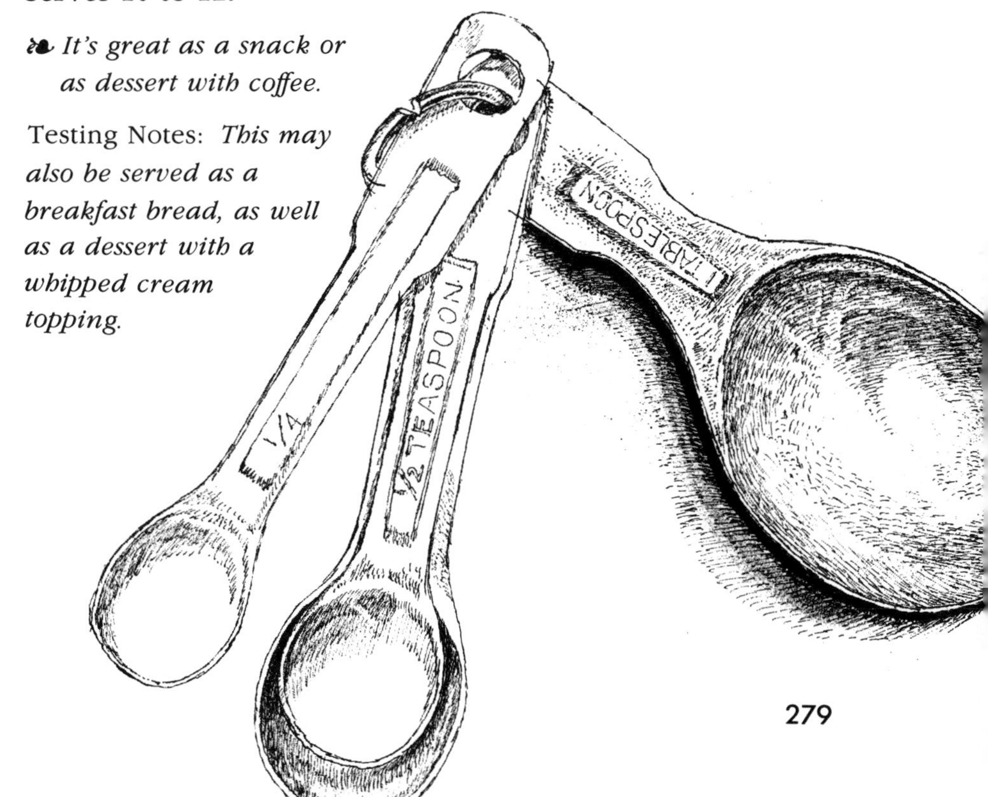

Mrs. Ernest J. Colant—San Francisco, CA
Donation to: Alzheimer's Association, Inc., Palo Alto, CA

Walnut Slice Cake

My mother, Edith Horner, guarded this recipe for over eighty years, and was famous for it in Santa Barbara. Now, it is treasured by her family, including great-granddaughters. We believe good things should be shared.

INGREDIENTS

1 cup *plus* **2 teaspoons** *flour*
½ cup *butter*
Cold water
2 *egg yolks, beaten*
1½ cups *brown sugar*
1 teaspoon *vanilla*
1 teaspoon *baking powder*
1 teaspoon *salt*
1 cup *coconut*
1 cup *finely chopped walnuts*
2 *egg whites, beaten*

DIRECTIONS

Thoroughly mix 1 cup flour and the butter with a few drops of cold water. Spread on the bottom of an 8-inch-square pan. Combine beaten egg yolks, sugar, vanilla, baking powder, 2 teaspoons flour, salt, coconut, and walnuts in a mixing bowl, stirring well. Gently fold in egg whites. Pour this mixture over dough and bake 35 minutes in a moderate 325° oven until done. When cake is completely cooled, prepare a butter icing and spread thinly over the top of the cake. Cut into small squares when cold.

Makes 16 squares.

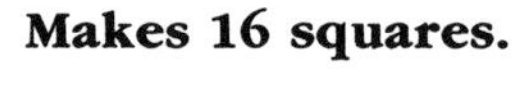

Brady White—Los Angeles, CA
Donation to: Children's Medical Center of Dallas, Dallas, TX

North Pole Pumpkin Cookies

Our "Santa to the Stars" (and InCircler) swears this cookie recipe "was left on Christmas Eve with a note to Santa explaining that the maid was off that day." (Ah, Christmas in Beverly Hills.)

INGREDIENTS

½ cup *raw sugar*
1 cup *brown sugar*
1 cup *plus* **3 tablespoons** *butter or margarine*
1 cup *canned pumpkin*
1 teaspoon *vanilla*
1 *egg*
2 cups *flour*
1 teaspoon *baking powder*
1 teaspoon *baking soda*
1 teaspoon *cinnamon*
1 teaspoon *pumpkin pie spice*
¼ teaspoon *salt*
1 cup *chocolate chips*
¼ cup *milk*
2 cups *powdered milk*

DIRECTIONS

Mix raw sugar, ½ cup brown sugar, and 1 cup butter; set aside. Mix pumpkin, vanilla, and egg; set aside. Stir together the flour, baking powder, baking soda, cinnamon, pumpkin pie spice, and salt. Combine the sugar, pumpkin, and flour mixtures; blend well. Stir in chocolate chips. Spray cookie sheets with PAM®. Drop by teaspoonfuls on cookie sheet and bake 10 to 12 minutes at 350°. In a saucepan, stir remaining butter and the remaining brown sugar; heat until thickened. Cool 10 minutes. Add milk and beat. Add powdered sugar a little at a time. Let glaze set 5 minutes to thicken. Spread on top of cooled pumpkin cookies. **Makes 4 dozen.**

Lenore J. Morris—Rolla, MO
Donation to: Alzheimer's Association, Inc., St. Louis, MO

Calla Lily Cookies

This is my most treasured recipe. It was given to me by an aunt from Chicago in the late forties with the understanding that I would not share it with anyone in the town where I lived. For that reason, it became an albatross around my neck; because if I served it, everyone wanted the recipe. That made me uncomfortable. So, for many years I avoided making this very special dessert. Now, I give it to anyone who asks, and some who don't.

INGREDIENTS

2 *egg whites*
2 *egg yolks*
1 cup *light brown sugar*
6 tablespoons *all-purpose flour*
1 cup *finely chopped pecans*
1 teaspoon *vanilla*
½ cup *heavy cream, sweetened and whipped*

DIRECTIONS

Beat egg whites until they form stiff peaks. Set aside. Clean mixer and beaters. Beat egg yolks until light yellow. Add sugar to yolks and beat long and hard. Remove from mixer and fold in egg whites, flour, pecans, and vanilla. Thoroughly grease and flour large baking sheets. Allow space for only 4 or 5 cookies per sheet. Drop batter with a tablespoon, allowing plenty of room for each cookie. Bake 10 to 12 minutes at 350° until very slightly browned on edges and bottom. Remove from oven. Working quickly, roll each cookie into a cone. Cool completely. Whip the cream; sweeten to taste. Unroll cooled cookies and fill with 1 tablespoon of whipped cream per cookie. If cookies are too brittle, place in slightly warm oven to soften. Refrigerate overnight at least 6 to 8 hours. Unfilled cookie shells freeze well. **Makes about 12.**

Melinda G. Jayson—Dallas, TX
Donation to: American Cancer Society, Inc., Dallas, TX

Pecan Icebox Cookies

The pecan icebox cookies have been made by my mother for years, and they are so easy. I can make them while doing other things.

INGREDIENTS

½ cup *brown sugar*
½ cup *white sugar*
2 sticks *butter or margarine*
1 *egg*
2 ½ cups *flour*
½ teaspoon *baking powder*
1 teaspoon *vanilla*
1 cup *finely chopped pecans*

DIRECTIONS

Cream sugars and butter together. Add egg, flour, baking powder, and vanilla. Divide dough in half and roll each out on wax paper. Sprinkle pecans over dough, roll up, wrap in wax paper, and refrigerate overnight or several hours. When well-chilled, slice dough ⅛-to ¼-inch-thick. Bake 15 minutes in a 350° preheated oven. If they are not lightly browned, bake another 5 minutes. **Makes 2 dozen.**

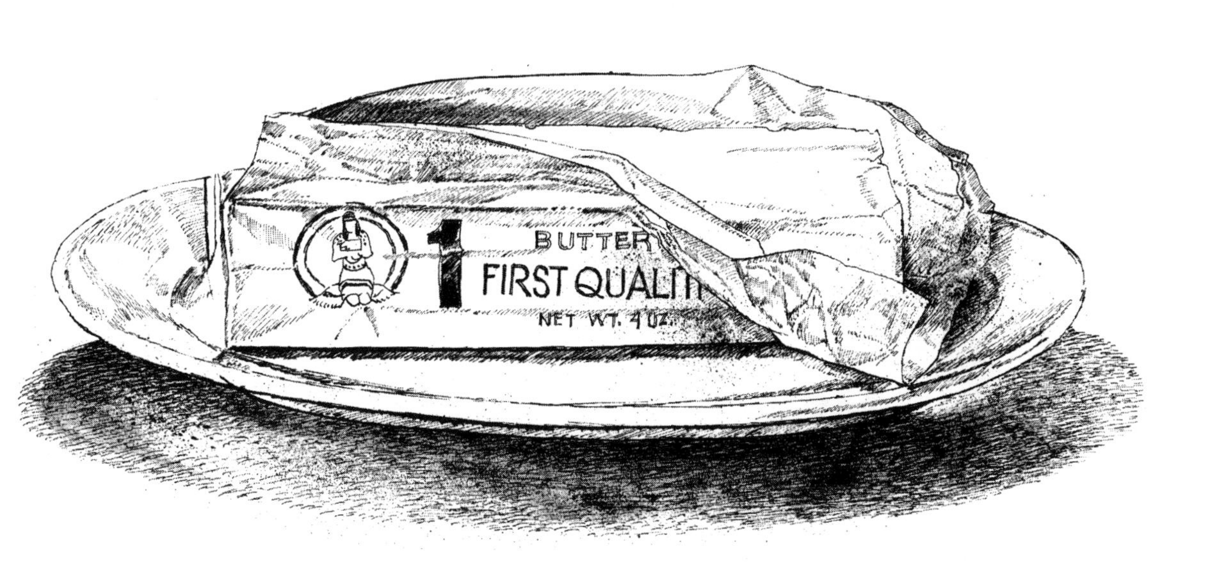

Joyce Konigsberg—Ross, CA
Donation to: National Neurofibromatosis Foundation, New York, NY

Chocolate Joycies

This is adapted from a neighbor's recipe which took second place at the San Francisco County Fair. It won a contest for Best Overall Cookie at my previous place of employment: they were well received and consumed.

INGREDIENTS

2 ounces *unsweetened chocolate*

12 ounces *semisweet chocolate, (TOBLER® or LINDT®)*

¼ cup *sifted flour*

¼ teaspoon *baking powder*

½ teaspoon *salt*

3 ounces *(¾ stick) sweet butter*

2 *large eggs*

¾ cup *sugar*

2 teaspoons *vanilla*

DIRECTIONS

Preheat oven to 350°. Cover 2 large cookie sheets with foil. Break 6 ounces of chocolate into chunks and set aside. Sift dry ingredients and set aside. Melt together butter and remaining chocolate. Beat eggs, sugar, and vanilla on high-speed until foamy. Add chocolate mixture and continue beating. Stir in dry ingredients. Stir in chocolate chunks. Drop 12 well-rounded tablespoons of batter per cookie sheet. Bake 12 to 13 minutes. Cool on racks. **Makes 2 dozen.**

Charles and Helen Nixon—Dallas, TX
Donation to: Trinity Ministry to the Poor, Dallas, TX

Grandmother's Sugar Cookies

Everybody has a favorite sugar cookie, but these are part of Charles' family heritage and are called for at every special occasion. They are crisp, extremely buttery, and coated with enough sugar to make a real mess when you eat them!

INGREDIENTS

1 ½ cups *flour*
1 teaspoon *cream of tartar*
Pinch of baking soda
1 cup *sugar*
1 ½ sticks *butter*
1 *egg*
1 teaspoon *vanilla*

DIRECTIONS

Combine flour, cream of tartar, and baking soda; set aside. Cream the sugar and butter. Add egg and vanilla, mixing well. Stir flour mixture into the butter mixture. (You may chill the dough to eliminate excessive flour being used in the rolling process.) Roll on a lightly floured surface, cut into shapes, and dust with sugar. Bake on an oiled cookie sheet 20 minutes at 350°. After removing from the oven, place cookies on a large paper bag. Cover with sugar while they cool. Store in an airtight container. **Makes about 2 dozen.**

❧ *Serve with champagne or milk.*

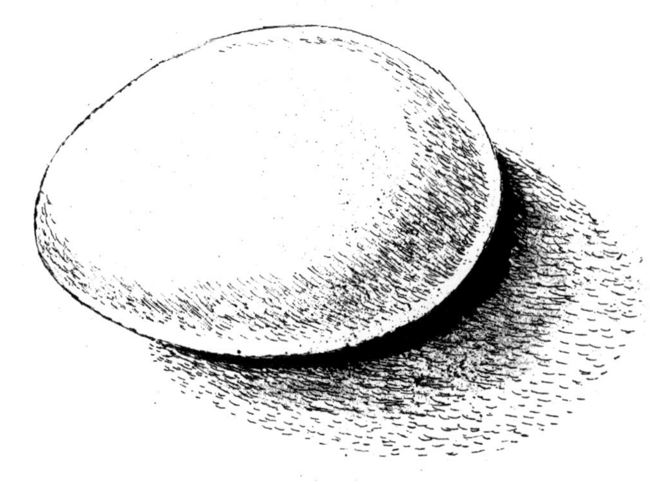

Madlyn Daniel—Chicago, IL
Donation to: Hospice-VNSW, White Plains, NY

Tiramisu

This is a successful recipe, which I've made numerous times.

INGREDIENTS

4 *large egg yolks*

1 cup *superfine sugar*

1 cup *crème fraîche or mascarpone*

1 cup *whole-milk ricotta cheese*

1 cup *well-chilled heavy cream*

3 tablespoons *cognac or other brandy*

48 *ladyfingers*

1 cup *strong coffee*

1 ½ teaspoons *unsweetened cocoa powder*

DIRECTIONS

Beat yolks with electric mixer. Add sugar, a little at a time, and beat mixture until thick and pale. In a small bowl, beat crème fraîche and ricotta cheese with an electric mixer until mixture holds soft peaks. In a chilled bowl, beat heavy cream until it holds soft peaks. Fold crème fraîche mixture and whipped cream gently into the yolk mixture. Fold in cognac. Dip ladyfingers into the coffee and arrange on bottom of serving dish. (The size of pan will determine how many ladyfingers are in each layer. Before dipping them into the coffee, determine how many you need. I prefer using a loaf pan or a dish no wider than the length of 2 ladyfingers.) Spread cream mixture on ladyfingers. Repeat layering, ending with cream mixture on top. Chill overnight. This recipe tastes better when made a day or two ahead. Sift cocoa through a fine sieve over top before serving.

Richard F. Friedeman, Jr.—Chicago, IL
Donation to: American Cancer Society, Inc., Nutley, NJ

Apple Crêpes

There's no special story. I just like to spend my time experimenting in the kitchen.

INGREDIENTS

4 *medium-sized apples, peeled, cored, and sliced*
4 tablespoons *butter*
Juice of 1 lemon
Grated rind of 1 lemon
½ cup *sugar, or more depending upon tartness of apples*
¼ cup *cider*
8 *medium-sized crêpes*

DIRECTIONS

Sauté apples over medium heat in 3 tablespoons butter until softened. Add lemon juice and grated rind, ¼ cup sugar, and cider. Let liquid reduce slightly. Place crêpe in pan, put some apple mixture on crêpe, and fold over. Repeat with remaining crêpes and apples. Reserve sauce. Melt remaining butter and paint tops of crêpes with it. Sprinkle remaining sugar over crêpes. Bake 15 minutes in a preheated 400° oven. Serve with reserved sauce, allowing 2 crêpes per person. **Serves 4.**

Sue Zelickson—Minneapolis, MN
Donation to: Twin Cities Down's Syndrome Association, Minneapolis, MN

Grandma's Strawberry Jam

My grandmother made the best everything, but her jam was something I helped her with. I brought her the strawberries, the bigger the better. (Well up into his nineties her brother made jam too.)

INGREDIENTS

1 quart *fresh strawberries, stemmed*
3 cups *sugar*
½ *medium lemon, sliced*

DIRECTIONS

Rinse strawberries. Drain well. Cover strawberries with sugar; let stand 8 hours or overnight. Place in large saucepan with lemon slices, cook until thick, skimming off foam. (Test small amount for thickness by refrigerating.) Let cool completely. Spoon into sterile jar. Seal or cover with hot paraffin. **Makes 1 jar.**

❧ *Serve on toast, fresh bread, bagels, or buttermilk pancakes.*

Neiman Marcus—THE RESTAURANT Palo Alto
Donation to: combined charities

Cocoa Pink Cuplets

Restaurant Manager Richard Wilson says he's considering adding these delicious little morsels to the menu. They were always a family favorite at the Wilsons'.

INGREDIENTS

2 cups *flour*
1 tablespoon *cocoa*
1 teaspoon *salt*
3/4 cup *shortening*
1 1/4 cups *sugar*
2 *eggs, unbeaten*
1 teaspoon *vanilla*
1 teaspoon *baking soda*
1 cup *cold water*
Chocolate chips
Pecan pieces

DIRECTIONS

Sift the flour, cocoa, and salt twice. Set aside. In a large mixing bowl, cream shortening and gradually add the sugar. Add eggs and vanilla. Mix well. Combine baking soda and water in a separate bowl. Alternately, add the dry mixture and the liquid mixture to the creamed sugar, beginning and ending with the dry mixture. Fill muffin cups 1/2 full and sprinkle generously with chocolate chips and pecan pieces. Bake 20 to 25 minutes in a preheated 375° oven. **Makes 12 muffins.**

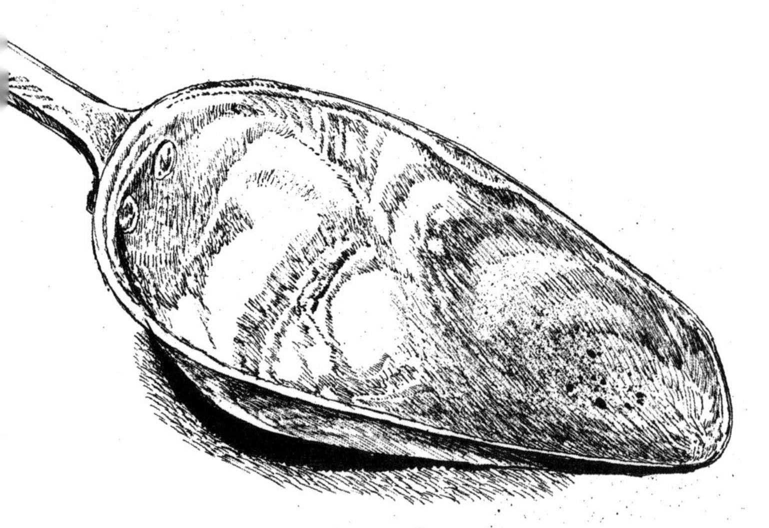

Lady Bird Johnson—Stonewall, TX
Donation to: National Wildflower Research Center, Austin, TX

Peach Ice Cream

If you were lucky enough to be invited to a summer dinner party at the LBJ Ranch on the banks of the Pedernales River, chances are this would be the dessert. The former first lady says, "made with our Stonewall peaches, this makes our favorite company dessert." If you're very lucky, maybe she will let you turn the crank.

INGREDIENTS

1 quart *heavy cream*
1 pint *milk*
3 *eggs*
1 cup *sugar*
½ gallon *soft peaches, mashed and well sweetened*

DIRECTIONS

Make a boiled custard of the cream, milk, eggs, and sugar. When cooled, add peaches. This **makes 1 gallon** of ice cream.

Mrs. John A. Harris—Potomac, MD
Donation to: Children's Hospital Foundation, Washington, D.C.

Glop

This came from my mother-in-law.

INGREDIENTS

24 *almond macaroons, dried and crumbled*
2 jiggers *bourbon whiskey*
1 package *(10 ounce) slivered almonds, blanched*
6 *HEATH® bars, crumbled*
2 quarts *coffee-flavored ice cream*

DIRECTIONS

Mix macaroons and bourbon together. Add almonds and HEATH® bars. Mix this with coffee ice cream and freeze. Before serving, top with crumbled HEATH® bars or shaved chocolate. Or, another variation is to line the bottom and sides of a springform pan with ladyfingers, add ice cream mixture and freeze. Unmold before serving.

❧ *Serve with lace cookies.*

Neiman Marcus—CLASSIC
Donation to: combined charities

Margarita Pie with Pretzel Crust

Another all-time favorite right out of the *Summer Suppers* recipe booklet and Bob Jones' repertoire.

INGREDIENTS

½ pound *corn-oil margarine*

2½ cups *(1 pound, 1 ounce package) pretzels*

⅛ cup *sugar*

3 quarts *vanilla ice cream, slightly thawed*

6 ounces *frozen limeade concentrate, thawed*

4 ounces *TEQUILA GOLD®*

1 ounce *COINTREAU® liqueur*

2 *whole limes, grated and juiced, plus* **1** *for garnish*

Fresh mint (optional)

DIRECTIONS

Melt margarine. Crush pretzels in food processor. Stir crushed pretzels and sugar into melted margarine. Mix well. Position mixture in two 9-inch pie pans, pressing firmly into sides and bottom of pans. Freeze 1 hour. Combine ice cream, limeade, tequila, COINTREAU®, grated lime peel, and lime juice in a mixer with a whip attachment. Whip at medium speed until well-mixed. Filling should be thick. Pile 5 heaping cups of filling into each crust. Freeze at least 4 hours until firm. Garnish pies with thin slices of lime, lime-peel curls, and fresh mint. **Makes two 9-inch pies.**

Patricia Renwick Lawler—Beverly Hills, CA
Donation to: American Cancer Society, Inc., Beverly Hills, CA

Auntie Chick's Lemon Cream Pie

My favorite aunt concocted this recipe. Every time I have this pie, I feel pampered, spoiled, indulged, and all sorts of good things.

INGREDIENTS

4 *egg yolks, beaten*
1 cup *sugar*
¼ teaspoon *salt*
½ cup *boiling water*
1 tablespoon *unflavored gelatin (1 envelope)*
¼ cup *cold water*
⅓ cup *lemon juice*
Grated rind of 1 lemon
4 *egg whites*
1 cup *heavy cream, whipped*
1 9-inch *deep-dish pie shell, baked*

DIRECTIONS

Beat egg yolks, ½ cup sugar, and salt until thoroughly combined. Put boiling water in top half of a simmering double boiler. Add egg yolk mixture and stir constantly until mixture thickens. Soften gelatin in cold water. Add to yolk mixture and stir until dissolved. Let cool until it begins to set. Stir in lemon juice and rind; continue to cool until thickened. Beat egg whites with remaining sugar and a pinch of salt until stiff peaks form. Whip cream. Fold egg whites into yolk mixture, then fold in whipped cream. Pour into baked pie shell. Cool. **Makes one 9-inch pie.**

Testing Notes: *Actually, this is more like a chiffon pie than a cream pie.*

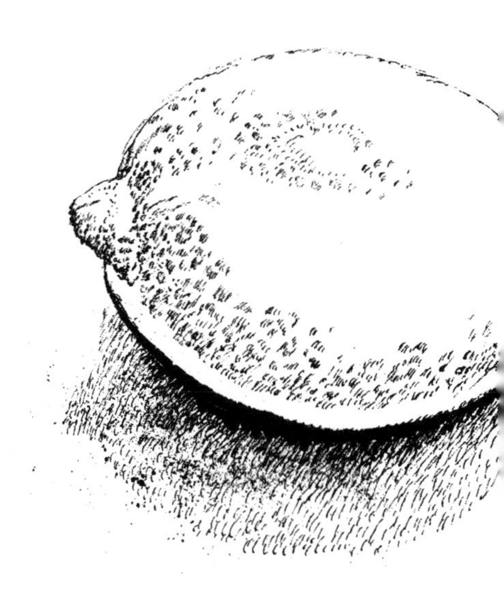

Nancie Wagner—Dallas, TX
Donation to: Dallas Easter Seal Society for Children, Dallas, TX

Best Key Lime Pie

I cut this recipe from a newspaper three or four years ago, and I've made it hundreds of times since. I'm known for my Key lime pie!

INGREDIENTS

5 tablespoons *butter, melted*

1 cup *WALKERS® shortbread cookies, crushed*

¼ cup *sugar*

½ cup *finely chopped macadamia nuts plus*
8 to 10 *macadamia nuts, coarsely chopped*

1 can *(14 ounce) BORDEN EAGLE® brand sweetened condensed milk*

4 *egg yolks*

1 package *(3 ounce) cream cheese*

½ cup *Key lime juice*

1 cup *heavy cream, whipped*

DIRECTIONS

Combine butter, cookies, sugar, and ½ cup macadamia nuts; press into a 9-inch pie plate. Put in freezer while making filling. Combine milk and egg yolks; add cream cheese. Slowly add lime juice. (I make this in the food processor.) Pour into chilled pie crust and refrigerate overnight. Top with whipped cream and 8 to 10 coarsely chopped macadamia nuts. Very rich. **Serves 8 to 10.**

Lois Jean MacFarlane—Kiawah Island, SC
Donation to: Save the River, Inc., Clayton, NY

Genora's Blueberry Pie

This is from my mother, Genora Hungerford, of Clayton, New York, who is now 93-years-old. I remember this recipe, and many more, as stand-bys for her luncheon and dinner parties. They have been mine for the past forty-four years.

INGREDIENTS

1 cup *sugar*

4 tablespoons *flour*

3 tablespoons *water*

1 quart *blueberries, cleaned and dried*

1 9-or 10-inch *deep-dish pie shell, baked*

DIRECTIONS

Cook sugar, flour, water, and ½ the blueberries until thickened. Put remaining berries into cooled pie shell. Pour boiling mixture over berries in pie shell. Chill and top with whipped cream. **Makes one 9-or 10-inch pie.**

Clarice Tinsley-Giles—Dallas, TX
Donation to: Sickle Cell Anemia Foundation of Dallas, Dallas, TX

Janet's Walnut-Coconut-Pumpkin Pie

The news anchor of KDFW-TV, Channel 4, tells us—"this yummy twist on an old favorite comes from my mother, Janet Tinsley." It's certainly a multi-flavored variation of the traditional holiday pie. Invite us for Thanksgiving soon, Clarice.

INGREDIENTS

- **1 can** *pumpkin pie filling (or homemade)*
- **1 9-inch** *deep-dish pie shell, unbaked*
- **½ cup** *chopped walnuts*
- **½ cup** *diced pineapple, drained*
- **½ cup** *finely shredded coconut*

DIRECTIONS

Prepare pumpkin pie filling, according to label directions. Combine walnuts, pineapple, and coconut with the pie filling. Blend well. Pour into pie shell. Bake 1 hour at 325°. **Makes one 9-inch pie.**

❧ *Serve plain or à la mode with ice cream, frozen yogurt, or whipped topping.*

Mrs. Robert R. Richardson—Atlanta, GA
Donation to: Shepherd Spinal Center, Atlanta, GA

Mystery Pecan Pie

It's a delicious, old family recipe from Georgia.

INGREDIENTS

- **1 package** *(8 ounce) cream cheese, softened*
- **⅓ cup** *plus* **¼ cup** *sugar*
- **2 teaspoons** *vanilla*
- **½ teaspoon** *salt*
- **4** *eggs*
- **1 9-or 10-inch** *deep-dish pie shell, unbaked*
- **1¼ cups** *chopped pecans*
- **1 cup** *light or dark corn syrup*

DIRECTIONS

Combine cream cheese, ⅓ cup sugar, 1 teaspoon vanilla, salt, and 1 egg. Pour into pie shell. Sprinkle with pecans. Combine remaining eggs, sugar, vanilla, and syrup. Pour carefully over pecans. Do not mix. Bake 40 to 45 minutes at 375° until center is firm. **Serves 6 to 8.**

❧ *Serve with whipped cream or vanilla ice cream on top.*

Neiman Marcus—THE RESTAURANT AND THE CLUBsm
Beverly Hills
Donation to: combined charities

Creamed Rice Pudding

Chef Roger Smith offers his own version of the ultimate comfort food.

INGREDIENTS

1 quart *half-and-half*
2 cups *heavy cream*
3/4 cup *long-grain white rice*
2/3 cup *sugar*
1/8 teaspoon *salt*
2 teaspoons *vanilla*
3 *egg yolks*
1/3 cup *raisins*
3 tablespoons *dark rum*
1 teaspoon *ground cinnamon*
1 teaspoon *almond extract*
Cinnamon sugar

DIRECTIONS

Combine the half-and-half and 1½ cups heavy cream in a large, heavy saucepan. Stir in rice, sugar, salt, and vanilla. Place pan over moderate heat and, stirring constantly, bring to a boil; but do not boil. Reduce heat to low and simmer, stirring frequently, for 35 minutes until as thick as oatmeal. Stir continuously for the last 10 minutes to avoid sticking. Remove pan from heat. Whisk egg yolks in a large bowl and gradually add about 1 cup of the pudding; then, add the remaining pudding. Stir in almond extract. Cover pudding with plastic wrap, placing the wrap directly on the pudding to prevent a skin from forming. Cool pudding, preferably overnight. Combine raisins and rum in a small bowl. Soak at least 1 hour, but preferably overnight. Whip remaining heavy cream until stiff. Carefully fold it into the chilled rice pudding. Drain raisins and spoon them into individual serving bowls. Sprinkle raisins with cinnamon; spoon in pudding. Top with cinnamon sugar and glaze under broiler until browned. **Serves 8 to 10.**

Linda McElroy Gibbons—Dallas, TX
Donation to: Children's Medical Center of Dallas, Dallas, TX

Clara's Chocolate Icebox Supreme

A dessert lover's downfall, this recipe will be cherished forever.

INGREDIENTS

1 package *(12 ounce) semisweet chocolate chips*
6 tablespoons *sugar*
1 stick *butter*
6 tablespoons *water*
6 *eggs, separated*
1 teaspoon *vanilla*
2 cups *whipping cream*
1 *large angel food cake*
½ cup *KAHLÚA® (optional)*
1 cup *sliced almonds, toasted*
½ cup *sliced maraschino cherries*

DIRECTIONS

Melt chocolate chips, sugar, butter, and water over hot water in double boiler. Blend well. Cool. Separate eggs. Beat egg yolks. Add to chocolate mixture. Beat egg whites until stiff. Fold egg whites into chocolate mixture. Add vanilla to mixture. Whip cream in separate bowl. Break cake into bite-sized pieces. In a silver or crystal bowl that has been buttered, layer as follows: cake, chocolate mixture, KAHLÚA®, whipped cream, and almonds. Repeat layers, ending with whipped cream. Decorate with almonds and cherries. Chill 6 to 8 hours or overnight. **Serves 8.**

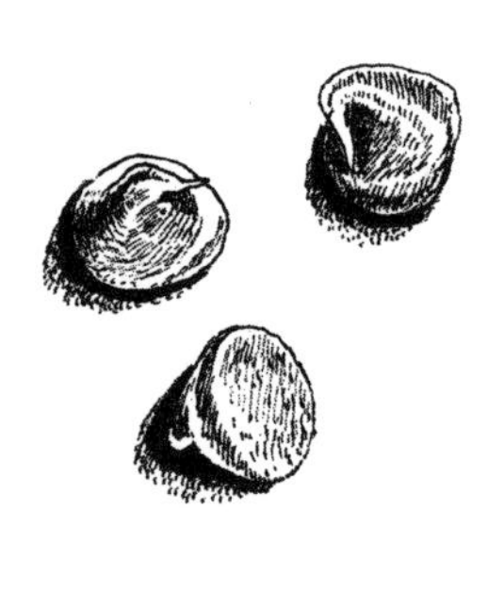

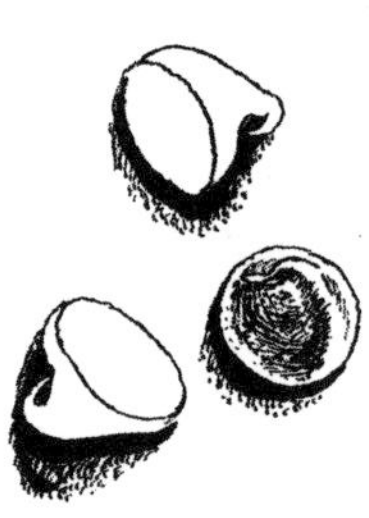

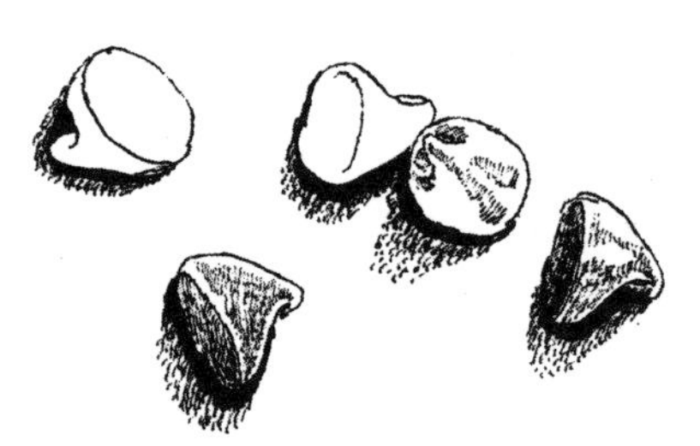

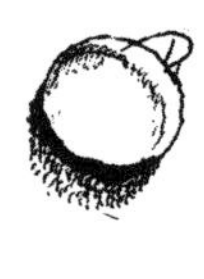

Betty Hochstadter—Northbrook, IL
Donation to: Lincoln Park Zoological Society, Chicago, IL

Gâteau au Chocolat

This is a lovely, very rich holiday dessert.

INGREDIENTS

- **14 ounces** *GHIRARDELLI® semisweet baking chocolate*
- **14 tablespoons** *unsalted butter*
- **1 1/2 cups** *sugar*
- **10** *egg yolks*
- **1 tablespoon** *GRAND MARNIER® liqueur*
- **1 teaspoon** *vanilla extract*
- **10** *egg whites*

DIRECTIONS

Butter and flour a 12-inch springform pan. Break chocolate into chunks and put in the top of double boiler along with the butter. Melt over simmering water, stirring occasionally. Stir 1 1/4 cups sugar into the melted chocolate mixture, and continue heating until the sugar is dissolved. Beat egg yolks in separate bowl. Beat some of the hot chocolate mixture into the yolks, then combine this with the chocolate mixture in double boiler. Cook over simmering water until slightly thickened, stirring constantly. Stir in GRAND MARNIER® and vanilla. Beat egg whites until they stand in soft peaks. Continue beating, gradually adding remaining sugar, until whites stand upright in stiff peaks when beater is removed. Fold egg whites and chocolate mixture together carefully. Pour mixture into the prepared pan. Bake 3 hours at 250°. Remove from oven. Cool at room temperature; cover and chill. Can be made a day or two in advance and refrigerated. Serve small wedges, as this is very rich.

❧ *Serve with unsweetened whipped cream or crème anglaise.*

Neiman Marcus—THE ZODIAC Atlanta
Donation to: combined charities

Chocolate Bread Pudding

Was there bread pudding before chocolate bread pudding? Not for chocoholics!

INGREDIENTS

1 loaf *brioche or egg bread, cut into 12 slices*

1 cup *sweet butter, melted*

½ pound *bittersweet chocolate (preferably CALLEBAUT®)*

3 cups *heavy cream*

1 cup *milk*

1 cup *sugar*

12 *egg yolks*

1 teaspoon *vanilla extract*

Pinch salt

DIRECTIONS

Preheat oven to 425°. Brush bread slices with melted butter and toast in oven until golden brown. Set aside. Chop chocolate into rough pieces and place in a bowl over hot water so it will melt slowly. Heat cream and milk in saucepan and bring almost to boil. Meanwhile, whisk sugar and yolks in a large bowl until well-blended. Slowly whisk in the cream-and-milk mixture. Strain and skim off any foam. Add yolk mixture to melted chocolate, whisking constantly. Stir in vanilla and salt. Break the bread into pieces and add to the milk-and-chocolate mixture. Bake 20 minutes. **Serves 6.**

Mrs. Paul Radin—Santa Barbara, CA
Donation to: The East African Wildlife Society, Nairobi, Kenya, East Africa

Hot Apricot Soufflé

My husband's business takes us often to Kenya where I first tasted this soufflé, made in our honor, at the lovely old Norfolk Hotel in Nairobi. The surprise . . . it eliminates the usual egg yolk-sauce base and, thus, eliminates both effort and calories. And, since it holds, unlike other soufflés, you can dare to serve it at dinner parties.

INGREDIENTS

12 ounces *apricot preserves*

2 tablespoons *GRAND MARNIER® liqueur*

1 tablespoon *fresh lemon juice*

Grated rind of 1 orange

8 *egg whites, room temperature*

¼ teaspoon *cream of tartar*

DIRECTIONS

Preheat oven to 400°. Butter the inside of a 2-quart soufflé dish and dust with sugar. Combine preserves, GRAND MARNIER®, lemon juice, and orange rind in a large mixing bowl. In a separate bowl, whip egg whites with the cream of tartar until soft peaks form. Gently fold ¼ of whipped egg whites into the apricot preserve mixture; fold in the remaining whites until the mixture is blended. Pour into the soufflé dish and smooth with a rubber spatula. Bake 10 to 12 minutes until top is puffed and golden. This soufflé, unlike others, holds well and can be left in the oven for 10 minutes or so, after turning off the oven.
Serves 6.

Vickie Carlton—Las Colinas, TX
Donation to: Irving Healthcare Systems Foundation, Irving, TX

Warm Caramel Soufflé with Caramel Custard

I first tasted a dessert like this at an affair catered by Captain White in Dallas. He served two dozen of these almost simultaneously out of a kitchen with only two ovens. I later found a similar recipe and the secret: bake it early and let it fall. It rises again when reheated, and you serve it out of the dish, like a delicious puff of air.

INGREDIENTS

2¾ cups *sugar*
3 tablespoons *butter*
7 *egg whites, stiffly beaten*
Pinch of salt
⅛ teaspoon *cream of tartar*
1½ cups *milk*
7 *egg yolks, beaten*
½ teaspoon *caramel extract*
½ pint *heavy cream, whipped*

DIRECTIONS

For the soufflé, heat 1¼ cups sugar gently in a heavy skillet over low heat until a light brown syrup forms. Pour half the caramel into a 2-quart soufflé dish, rotating quickly to coat bottom and sides. Be careful; the caramel is super hot. Cool. Rub 2 tablespoons butter over the caramel and set aside. Beat egg whites until foamy; add salt and cream of tartar. While beating constantly, add 1 cup sugar gradually, until stiff peaks form. Return skillet to heat to liquify remaining caramel. Add this to egg white mixture, beating constantly. Continue beating at medium speed for 5 minutes (very important). Pour into the prepared soufflé dish. Bake 1 hour in a pan of hot water at 300° until firm, but light. Remove from oven. This can be done early in the day. For the custard, cook ½ cup sugar and milk in top of double boiler until sugar melts. Add remaining butter and slowly add this mixture to the egg yolks while beating. Return to heat and cook until mixture is thickened, stirring constantly. Cool. Add caramel extract and whipped cream. Refrigerate until serving time. When ready to serve, bake the soufflé 15 minutes at 350° because soufflé must be warm to come out of the dish. Invert soufflé onto a large serving dish and allow caramel to run down the sides. Serve custard in a separate crystal bowl, for spooning over individual portions. **Serves 8.**

Marian Marshall—New York, NY
Donation to: Thomas H. Seebode Environmental Education Fund, Decatur, GA

Lemon Bars

All my recipes are from family and friends, and over the years I have added ingredients and changed measurements to enhance the results.

INGREDIENTS

½ cup *butter*
1 cup *plus* **2 tablespoons** *flour*
¼ cup *confectioners' sugar*
2 *eggs, slightly beaten*
1 cup *granulated sugar*
3 tablespoons *lemon juice*
¼ teaspoon *salt*
Grated rind of 1 lemon

DIRECTIONS

Mix together the butter, 1 cup flour, and confectioners' sugar. Put into an 8-inch-square pan and press with fingers to form an even layer of crust. Bake 15 minutes at 350°. Mix eggs, granulated sugar, lemon juice, salt, remaining flour, and grated lemon rind. Pour over hot crust. Bake 20 minutes. Sift confectioners' sugar over lemon bars when cooled.
Makes 16 to 20 bars.

Serve with a big glass of milk, hot cup of tea, or coffee.

Neiman Marcus—THE RESTAURANT AND THE CLUB
Beverly Hills
Donation to: combined charities

Tarte Tatin

Restaurant General Manager Guy Veletzos says these tarts disappear off the dessert cart like nobody's business. They're that good.

INGREDIENTS

6 ounces *butter, sliced*

14 ounces *sugar*

8 *Granny Smith apples, peeled, cored, and halved*

1 *chilled puff pastry, 1/8-inch-thick*

DIRECTIONS

Place butter slices on the bottom of a frying pan and sprinkle with sugar. Arrange apples, tightly packed, on top of the sugar. Heat on the stove until the caramel is golden. Remove from heat. Place a springform pan around apple halves and tighten. Let cool a bit and cover with a circle of chilled puff pastry; tuck in the pastry edges. Bake 20 to 25 minutes at 350° to 400° in the frying pan until crisp. Serve warm with some crème fraîche. **Serves 10.**

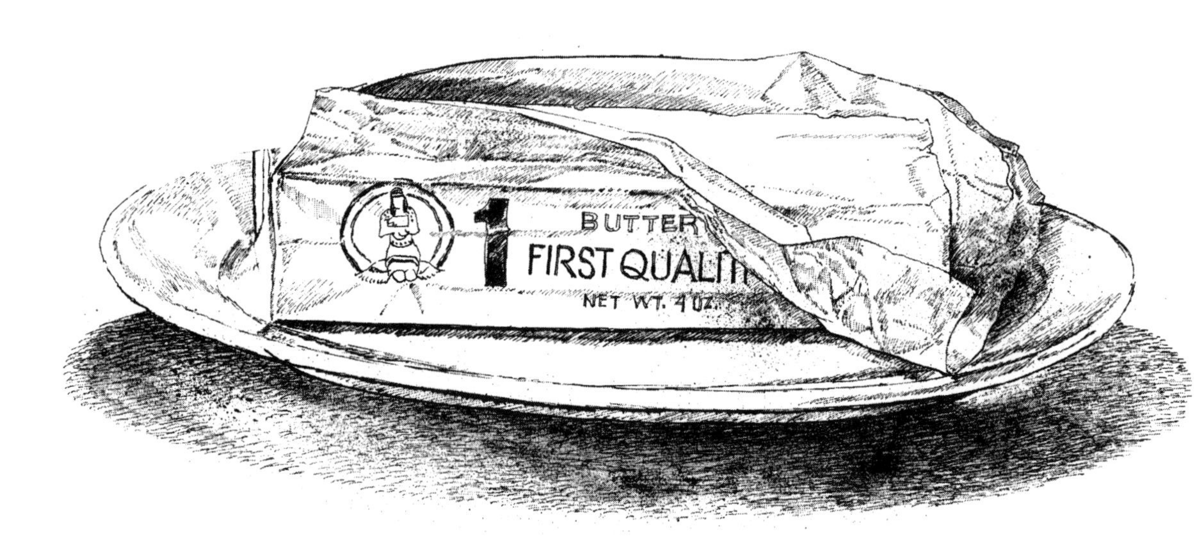

Marlene Schell—Huntington Beach, CA
Donation to: Interval House, Seal Beach, CA

Pralines

This is an easy recipe that people love.

INGREDIENTS

1 package *(3 ounce) vanilla-flavor pudding and pie filling mix*

1 1/2 cups *light brown sugar, firmly packed*

6 ounces *evaporated milk*

1 tablespoon *butter*

2 cups *pecan halves*

DIRECTIONS

Combine pudding mix, brown sugar, evaporated milk, and butter in medium-sized heavy saucepan. Heat slowly until sugar dissolves, stirring constantly. Now, cook without stirring until mixture reaches 238° on a candy thermometer (or a teaspoon of syrup forms a soft ball when dropped in cold water). Remove from heat at once. Stir in pecans and beat 2 to 3 minutes with a wooden spoon until mixture starts to thicken. Drop by tablespoonfuls, 2-inches apart, on wax paper. (If mixture hardens as you work, set pan over hot water.) Let pralines stand until firm. **Makes 3 1/2 dozen.**

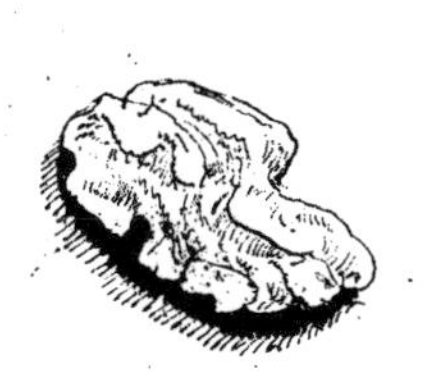

Pure and Simple Cooking Terms Defined:

Consommé	A clear broth flavored by a specific meat, fish, fowl, or vegetable.
Stock	A mixture of water and specified meat, fish, or fowl, including bones and vegetables that are boiled together until the stock is flavored.
Vegetable stock	Made only with onions, celery, carrots, parsley, and herbs.
Chicken stock	Made with chicken and chicken bones, onions, celery, carrots, parsley, and herbs.
Fish stock	Made with fish and onions, celery, carrots, parsley, and herbs.
White veal stock	Made with veal and veal bones, onions, celery, carrots, parsley, and herbs.
Brown stock	Made with any meat, bones, water, onions, celery, carrots, parsley, and herbs.
	Specific stocks may be used as the foundation for soups, sauces, and gravies. Adding red wine to white stock creates a blush version of that specific stock.
Essence of stock	A concentrated form of a specific flavor such as beef base, chicken base, fish base, or vegetable base (such as mushroom or tomato).
Glaze	A reduction of stock until it takes on a gelatinous texture. Used to add a shiny finish to ham, turkey, salmon, etc., for buffet service.
Roux	Thickening agent for soups, sauces, and gravies. Three types: white, pale, and brown. Roux is made in a thick skillet with flour and oil, or clarified butter. The types are created by cooking over slow heat until the desired color is achieved.
Brown sauce, or Espagnole	Brown sauce, or espagnole, is a meat stock thickened with brown roux. You can make a brown fish sauce with only fish stock. Sauces are seasoned to taste.
White sauce, or Velouté	A white stock of a specific flavor, thickened with a pale roux, such as fish velouté, poultry velouté, or veal velouté. Seasoned to taste.
Cream sauce, or Béchamel	Made by adding boiling milk to white roux. Cream sauces can be light, medium, or heavy. Flavor may be added by using essences of the desired flavor. Seasoned to taste.

Note: The brown, white, and cream sauces are the basic sauces from which the majority of sauces are made. Exceptions: hollandaise, Béarnaise, butter, and fruit sauces, as examples.

MENU SUGGESTIONS

What a potpourri—from the most sophisticated menus, devised by Neiman Marcus' Vice President Bob Jones, to the purest and simplest of all, offered at the conclusion of this section, by our good friend, fishing buddy, and veteran sportscaster, Curt Gowdy.

Seated Brunch

Broiled Pink Grapefruit
Section fruit and top with brown sugar and sherry. Broil until top is slightly browned.

Shirred Eggs in Tomato
Scoop out the pulp of a large tomato. Crack two eggs into cavity, season with salt and pepper, and dust with bread crumbs. Bake at 350° until tomato is tender and eggs are set.

Grilled Canadian Bacon
Lyonnaise Potatoes
Miniature Bran Muffins
Butter and Orange Marmalade
Capuccino or Coffee with Cinnamon Stick

Buffet Brunch

Fresh Fruit Bowl
Use four of the freshest, ripe fruits available. Slice and layer them; decorate with fresh mint.

Knobly Apple Coffee Cake .... See page 277

Orange French Toast
Prepare French toast for 8 by dipping bread into a batter of 2 slightly beaten eggs, the grated rind of 1 orange, ¼ teaspoon salt, 1 cup milk, 1 tablespoon rum, and an optional ¼ cup orange juice. Serve with warmed, pure-maple syrup.

Mixed Grill
Crisp bacon, sausage, and small lamb chops

Margarita Pie with Pretzel Crust .... See page 290

Coffee

Seated Luncheon

Hot Mah-Jongg Chicken Salad .... See page 70

Scones with Strawberry Butter .... See page 260

Iced Russian Chocolate Coffee
Allow hot, strong coffee to cool; pour into a 12-ounce glass. Add two tablespoons of chocolate syrup, ¼ cup soft-serve vanilla yogurt, and ice cubes. Top with powdered cinnamon.

Or Spiced Tea

Glop .... See page 289

Buffet Luncheon

Crab Meat Quesadillas .... See page 12

Romaine Salad with Pink Grapefruit

Section fruit, add walnuts, Roquefort pieces, and clear lemon French dressing.

Tomato Aspic with Avocado Dill Mayonnaise

Mash ½ of a ripe avocado. Thoroughly combine with 1 cup mayonnaise and 1 tablespoon chopped fresh dill. Chill and serve with aspic.

Baked Chicken Supreme .... See page 160

Broccoli with Mushrooms and Pimiento Butter

Corn Casserole .... See page 237

Assorted Breads or Fold-over Yeast Rolls

Baked Apples with Vanilla Sauce

Choose medium-sized Red Delicious apples.

Brownie Fingers

Seated Dinner

Brownwood Texas Black Bean Soup .... See page 41

Mixed Field Greens with Oil and Vinegar and Roquefort Pieces

Oven-Fried Lemon Marinated Chicken .... See page 161

Wild Rice with Fresh Corn .... See page 238

Sautéed Buttered Carrots with Fresh Mint

Monkey Bread .... See page 267

Margarita Pie with Pretzel Crust .... See page 290

Dinner Buffet

Roast Beef Au Jus

Tuna Loaf with Cucumber Sauce .... See page 138

Lemon Broiled Chicken

Confetti Squash .... See page 255

Gourmet Spinach Ring .... See page 251

Crusty Potato Balls .... See page 248

Fresh Fruit Salad with Poppy Seed Dressing

Vegetable Perfection Aspic .... See page 81

Salad Broccoli with Sour Cream Dressing .... See page 57

Carrot-Pineapple Salad Mold .... See page 65

Club Salad .... See page 68

Selection of Seven Desserts

Cocktail Dinner Buffet

Roast Tenderloin of Beef with Pocket-Sized Yeast Rolls
Serve with mayonnaise and horseradish.
Tomato Aspic with Shrimp
Cold, Decorated, Poached Salmon
Thinly Sliced Baked Ham in Parsley Biscuits
Assorted Tray of Four Vegetable Crudités
Cheese Ball with Assorted Crackers
Coffee
Assorted Miniature Sweets

How To Time A Perfect Party

The Occasion:	**Invite Guests to Come:**		
Breakfast	8:00 a.m.	until	9:30 a.m.
Midnight Breakfast	Midnight		
Brunch	10:30 a.m.	until	Noon
Luncheon	11:30 a.m.	until	1:30 p.m.
Afternoon Shower	2:00 p.m.	until	3:00 p.m.
Cream Tea	2:30 p.m.	until	4:00 p.m.
High Tea	4:00 p.m.	until	6:00 p.m.
Cocktails Only	5:00 p.m.	until	6:00 p.m.
Cocktails/Hors d'Oeuvres	6:30 p.m.	until	7:00 p.m.
Cocktails with Light Dinner (no plates)	6:30 p.m.	until	7:30 p.m.
Buffet Dinner	7:00 p.m.	until	8:00 p.m.
Formal Seated Dinner	8:00 p.m.	until	8:15 p.m.
Dessert and Champagne	9:00 p.m.	until	10:00 p.m.

Rules Of Thumb For Beverage Service

Gallon	128 ounces	*Serves*	*30*	*coffee punch cups*
Half-Gallon	64 ounces	*Serves*	*15*	*coffee punch cups*
Quart	32 ounces	*Serves*	*8*	*4-ounce juice glasses*
Fifth	25.6 ounces	*Serves*	*18*	*highballs*
		or	*12*	*rocks*
		or	*5*	*champagnes*
		or	*5*	*wines*
Pint	16 ounces	*Serves*	*10*	*highballs*
		or	*8*	*rocks*
		or	*4*	*champagnes*
		or	*4*	*wines*
Tenth	12.8 ounces	*Serves*	*7*	*highballs*
Split	6.8 ounces	*Serves*	*2*	*champagnes*
		or	*2*	*wines*

Curt Gowdy– Boston, MA
Donation to: American Heart Association, Inc., N. Palm Beach, FL

This is what the legendary sportscaster and everyone's favorite American Sportsman told us about his "Riverbank Lunch:" "I love outdoor cooking and one of my favorite meals is a streamside lunch prepared by a young guide, Jack Dennis, who used to float me down the Snake River near Jackson Hole, Wyoming. Most of the preparation is done before we cast off. The cleanup is easy. Just put the foil back in your cooler or in a garbage disposal, if one is handy. It's a real treat in the outdoors on a beautiful river, or anywhere."

Riverbank Trout
Barbecue Beans
Ground Beef Patties with Jack's Western Barbecue Sauce
Tater Tots® with Peppers, Onions, and Mushrooms
Green Salad with Western French Dressing

Riverbank Trout

INGREDIENTS

Trout
Seasoned salt
Bacon
Bacon grease
Sliced onion
Butter
Salt and pepper
Juice of 1 lemon
Lemons, thinly sliced
Limes, thinly sliced

DIRECTIONS

Sprinkle seasoned salt on fish. Lay fish on foil. Cook bacon slightly. Rub cavity of trout with bacon grease, then fill cavity with onion, bacon, butter, salt, pepper, and juice of lemon. Butter outside of trout and place lemon and lime slices on it. Wrap tightly in foil. Place on coals and cook 5 minutes on each side. Do not overcook. **Serves 1.**

Barbecue Beans

INGREDIENTS

2 cans *(16 ounces each) CAMPBELL'S PORK & BEANS®*
1 can *(16 ounce) BOSTON BRICK BEANS®*
1 can *(15 ounce) tomato sauce*
1 large *onion, diced*
1/4 pound *brown sugar*
1/2 cup *KARO® dark corn syrup*
2 tablespoons *Worcestershire sauce*
1 can *(16 ounce) crushed pineapple*
1/2 tablespoon *pepper*
1/2 tablespoon *dry mustard*
1/4 cup *sweet-pickle relish*
4 tablespoons *wine vinegar*
TABASCO® sauce
Seasoned salt

DIRECTIONS

Place all ingredients in a cast-iron kettle at the campsite and cook until seasonings are well blended, stirring occasionally. **Serves 4.**

Ground Beef Patties with Jack's Western Barbecue Sauce

INGREDIENTS

3 cans *(15 ounces each) tomato sauce*
½ **cup** *lemon juice*
¼ **cup** *Worcestershire sauce*
¼ **cup** *KARO® dark corn syrup*
3 dashes *TABASCO® sauce (optional)*
1 tablespoon *salt*
2 tablespoons *seasoned salt*
½ **tablespoon** *oregano*
1 tablespoon *garlic salt*
2 onions, *finely chopped*
½ **pound** *brown sugar*
1 can *(16 ounce) crushed pineapple*
4 pounds *lean ground beef (½ pound per person)*

DIRECTIONS

Empty tomato sauce into a large pan. Add lemon juice, Worcestershire sauce, and corn syrup. Stir and cook 10 minutes. Add TABASCO® sauce, both salts, oregano, and garlic salt. Cook 10 minutes. Add onions, brown sugar, and pineapple. Stir and cook 15 minutes. Cool the sauce and put in jars to take on the river trip. Shape meat into ½-pound patties and place on individual squares of foil. Pour barbecue sauce over meat patties; wrap and seal securely. Place on coals and cook 15 minutes on each side. **Serves 8.**

Tater Tots® with Peppers, Onions, and Mushrooms

INGREDIENTS

½ *yellow onion, thinly sliced*
1 can *(16 ounce) sliced mushrooms*
1 *green pepper, thinly sliced*
Salt
Pepper
1-1½ sticks *of butter (allow 2 tablespoons per packet)*
1 package *(12 to 16 ounce) TATER TOTS®*

DIRECTIONS

Divide ingredients in packets of double foil. Seal and cook 15 minutes. Open foil and shake. Close foil and cook 15 minutes more. Another variation is to sauté TATER TOTS® in a pan with finely chopped green peppers, onions, and mushrooms. **Serves 4 to 6.**

Green Salad with Western French Dressing

INGREDIENTS

1 *head lettuce, cut into bite-sized pieces and chilled*
1 can *(15 ounce) tomato sauce*
1 onion, *chopped*
1 tablespoon *pepper*
1 tablespoon *Worcestershire sauce*
1 tablespoon *seasoned salt*
1 cup *sugar*
½ **cup** *salad oil*
¼ **cup** *vinegar*

DIRECTIONS

Prepare the lettuce and the dressing prior to leaving on the river trip. Wrap lettuce tightly in foil and pack in the cooler. Blend tomato sauce, onion, pepper, Worcestershire sauce, and seasoned salt in an electric mixer. Add ½ cup sugar and the oil; blend. Add vinegar and ½ cup sugar. Blend about 30 seconds to create a smooth dressing. Add dressing to lettuce just before serving. **Makes 1 quart.**

GOOD THINGS TO REMEMBER WHEN COOKING PURE AND SIMPLE

Four basic rules:

1. Measure ingredients accurately.
2. Use recommended cooking temperatures.
3. Use recommended cooking times.
4. Test any new recipe before serving it to guests.

- Hot foods should be served on a warm platter or dish.
- Cold foods should be served on a cold platter or dish.
- To keep scrambled eggs creamy and moist for a buffet brunch, add a lightly seasoned cream sauce.
- Do not overwork pie dough; use a knife.
- Before baking meat or fish pies, brush crust with egg white.
- When frying eggs, dust skillet with flour to keep grease from popping onto the floor, stove, or you.
- When cooking pasta or rice, add a touch of olive oil to the water.
- To prevent scalded milk from sticking to the saucepan, place pan in cold water before you add the milk.
- When preparing hard-cooked eggs, first rinse them in cold water to prevent cracking when placed in boiling water.
- To make any vegetable crisp, place it in ice water.
- Food must have eye appeal. Experiment with your presentation.

Basic Cooking Measurements

1 quart = 4 cups = 64 tablespoons = 32 ounces
1 pint = 2 cups = 32 tablespoons = 16 ounces
½ pint = 1 cup = 16 tablespoons = 8 ounces
1 tablespoon = 3 teaspoons = 3 ounces
Dash = less than ⅛ teaspoon

Metric liquid measurements:

3.785 liters = 1 gallon
.9463 liters = 1 quart
.4732 liters = 1 pint
¼ liter, approximately = 1 cup

Metric dry measurements:

1.101 liters = 1 quart
.551 liters = 1 pint

Metric weights:

30 grams, approximately = 1 ounce
454 grams, approximately = 1 pound

Some practical advice on cooking fish from the kitchens of Neiman Marcus.

1. Do not overcook fish. Give it your undivided attention as it cooks.
2. Fish is done when it flakes easily and is no longer translucent.

Here is a good all-round recipe for basting fish when you are baking in the oven. It will season eight, 6-ounce fish fillets.

¼ cup olive oil
1 teaspoon lemon pepper
1 tablespoon dill (fresh, if possible)
¼ cup white wine

INDEX

ALPHABETICAL LISTING OF CONTRIBUTOR OF RECIPE

Beverly Wade (Mrs. Roy Lee) Aach—
Baldwin, MO, 23
Carol Adamek—Dallas, TX, 20
Carmen M. de Alejos—Miami, FL, 87
JoDale Ales—Baton Rouge, LA, 209
Edna Marie Allen—Shreveport, LA, 276
Danna Almon—Richardson, TX, 255
Debra Alper—Chicago, IL, 187
Michèle d'Arlin—Los Angeles, CA, 260
Bonnie Baker—Playa del Rey, CA, 47
Trish Ballard—Atlanta, GA, 41
Mrs. William Terry Barbee—Weslaco, TX, 16
Susan Barnes—Phoenix, AZ, 19
Joyce Baseman—Alexandria, VA, 33
Pamela K. Baxter—New York, NY, 108
Jill Bee—Dallas, TX, 144
Barbara Berdy—New City, NY, 239
Tina Berman—Framingham, MA, 237
Mrs. Leonard Bernstein—Los Angeles, CA, 177
Mrs. Thomas S. Beyt—New Iberia, LA, 75
Georgie Bixler—Tallahassee, FL, 167
Debra Blauwiekel—Geneva, IL, 126
Joan Fanaberia Bloom—
Montreal, Quebec, Canada, 185
Janet Newlan Bower—La Mesa, CA, 173
Catherine E. Brackbill—Dallas, TX, 111
Mrs. C. A. Brawner—Dallas, TX, 247
Barbara Breckur—Colleyville, TX, 201
Nancy Brinker—Dallas, TX, 141
Susan Brodarick—St. Louis, MO, 234
Princess Marie-Blanche de Broglie—59
Cissy Brottman—Northfield, IL, 102
Jo-Ann M. Brown—Bronxville, NY, 136
Marilyn E. Brown—Houston, TX, 113
Mrs. Joel T. Broyhill—Arlington, VA, 270
June R. Bumpas—Dallas, TX, 148
Linda L. Burk, M.D.—Dallas, TX, 261
Mrs. Frank J. Bush, Jr.—St. Louis, MO, 272
Catherine A. Byles—Dallas, TX, 220
Mrs. Patsy Cantrell—Cresson, TX, 24
Mrs. L. E. Caraway—Houston, TX, 81
Vickie Carlton—Las Colinas, TX, 300
Mrs. William M. Carpenter—Los Angeles, CA, 111
Mrs. Susan Carroll—Elgin, IL, 29
Lisa J. Cave—Clearwater, FL, 34
Ellen G. Chamberlin—Corona del Mar, CA, 72
Joanna M. Champlin—Oklahoma City, OK, 164
Mrs. Jack M. Chinn—Dallas, TX, 119
Frances L. Chu—Briarcliff Manor, NY, 242
Inez Cohen—Winnetka, IL, 22
Susan S. Cohon—Toronto, Ontario, Canada, 161
Mrs. Ernest J. Colant—San Francisco, CA, 280
Mrs. Janice M. Comis—Westport, CT, 215
Carol R. Cooper—West Bloomfield, MI, 15
Shirley Copeland—Grants Pass, OR, 76
Carla Cotropia—Galveston, TX, 102
David W. Cowles—Las Vegas, NV, 124
Mrs. A. D. (Sandra) Crawford—
Mineral Wells, TX, 224
Mrs. J. A. Cronic—Griffin, GA, 56
Renée Crown—Wilmette, IL, 254
Diane M. Cummins—Columbus, OH, 94
Gwen Cupp—Hot Springs, AR, 40
Madlyn Daniel—Chicago, IL, 286
Amy Davenport—Dallas, TX, 278
Norma Sue Davis—Arlington, TX, 64
Steven P. Davis—Dallas, TX, 204
Emma DeLucas—Peru, NY, 221
Naomi Denison—W. Bloomfield, MI, 176
Mrs. Sharon H. Dewberry—Dallas, TX, 39
Susan Z. Diamond—Melrose Park, IL, 46
Beth Donnell—Houston, TX, 27
M. Susan Douglas—Topeka, KS, 128
Mrs. James H. Dudley—Comanche, TX, 182
Happy Dumas—Hillsborough, CA, 212
Sara Dunham—Marfa, TX, 12
Linda R. Dunn—Swampscott, MA, 198
Martha S. Durrett—Simsboro, LA, 120
José Eber—Los Angeles, CA, 165
Diane C. Eberly—Plano, TX, 213
Anton Edelmann—122
Caroline Hite Edens—Dallas, TX, 237
Kaye C. Edwards—San Antonio, TX, 41
Anneliese Eisenberg—Des Plaines, IL, 79
Nancy R. Engerman—Highland Park, IL, 168
Judith Enright—Brighton, MI, 38
Mrs. Claude R. Erickson—Livingston, MT, 54
Patti Estabrooks—Laguna Beach, CA, 225
Ellise Dobson Falkoff—Union City, TN, 35
Carolyn Farb—Houston, TX, 137
Dean Fearing—Dallas, TX, 18
B. Rhoads Fearn—San Francisco, CA, 154
Esther Feder—Suffern, NY, 180
Dawn Fine—Miami, FL, 216
Kathryn A. Fiore—Saugus, MA, 175
Christine Fluor—Newport Beach, CA, 58
Allan H. Fradkin, M.D.—Galveston, TX, 143
Marcy Friedman—Carmichael, CA, 184
Mrs. Herbert (Joanne) Friedman—Scarsdale, NY, 208
Richard F. Friedeman, Jr.—Chicago, IL, 287
Mrs. Ted R. (April) Gamble—Carmel Valley, CA, 236
Selene (Mrs. Marvin) Ganek—Glencoe, IL, 274
Reidun V. Gann—Beverly Hills, CA, 51
Carol Garfield—Riverdale, NY, 195
Francine Gerson—Dallas, TX, 174
Linda McElroy Gibbons—Dallas, TX, 296
Herbert L. Goldberg—Dallas, TX, 162
Mrs. Rachel P. Goldman—Fort Worth, TX, 130
Mrs. Bram Goldsmith—Beverly Hills, CA, 133
Marsha Goldstein—Northbrook, IL, 71
Mrs. Ronald Goldstein—Atlanta, GA, 78
Roslyn Goldstine—Beverly Hills, CA, 242
Suzanne M. Goodman—Santa Ana, CA, 147
Curt Gowdy—Boston, MA, 308
Dolly Granatelli—Montecito, CA, 145
Karen Green—Irvine, CA, 268
Ferde Grofe—Malibu, CA, 28
Mrs. Joyce Grunauer—Beverly Hills, CA, 217
Fran Gunner—Bakersfield, CA, 206
Jacqueline Gutman—Key Colony Beach, FL, 235
Dana W. Hagen—Pompano Beach, FL, 107
Marlene Hammerman—St. Louis, MO, 200
E.O. Hand—Chicago, IL, 211
Marilyn Harbison—Dallas, TX, 93
Nancy Harrell—Houston, TX, 45
Mrs. John A. Harris—Potomac, MD, 289
Kit W. Harrison—Houston, TX, 24
Mary M. Harvey—Houston, TX, 92
Mrs. Hayden Hatcher—Fort Worth, TX, 86
Mrs. G. A. Hawkins—Graham, TX, 88
L. R. Herkimer—Dallas, TX, 121
Frances Heyne—Houston, TX, 256

ALPHABETICAL LISTING OF CHARITIES

Aid for Cancer Research, Natick, MA
AIDS Action Committee of Massachusetts, Inc., Boston, MA
AIDS Arms Network, Inc., Dallas, TX
AIDS Project L.A., Los Angeles, CA
AIDS Research Institute, San Francisco, CA
Aldeas Infantiles, S.O.S., Mixco, Guatemala
Alton Area Animal Aid Association, Godfrey, IL
Alzheimer's Association, Inc., Chicago, IL
Alzheimer's Association, Inc., Dallas, TX
Alzheimer's Association, Inc., Palo Alto, CA
Alzheimer's Association, Inc., St. Louis, MO
American Cancer Foundation, Dallas, TX
American Cancer Foundation, Houston, TX
American Cancer Society, Inc., National Headquarters, Atlanta, GA
American Cancer Society, Inc., Batavia, IL
American Cancer Society, Inc., Beverly Hills, CA
American Cancer Society, Inc., Boca Raton, FL
American Cancer Society, Inc., Dallas, TX
American Cancer Society, Inc., Las Vegas, NV
American Cancer Society, Inc., Los Angeles, CA
American Cancer Society, Inc., N. Palm Beach, FL
American Cancer Society, Inc., New York, NY
American Cancer Society, Inc., Nutley, NJ
American Cancer Society, Inc., Pompano Beach, FL
American Cancer Society, Inc., Portland, OR
American Cancer Society, Inc., St. Louis, MO
American Cancer Society, Inc., Washington, D.C.
American Diabetes Association, Dallas, TX
American Heart Association, Inc., Chicago, IL
American Heart Association, Inc., Colorado Springs, CO
American Heart Association, Inc., Dallas, TX
American Heart Association, Inc., Fort Worth, TX
American Heart Association, Inc., Houston, TX
American Heart Association, Inc., Los Angeles, CA
American Heart Association, Inc., Miami, FL
American Heart Association, Inc., N. Palm Beach,FL
American Heart Association, Inc., St. Louis, MO
American Heart Association, Inc., Tallahassee, FL
American Heart Foundation, Des Moines, IA
American Heart Foundation, Inc., Stamford, CT
American-Israel Cultural Foundation, Manhattan, NY
Amie Karen Cancer Fund for Children, M. Freedman, Beverly Hills, CA
The Andrews Adult Literacy Council, Andrews, TX
The Ark, Chicago, IL
Asian Art Museum Foundation of San Francisco, San Francisco, CA
Ballet Theatre Foundation, Inc., New York, NY
Bayou Bend Collection, Houston, TX
Botsford General Hospital, Farmington Hills, MI (Memorial Fund)
Bryan's House, Dallas, TX
California Special Olympics, Inc., Santa Monica, CA
Cancer Patients Services, Inc., Laredo, TX
Cancer Research Foundation of North Texas, Arlington, TX
Cancer Research Institute, Inc., New York, NY
Carlsbad Association for Retarded Citizens Farm, Inc., Carlsbad, NM
Carmel Valley Community Youth Center, Inc., Carmel Valley, CA
Child Help, Inc., Temple, TX
Children's Cancer Research Institute, San Francisco, CA
Children's Hospital Branches, Inc., Oakland, CA
Children's Hospital Foundation, Washington, D.C.
The Children's Hospital League Corp., Boston, MA
Children's Hospital of Los Angeles, Los Angeles, CA
Children's Leukemia Foundation of Michigan, Southfield, MI
Children's Medical Center of Dallas, Dallas, TX
Children's Memorial Hospital, Chicago, IL
Children's Museum, Inc., Houston, TX
Children's Museum of the Desert, Rancho Mirage, CA
Children's National Medical Center, Washington, D.C.
Children's Wish Foundation International, Inc., Atlanta, GA
Cleo Parker Robinson Dance Ensemble, Denver, CO
Comanche Public Library, Comanche, TX
Community Rehabilitation Industries, Long Beach, CA
Concern Foundation, Los Angeles, CA
Cook-Fort Worth Children's Medical Center, Fort Worth, TX
Covenant House Florida, Fort Lauderdale, FL
Crocker Art Museum Foundation, Sacramento, CA
Cystic Fibrosis Foundation North Texas, Fort Worth, TX
Dallas Children's Theater, Inc., Dallas, TX
Dallas Easter Seal Society for Children, Dallas, TX
Dallas Garden Center, Inc., Dallas, TX
Dallas Museum of Art, Dallas, TX
Dallas Opera, Dallas, TX
Dallas SPCA, Dallas, TX
Dallas Summer Musicals, Inc., Dallas, TX
Dallas Symphony Orchestra Guild, Dallas, TX
Dana Farber Cancer Institute, Boston, MA
Deborah Hospital Foundation—Sonia Sobelman Chapter, Browns Mills, NJ
Delnor Community Hospital Foundation, Geneva, IL
Detroit Symphony Orchestra Hall, Inc., Detroit, MI
Ditka Foundation, Chicago, IL
Ducks Unlimited, Inc., Long Grove, IL
The East African Wildlife Society, Nairobi, Kenya, East Africa

Easter Seals Society for Children, Carrollton, TX
Egleston Children's Hospital at Emory University, Atlanta, GA
Family Place, Inc., Dallas, TX
Fight for Sight, Inc., Baltimore, MD,
Finley Hospital, Dubuque, IA
Fort Worth Symphony Orchestra, Fort Worth, TX
Founder's Society, Detroit Institute of Art, Detroit, MI
Freedoms Foundation, Valley Forge, PA
Friends of Breakhart Reservation, Saugus, MA
Friends of Kern County Multiple Sclerosis Patients, Inc., Bakersfield, CA
Friends of the Topeka Zoo, Inc., Topeka, KS
Fulton County Library District, Fulton, KY (Hickman, KY)
Galveston Arts Center, Inc., Galveston, TX
Garfield Farm Museum, LaFox, IL
Georgia Special Olympics, Inc., Atlanta, GA
Georgians for Clean Water, Inc., Newnan, GA
Good Shepherd Foundation, Longview, TX
The Graham Public Library, Graham, TX
The Grand 1894 Opera House, Galveston, TX
Gymnastics Olympica USA, Inc., Van Nuys, CA
Hadassah Hospital, Israel
Harlem Valley Psychiatric Center, Wingdale, NY
High Museum of Art, Atlanta, GA
Highland Park Hospital Foundation, Highland Park, IL (Social Services)
Hoag Hospital, Newport Beach, CA (Sandpipers of Hoag Hospital)
Hoag Hospital Foundation, Newport Beach, CA
Hope and Cope, Montreal, Quebec, Canada
Hospice Care of Clinton County, Inc., Plattsburgh, NY
Hospice of Florida Keys, Inc., Key West, FL
Hospice-VNSW, White Plains, NY
Hot Springs Art Center, Hot Springs, AR
Houston Area Parkinsonism Society, Houston, TX
Houston Foto Fest, Inc., Houston, TX
Houston Grand Opera Association, Inc., Houston, TX
Humane Society of Santa Clara Valley, Santa Clara, CA
Infantry for Project Newborn University of Miami, Jackson Memorial, Miami, FL
Institute for Cancer and Blood Research, Beverly Hills, CA
Institute for Research in Behavioral Neuroscience, Inc., New York, NY
Interval House, Seal Beach, CA
Iowa Natural Heritage Foundation, Des Moines, IA
Irving Healthcare Systems Foundation, Irving, TX
The Jewish Museum, New York, NY
John Wayne Cancer Clinic Auxiliary, Los Angeles, CA
Keep Mineral Wells Beautiful Campaign, Mineral Wells, TX
Lakeview Museum of Arts & Sciences, Peoria, IL
Lincoln Park Zoological Society, Chicago, IL
Livingston Memorial Hospital League, Livingston, MT
Lucile Salter Packard Children's Hospital at Stanford, Palo Alto, CA
Lupus Foundation of America, Connecticut Chapter, West Hartford, CT
Lupus Foundation of America, Inc., Dallas Chapter, Dallas, TX
Lyric Opera of Chicago, Chicago, IL
M. D. Anderson Cancer Center Outreach Corporation, Houston, TX
Magnolia Avenue School Student Body Library Account, Los Angeles, CA
Make-A-Wish Foundation of the Texas Gulf Coast, Inc., Houston, TX
Marian Medical Center Foundation, Santa Maria, CA (Dialysis Treatment)
Mary Bird Perkins Cancer Center, Baton Rouge, LA
Mission Arlington Health Clinic, Arlington, TX
Missouri Chapter of the Lupus Foundation, Inc., St. Louis, MO
Moncrief Radiation Center, Fort Worth, TX
Mother's Against Drunk Driving, Santa Ana, CA
Motion Picture & Television Fund, Woodland Hills, CA
Mt. Baker Theater Center, Bellingham, WA
Muscular Dystrophy Association, New York, NY
Museum of Art, Inc., Fort Lauderdale, FL
Museum of Contemporary Art, Chicago, IL
Museum of Contemporary Art, Los Angeles, CA
Nathan Adelson Hospice, Inc., Las Vegas, NV
National Foundation for Ileitis and Colitis, Inc., New York, NY
National Multiple Sclerosis Society, Chicago, IL
National Neurofibromatosis Foundation, New York, NY
National Wildflower Research Center, Austin, TX
National Wildlife Federation, Washington, D.C.
New Canaan Nature Center Association, Inc., New Canaan, CT
New Iberia Humane Society, Inc., New Iberia, LA
Newport Harbor Art Museum, Newport Beach, CA
North Shore Animal League, Inc., Port Washington, NY
Northshore Senior Center Alzheimer's Patients, Winnetka, IL (House of Welcome)
The Oceanarium, Chicago, IL
Old Globe Theatre, San Diego, CA
The Opera Association of Central Ohio, Columbus, OH
Otis Parsons Art Institute, Los Angeles, CA
Pacific Vision Foundation, San Francisco, CA
Phelps Memorial Hospital Association, North Tarrytown, NY
Presbyterian Hospital of Dallas, Dallas, TX
Project Open Hand, San Francisco, CA
Project Wildlife, San Diego, CA
Rockland Family Shelter, Inc., Spring Valley, NY
Ronald McDonald House, Dallas, TX
Ronald McDonald House, Houston, TX
Ronald McDonald House, Palo Alto, CA
Rose Resnick Center for the Blind & Visually Impaired, San Francisco, CA
Roye Levin Adopt-A-Pet, Miami, FL
The Salvation Army, Houston, TX
The Salvation Army, New York, NY
The Salvation Army, St. Louis, MO
San Antonio Art Institute, San Antonio, TX

Save the River, Inc., Clayton, NY
Save the Whales, Inc., Venice, CA
Schenectady Civic Playhouse Theater,
Schenectady, NY
Schomburg Center for Research in
Black Culture, New York, NY
Scottish Rite Hospital for Crippled Children, Inc., Atlanta, GA
Scottish Rite Hospital for Crippled Children, Inc., Dallas, TX
Shepherd Spinal Center, Atlanta, GA
Shreveport Symphony Society, Shreveport, LA
Sickle Cell Anemia Foundation of Dallas, Dallas, TX
Sloan-Kettering Institute for Cancer Research,
New York, NY
South Coast Medical Center, South Laguna, CA
Special Camps for Special Kids, Dallas, TX
Special Olympics Productions, Inc., Washington, D.C.
St. Elizabeth Hospital, Beaumont, TX
St. Elizabeth's Hospice Medical Center,
Yakima, WA
St. Jude's Children's Research Hospital,
Memphis, TN
St. Jude's Ranch for Children, Inc.,
Boulder City, NV
St. Louis Symphony Orchestra, St. Louis, MO
St. Louis Symphony Society, St. Louis, MO
Starlight Foundation, New York, NY
Susan G. Komen Foundation, Inc., Dallas, TX
Tampa Museum of Art, Inc., Tampa, FL
Texas Heart Institute, Houston, TX
Texas Neurofibromatosis Foundation, Dallas, TX
Thomas H. Seebode Environmental
Education Fund, Decatur, GA
Trinity Ministry to the Poor, Dallas, TX
Twin Cities Down's Syndrome Association, Minneapolis, MN
United Way of Metropolitan Tarrant County,
Fort Worth, TX (Human Services)
University of Alabama Diabetes Research and
Education Hospital, Birmingham, AL
University of Washington Foundation,
Seattle, WA (Diabetes Research)
Upper Raritan Watershed Association, Gladstone, NJ
The Variety Village Sports & Fitness Center,
Scarborough, Ontario, Canada
Virginia Mason Medical Association, Seattle,
WA (Virginia Mason Society)
Visiting Nurse Association, Pasadena, CA
Voices for Children, San Diego, CA
Wolf Trap Foundation for the Performing Arts,
Vienna, VA
Women's American ORT, Skokie, IL
Women's Auxiliary Cancer Fund, ABC Hospital,
Mexico City, D.F.
The Women's Board of The Lincoln Park
Zoological Society, Chicago, IL
World Neighbors, Inc., Oklahoma City, OK
World Wildlife Fund, Inc., Washington, D.C.
Zionist Organization of America, Richardson, TX